CW00384701

Gift Aid

20 70893836 5912

A Dictionary of COOKERY TERMS

compiled by
Sarie Forster

A Dictionary of

COOKERY TERMS

compiled by
Sarie Forster

InPrint

InPrint Publishing is registered with the Publishers Licensing Society in the UK and the Copyright Clearance Center in the USA.

British Library Cataloguing in Publication Data: a catalogue record for this book is available for the British Library.

ISBN 1 873047 17 7

Design & Layout by Facing Pages
Printed by TJ International Ltd, Padstow, Cornwall, UK.

First published 1998

InPrint Publishing Ltd
38 Ship Street
Brighton
BN1 1AB
UK

Preface

Work on this book began nearly 20 years ago when I was at home with my first baby. Every time I thought I had finished, I would discover important new developments in cooking and eating that meant many new terms had to be included. This could have gone on indefinitely: the book would carry on growing but never be published. This is as good a moment to stop as any, so here is the first edition.

Although I have tried to be exhaustive, there will inevitably be oversights and omissions, for which I apologise and promise to include in the next edition, if they are brought to my attention. My criterion for inclusion is as follows: all recipe instructions that may need clarification, unusual utensils, classic garnishes and sauces, cooking methods, plus international terms that may puzzle or confuse someone reading a menu in a restaurant or a recipe in a cookery book. Since a line had to be drawn somewhere, I decided not to include ingredients, unless they have undergone some process which requires explanation: thus you will find *tofu*, but not *soya bean* which tofu is derived from. Finally, bearing in mind the need to keep the reader awake, I have included as many anecdotes as I could about the creation of dishes, regardless of how improbable they are.

Sarie Forster, 1998

AALSUPPE — Eel soup flavoured with pears, and sometimes other fruit as well, which is a speciality of Hamburg in Germany.

ABAISSE — French pastry-making term, for which there is no exact equivalent in English, meaning a piece of pastry which has been rolled out to a certain thickness, according to the recipe in question. Abaisse is also used to describe the undercrust of pastry and, occasionally, a layer of cake.

ABAT-FAIM — French for hunger-killer. This term refers to a substantial first-course or other dish served early in the meal.

ABATS — French term for giblets.

ABATTE — Broad double-edged knife used to bat or flatten meat before cooking. The word comes from the French battre, meaning to beat.

ABERNETHY BISCUIT — Sweet biscuit flavoured with caraway seeds. It was invented in the early nineteenth century, when Dr. Abernethy of St. Bartholomew's Hospital in London suggested to a baker that he add sugar and caraway to a plain biscuit.

ABRICOTER — French pâtisserie term meaning to brush a layer of reduced, strained apricot jam or redcurrant jelly over a pastry or cake base.

ACCOLADE, IN — A style of presenting cooked food to serve. Two or more items of the same type, eg. two chickens, are arranged back to back.

ACCRAT — Caribbean fritter made with a yeast batter, enclosing meat, fish, vegetables or fruit.

ACHAR/ACHARD — Spicy Indian pickle made with either fruit or vegetables.

ACID DROP — Boiled sweet made with sugar and citric acid.

1

ACIDIFY — To add acid to food. The acid is usually in the form of lemon juice or vinegar.

ACIDITY — The unpleasantly sharp taste which exists naturally in certain vegetables and fruit. Acidity can be treated by blanching.

ACIDULATED WATER — Cold water to which lemon juice or vinegar has been added. It is used to prevent peeled vegetables and fruit from the discoloration which takes place when they are exposed to air for more than a few minutes.

ACINO DI PEPE — Italian name for small squares of pasta which are used as a garnish for soup.

ACORDA — Portuguese soup made with bread, garlic, parsley and coriander.

ADELE — French soup. It is a chicken consommé, garnished with peas, cubed carrots and chicken quenelles.

ADELINA PATTI — French soup named after the opera singer. It is a chicken consommé garnished with royale, carrots and chestnut purée.

ADOBO — Spicy stew from the Philippines. It is usually made with pork, which has been marinated in vinegar, garlic, bayleaf, salt and pepper. Chicken or fish may replace the pork. Adobo is also the name of a Mexican chili paste used for pickling and marinating meat.

ADOUCIR — French term meaning to reduce bitterness by long slow cooking, or to reduce saltiness by adding liquid.

AEBLEKAGE — Danish apple cake. Made with breadcrumbs and stewed apples, which are arranged in layers, pressed flat and served cold with cream.

AEGIR SAUCE — Hollandaise sauce with a little mustard added.

A.F.D — Accelerated freeze dried. This is a method of preserving food by freezing to a very low temperature, then heating the food; this causes loss of most of its moisture through vaporization. A.F.D. food has to be reconstituted with boiling liquid.

AFELIA/APHELIA — Greek pork stew. Cubes of pork are marinated in red wine and coriander seeds before cooking in the marinade until tender.

AFFRIANDER — French culinary term, meaning to whet the appetite by means of an attractive appearance.

AFRICAINE, A L' — Descriptive term meaning in the African style: in cookery it is generally understood to mean that the food in question is served with a demi-glace sauce, flavoured with cayenne pepper, Madeira, onion and truffles. However, Crème à l'Africaine is a curried chicken soup with rice, aubergines and artichoke bottoms as a garnish.

AGAR-AGAR — Seaweed product with strong setting properties, which is used by vegetarians in place of gelatine.

AGITATE — To move the contents of a pan in order to cook the food evenly without stirring it. With a saucepan, the movement is up and down; with a frying pan, it is backwards and forwards.

AGLIATA, ALL' — Italian way of serving meat, poultry or fish with a sauce of pressed garlic, breadcrumbs and wine vinegar.

AGNES SOREL — Mistress of King Charles VIII of France. Two dishes have been named after her: one is a chicken and mushroom cream soup, garnished with diced chicken and ox tongue; the other is a garnish for poultry consisting of tartlets filled with chicken mousse, ox tongue and mushrooms.

AGNOLOTTI/ANOLINI — Italian crescent or oblong-shaped pasta, which is stuffed with a meat or vegetable mixture before boiling. It is served with grated Parmesan cheese or as a garnish for soup.

AGRODOLCE — Italian for bittersweet. In agrodolce means cooked in a sauce made with brown sugar, currants, chocolate, candied peel, capers and vinegar. It is not to be confused with sweet and sour, as the emphasis is on the bitterness rather than the sweetness; it is used to counteract richness, in game for example.

AIGRE-DOUX, A L' — The French equivalent of agrodolce.

AIGRETTE — Small, light pastry, fried in oil. It is savoury, most often flavoured with cheese.

AIGUILLETTE — A thin slice cut lengthwise on the breast of poultry and game birds. Aiguillette de boeuf is a French term for the top part of the rump of beef; it is usually braised or poached. In Britain aiguillette of beef is part of the round.

AIGUISER — French word meaning to make sharp by adding lemon juice.

AIL, A L' — French for with garlic. As garlic is often used in French cuisine, specific mention of it indicates that the flavour is more pronounced than usual.

3

Ai

AILLADE — A sauce made with oil, vinegar and garlic, which is served with potatoes, or cold meat or fish. Also a garlic and walnut or hazelnut-flavoured mayonnaise, usually served with fish. A l'aillade is a term describing toasted French bread, rubbed with garlic and sprinkled with olive oil.

AIOLI — Garlic-flavoured sauce from Provence. Basically it consists of garlic pounded in a mortar and blended with olive oil and lemon juice, but there are many variations, including aiolis made with eggs, cream cheese and nuts. Aioli made with egg yolks is similar to mayonnaise in consistency: it is traditionally eaten with boiled fish, or, in a dish called Aioli Garni, it is served in a bowl in the middle of a large platter, on which is arranged boiled octopus, hard-boiled egg, snails, chick peas and various boiled vegetables. Aioli à la grecque is a sauce of garlic, oil, vinegar, lemon juice, breadcrumbs and ground nuts, which is served with fish.

AITCHBONE — Joint of beef suitable for braising. In Britain it is cut between the buttocks and rump; in the United States it is cut across the pelvis and includes part of the rump and top and bottom round.

AJADA — Spanish sauce of garlic and breadcrumbs.

AJOUTEES — Small garnish served with the vegetable course.

A LA — French for in the style of.

ALASKA, BAKED OR BOMBE — A dessert consisting of a sponge cake topped with ice cream and covered with meringue. The meringue must totally cover the ice cream and the dish must be cooked very fast, as otherwise the ice cream will melt and ruin the dessert. It was created at Delmonico's, the famous New York restaurant, to commemorate the purchase of Alaska by the United States, but it is based on the French dish, Omelette à la Norvégienne.

ALBERTINE — Way of serving poached fish with white wine sauce, flavoured with mushrooms, truffles and parsley.

ALBERT SAUCE — Butter sauce with horseradish, mustard, cream, consommé and breadcrumbs, thickened with egg yolk. It is served with beef. Named after Queen Victoria's consort, Prince Albert.

ALBIGEOISE — Classic garnish for meat dishes consisting of stuffed tomatoes, croquette potatoes and (sometimes) chopped ham.

4

ALBONI SAUCE — Demi-glace flavoured with game stock, juniper berries, pine kernels and redcurrant jelly. It is served with venison.

ALBUFERA — Several dishes are named after Marshal Suchet of France, who was created Duc d'Albuféra in 1812 after his victories in the Peninsular War. Albuféra sauce is a suprême sauce with veal stock and pimento butter added: it is served with poultry and sweetbreads.

ALBUMEN — The white of an egg.

ALBUMIN — A protein in blood, milk and egg white, which is soluble in water and coagulates when heated.

ALBUNDIGA — Spicy meatball made with ground beef and pork. Popular in Spain and Portugal.

ALCAZAR — Famous French pastry consisting of an almond and kirsch- flavoured sponge spread on apricot jam inside a pastry case. It is decorated with a lattice of almond paste, apricot jam and pistachio nuts or almonds. It is named after a Spanish castle.

AL DENTE — An Italian expression which literally means to the teeth. It describes the point at which food, usually pasta or rice, is completely cooked yet firm to the bite, not soft.

ALEXANDRA — This name has been given to a number of well-known dishes. It is a way of preparing fillet steak by sautéeing it and garnishing it with truffles and quartered artichoke bottoms; a suprême sauce with truffles for sautéed chicken; a mayonnaise with sieved hard-boiled egg yolk, chervil and mustard; a cold Mornay sauce with truffles and asparagus for fish or cold chicken; a chicken consommé with a garnish of shredded lettuce, shredded chicken and chicken quenelles; a tartlet filled with lobster mousse, cold poached egg and aspic; and a salad of lettuce, artichoke hearts, beetroot and celery in mayonnaise.

ALFREDO — Name given to pasta, especially fettucine, which has been tossed in cream, butter and grated Parmesan cheese. It was invented at the restaurant Alfredo of Rome, where Alfredo himself used to toss the pasta at the table, using a gold spoon and fork presented to him by an appreciative customer.

ALGERIENNE, A L' — Classic garnish for small cuts of meat consisting of sautéed whole tomatoes, sweet peppers and sweet potato croquettes. Eggs à l'Algérienne are fried and served with a purée of tomatoes, peppers and aubergines in tomato sauce. This name is also given to a salad of courgettes, tomatoes and sweet potatoes in aioli; sautéed chicken and aubergine in tomato sauce; and a sweet potato and hazelnut cream soup.

ALGONQUIN — Salad from the famous New York hotel, consisting of lettuces cut in half, grapefruit, pears, strips of green pepper, chopped egg white and vinaigrette.

ALHAMBRA — Bombe Alhambra is a strawberry ice cream with kirsch-soaked strawberries inside a vanilla ice. Alhambra is also the name of a garnish for meat of artichoke hearts, peppers and tomatoes, and it is a salad of beetroot, celery, artichoke hearts and lettuce in mayonnaise.

ALICE — A potato and turnip cream soup; a salad of orange, apple, grapefruit, nuts, cherries and peppers in vinaigrette; eating apples filled with chopped apple, redcurrants, walnuts and cream.

ALICUIT — A stew of turkey giblets and wings from the Languedoc region of France.

ALIGOT — Traditional dish of mashed potatoes mixed with a large amount of Cantal cheese, from the Auvergne region of France.

ALIOLI — Spanish version of Aioli. The Spanish claim to have invented the sauce, which is very ancient in origin, but it is better known to the world by the Provencal name.

ALIVENCI — Rumanian dish of cabbage leaves stuffed with a milk, cornflour and dill mixture, then baked. It is served with sour cream.

ALKANNA — Red food dye obtained from the roots of a plant of the borage family.

ALLA/AL' — Italian for in the style of.

ALLEMANDE — French for German. This is the more frequently used name for a sauce also known as sauce Parisienne, a white sauce enriched with egg yolks and cream, which is served with poultry, veal or egg dishes. The name is due to the blond colour of the sauce, not its origin, to distinguish it from Espagnole. A l'Allemande is a term applied to dishes involving German ingredients such as sauerkraut, smoked sausage, pickled pork or potato dumplings. It is also used to describe a garnish for meat of calf's kidney, peppers and onions with Madeira. Beef consommé à l'Allemande is garnished in France with red cabbage and frankfurters, but in Germany with tarragon and chervil quenelles.

ALLUMETTES — French for matchsticks. The word is used in cookery to describe potatoes which have been cut into little sticks like matchsticks, or tiny chips, and then deep-fried until crisp. The term can also mean strips of pastry stuffed with a savoury filling and served as an appetizer or party snack. There are also cakes called allumettes, which are strips of puff pastry spread with royal icing and baked.

ALMIBAR — Syrup essential in Spanish pâtisserie.

ALMOND PASTE — U.S. for marzipan.

ALMONDINE — *see* AMANDINE.

ALOUETTES SANS TETES — Literally larks without heads. This traditional French dish is stuffed rolls of beef in a tomato sauce. The rolls (ie. thin slices of meat rolled up) are placed upright in the serving dish suggesting headless birds.

ALPHONSO POTATOES — Cooked potatoes, diced and baked with milk, minced green pepper and grated Parmesan cheese on top.

ALSACIENNE — A sauce of mayonnaise made with soft-boiled eggs and flavoured with shallots, capers and herbs, which is also known as Sauce de Sorges. A l'Alsacienne is a term applied to dishes containing typically Alsatian ingredients like sauerkraut, ham, Strasbourg sausage and foie gras. Alsace is a region famous for its charcuterie.

AMANDINE — French garnish of flaked or shredded almonds, either toasted or lightly sautéed in butter. It is often accompanying fish, particularly trout, green vegetables such as broccoli or green beans, or sprinkled over soup.

AMATRICIANA, ALL' — Classic Italian way of serving spaghetti in a sauce of pancetta, tomatoes and onions.

AMAZONE — Garnish for meat of lentil fritters stuffed with morels and chestnut purée.

AMBASSADEUR — Garnish for meat of pommes duchesse and artichoke hearts filled with puréed mushrooms and grated horseradish. It is also a chicken broth garnished with puréed truffles, chopped mushrooms and chicken.

AMBASSADOR — Pea soup, enriched with egg yolk, to which rice shredded lettuce and chervil are added.

7

Am

AMBASSADRICE — Several dishes have been named in honour of ambassador's wives. A chicken-flavoured suprême sauce mixed with whipped cream. A garnish for braised chicken of suprême sauce, asparagus tips, lamb's sweetbreads larded with truffles, pastry barquettes filled with chicken livers, cock's combs and truffles. A garnish for steak of pounded chicken livers, sautéed mushrooms, pommes Parisienne, kidneys and braised lettuce. A chicken consommé garnished with cubes of chicken, mushrooms, truffles and peas. A soufflé flavoured with macaroons, rum, vanilla and almonds.

AMBIGU — Cold buffet containing more than one course served at the same time. The name refers to an evening meal, particularly to a supper served during the course of a party.

AMBROSIA — Simple dessert from the southern states of America, consisting of oranges and fresh coconut mixed together. In Greek mythology, Ambrosia was the food of the gods.

AMBROSINE, COUPE — Kirsch-soaked peaches mashed with raspberry ice cream, decorated with crème Chantilly and chopped roasted almonds.

AMELIE — Garnish for fish of white wine sauce lightly coloured with tomato purée, diced truffles mushrooms and potato croquettes.

AMERICAINE — Several dishes are described as being in the American style, the best known of which is Lobster à l'Américaine. This is a luxurious recipe, in which pieces of lobster are poached in a rich tomato, sherry and herb sauce. It was invented by a Parisian restaurateur, Pierre Fraisse, for an American customer. Other shellfish are sometimes treated in this way. Bombe Américaine is tangerine ice cream with pistachio nuts, inside a strawberry ice cream. Salade Américaine is a salad in which raw fruit is included.

AMIRAL — The name Amiral has been given to a number of fish dishes. A sauce for boiled fish of pounded anchovies, chives, capers, butter, lemon juice and peel. Scrambled eggs with lobster sauce with pieces of lobster in it. A garnish for fish of oysters, mussels, mushrooms, truffles and sauce Normande flavoured with crayfish. A fish consommé thickened with arrowroot and garnished with fish quenelles, diced lobster, sliced mushrooms, oysters, truffles cooked in Madeira and chervil.

AMOURETTE — Culinary name for the bone marrow from the spine of calves and sometimes oxen. It is very delicate in flavour and is usually poached. It may be used in pies or croquettes or as a garnish.

8

AMUSE-GUEULES — French term for hors d'oeuvres or cocktail snacks.

ANADAMA — Hearty yeast bread made with cornmeal and molasses, which gives it its characteristic yellow-brown colour. Early American in origin, the legend is that it was invented by a fisherman who had a lazy wife and therefore had to do his own baking. He named his bread after his wife, "Anna, damn her," and this has been modified to Anadama over the centuries.

ANCHOIADE/ANCHOYADE — Hors d'oeuvre from Provence, in the form of anchovy paste spread on a slice of bread, which has been toasted on the underside. A more elaborate version, Anchoiade à la Nicoise, has onions and tomatoes on top of the anchovy paste.

ANCIENNE, A L' — Meaning in the old style. As a culinary term it is used to describe braised dishes, ragouts, blanquettes and fricassées, and denotes a mixed garnish.

ANDALOUSE — A sauce of mayonnaise mixed with tomato purée and diced peppers. A l'Andalouse is a garnish for meat or poultry of rice-shaped pepper halves, sliced aubergines and tomatoes, and sometimes small sausages. Andalouse is also a chicken consommé with tiny dumplings, rice, tomatoes and ham. Coupe Andalouse is orange segments soaked in maraschino, covered with lemon ice.

ANDOUILLE — Large black-skinned sausage from Normandy. It is made from the large intestines and stomach of a pig. Usually sold cooked and eaten cold, cut into thin slices, it is occasionally sold uncooked, in which case it is poached and then grilled at home.

ANDOUILLETTE — French sausage made from the small intestine of a pig. Mild flavoured, andouillettes are normally sold poached and then grilled at home.

ANGEL CAKE — American cake which is pure white in colour and very light in texture. It is made with stiffly beaten egg whites, flour and sugar, and is decorated with swirls of white frosting.

ANGEL ON HORSEBACK — Hot appetizer consisting of an oyster wrapped in a rasher of bacon, grilled, then served on toast.

ANGLAISE, A L' — In the English style can mean two quite different cooking methods. Either food cooked in water and stock, such as boiled vegetables, or food, especially fish, which has been dipped in beaten egg, coated with breadcrumbs, then fried.

ANIMELLE — Culinary term for ram's testicles. These were once popular in Southern Europe and are still eaten in the Middle East.

ANJOU — Game consommé with asparagus tips, game quenelles and rice.

ANNA, POMMES DE TERRE — Raw potatoes thinly sliced and layered in a casserole with plenty of butter and seasoning, then baked until golden brown. The resulting potato cake is turned out to serve and cut into wedges like a cake. Named after Anna Deslions, a famous courtesan, by chef Dugléré of the Café Anglais in Paris.

ANNATTO — Orange-yellow food dye obtained from a South American tree.

ANNETTE, POMMES DE TERRE — Variation of pommes de terre Anna, with the potatoes cut into julienne strips instead of sliced.

ANOLINI — *See* AGNOLOTTI.

ANSJOVISOGA — Swedish for anchovy eye. A raw egg yolk is placed in the centre of a plate and surrounded with chopped tomato, radish, hard-boiled egg white and anchovy fillets. The diner then mixes the ingredients himself. Served as an hors d'oeuvre.

ANTIBOISE — Mayonnaise with tomato purée, anchovy essence and tarragon. Served with fish.

ANTIN — Madeira sauce with shallots, mushrooms, truffles and parsley.

ANTIPASTO — Italian for before the pasta: in other words, hors d'oeuvre. Antipasto can consist of any of a wide variety of ingredients including salami, prosciutto, parma ham, tuna, and pickled vegetables, lightly dressed in oil and vinegar, and arranged on one large serving platter.

ANTOINETTE — Method of preparing fish with herb sauce, anchovy butter, capers and shrimps.

ANVEROISE, A L' — Garnish for meat, especially sweetbreads, and eggs, of hop stalks in butter or cream and potatoes fried in butter.

ANZAC BISCUITS — Coconut and oat biscuits from New Zealand.

APERITIF — French term for a drink taken before a meal to stimulate the appetite.

APHELIA — *See* AFELIA.

APLATIR — French culinary term meaning to beat meat with a mallet to tenderize it.

APPAREIL — French term used to describe the mixed preparations necessary for the making of a dish; for example, a cake mixture before cooking.

APPRET — French term for a finished culinary preparation. It also means the length of time needed for a yeast dough to rise.

APRICOTING — *See* ABRICOTER.

ARBROATH SMOKIE — Smoked haddock in the form of a beheaded and gutted, but otherwise whole fish. It is hot smoked, but heated to serve. It has a particularly creamy texture.

ARCHIDUC — A supreme sauce with champagne added. A l'Archiduc is a garnish for meat of duchess potatoes, croquettes of calves' brains, truffles and a sauce of sherry, cream, stock and paprika.

ARCHIDUCHESSE, A L' — Garnish for hard-boiled or scrambled egg of diced ham, mushrooms, paprika, potato croquettes and asparagus tips.

ARDENNAISE, A L' — A way of preparing pork chops with juniper berries, onion and potato. This expression may also be used to mean thrush, blackbird or other small bird cooked in a casserole with juniper berries. Two soups are described as in the Ardennes style, a thick soup of leeks, endives and potato, and a pheasant soup flavoured with kidney and port.

ARGENTEUIL — Asparagus from the region of the same name in France is regarded as the finest in the world: as a culinary term the word applies to a garnish of asparagus.

ARIEGEOISE,A L' — A garnish of pickled pork, kidney beans and cabbage. The Ariège region of France is famous for its pork, ham and geese.

ARLESIENNE, A L' — In the Arles' style may mean one of three different garnishes involving tomatoes. One consists of slices of fried tomatoes, aubergines and onions; another is tiny whole tomatoes fried in butter and pickled chicory hearts sauteed in oil; the third is tomatoes stuffed with rice and accompanied by new potatoes and olives filled with a chicken and anchovy mixture. Potage à l'Arlesienne, however, is a soup of haricot beans and tapioca.

ARMENIENNE, A L' — Armenian style often refers to a sauce or stuffing containing pine kernals and currants.

11

ARMENONVILLE — A garnish for large cuts of meat of sautéed potato balls, quartered artichoke hearts, tomatoes and French beans. Pommes de terre Armenonville is pommes de terre Anna with morels. The name is also given to a thick soup of peas and chervil.

ARMORICAINE, A L' — Armorica was the old name for Brittany. This term is usually applied to shellfish and is often confused with A l'Americaine: the ingredients (olive oil, garlic and tomatoes) are the same and are not typical of Brittany.

ARNOLD BENNETT — Omelette Arnold Bennett is a rich omelette filled with smoked haddock and cheese sauce, which is browned under the grill just before serving. It was first made for the novelist Arnold Bennett at the Savoy Grill in London. Soufflé Arnold Bennett is one of the derivatives of the famous omelette, using the same ingredients.

AROMA — The characteristic fragrance of a dish or an item of food.

AROMATICS — Substances which give out an odour of varying degrees of sweetness and which are used to add flavour to food, eg. herbs, spices, chocolate, coffee, flower water, zest etc.

ARROSER — French culinary term meaning to baste.

ARTESIENNE, A L' — The name given to a soup of haricot beans and tapioca.

ARTOIS, D' — A garnish for small cuts of meat of potato cases filled with green peas and covered with Madeira sauce. It is also a garnish for poultry of glazed carrots, onions and artichoke hearts.

ASBESTOS MAT — A square of asbestos placed under a saucepan when a very low heat is required or to stop an ovenproof but not fireproof casserole cracking when it is used on top of the stove.

ASCORBIC ACID — Vitamin C.

ASHLEY BREAD — Bread made with rice flour from the southern states of America.

ASPIC — Savoury jelly made from strong chicken, beef, veal or fish stock. Normally the bones make the stock very gelatinous, but if extra setting properties are needed a little gelatine may be added. Aspic is transparent and is used mainly for decorative purposes, so it is usually clarified before being allowed to set. It can be used like a glaze over cold dishes or allowed to set, then chopped up and used to make a decorative border.

ASSIETTE ANGLAISE — A French expression which literally means English plate, but as a culinary term it describes a selection of cold meats served on one plate. It usually consists of a slice of roast beef, a slice of ox tongue and a slice of brawn or galantine. It is a luncheon dish.

ASSIETTE VOLANTE — A selection of cold, salty foods, cut in thin slices and arranged on one plate as an hors d'oeuvre.

ATHENIENNE, A L' — Athenian style is typified by onions, aubergines, tomatoes, sweet peppers and olive oil in the recipe.

ATTELET — A skewer with an ornamental top used for purely decorative purposes.

ATTENDU — French culinary term which is applied to food for which one has to wait to eat while it improves in flavour; for example, game is hung before being cooked and eaten.

ATTEREAU — Pieces of food threaded on skewer, then dipped into a sauce, rolled in breadcrumbs and, usually, deep-fried. The food may be sweet or savoury.

AUFSCHNITT — German term for a variety of cold meats and sausages.

AUGUSTA, D' — Garnish for fish poached in white wine of sliced boletus (a fungus) and chopped shallots in Mornay sauce.

AULAGNIER, D' — The name of a clear beef soup garnished with cabbage and peas.

AUMALE, D' — Method of scrambling eggs with ox tongue and truffles. It is served with veal kidneys and Madeira sauce.

AUMONIERE, OEUFS FRIT EN — Fried egg with fried bread, cheese and ham, wrapped in a pancake to resemble an almsgiving purse.

AURORE — A velouté sauce, flavoured with tomato purée, which is good with fish, meat, eggs or vegetables. It is named after the mother of gourmet Brillat-Savarin.

AUTRICHIENNE, A L' — Austrian style is characterized by the prescence of paprika and/or sour cream and sometimes fennel in the dish.

AUVERGNATE, A L' — The name of a soup made from a pig's head, lentils, leeks and potato.

Au

AVGOLEMONO — A sauce of egg yolks and lemon juice from Greece. The sauce is often used as the basis for a soup of the same name.

AXONGE — French term for rendered down fat from round the kidneys of a pig. It is considered to be especially good for frying.

BABA — A cake made with a yeast dough mixed with raisins, which is steeped in rum or sometimes kirsch after cooking. It is said to have been invented in the eighteenth century by King Stanislaus Leszcynski of Poland, during his exile in France, when he sprinkled a Kugelhopf with rum and set it alight. He named his creation after Ali-Baba, hero of his favourite book, *1001 Nights*. A baba is made in a deep fluted mould and may be large or small. The ring-shaped cake without raisins often called a Rum Baba is technically a small Savarin.

BACALAO/BACALHAU — Spanish/Portuguese dish of salt cod. There are reputedly 365 different ways of cooking what was once a staple food – one for every day of the year.

BACON — The cured side of a pig.

BAECKENOFFE — German for baker's oven. This dish, which is popular in Alsace-Lorraine as well as Germany, consists of layers of mixed meats and vegetables cooked very slowly after being marinated. Traditionally a baker's oven was used as it stayed warm for hours after the bread had been baked.

BAGEL — Jewish bread roll in the shape of a ring, the dough is dropped in boiling water for a few seconds to puff it up before baking. Poppy seeds or rock salt crystals are sprinkled over.

BAGNA CAUDA — Italian for hot bath. This speciality from the Piedmont district of Italy is a sauce of butter, oil, garlic and crushed anchovy fillets. It is served at the table in a bowl over a spirit lamp to keep it hot. A selection of raw vegetables are dipped into it and eaten as an hors d'oeuvre.

BAGRATION — The name of a Russian general who fought against Napoleon has been given to a veal soup and a vegetable salad. Both dishes contain macaroni.

BAGUETTE — French for stick. A long (25 in., 65 cm.) thin loaf of French bread with diagonal slashes on top, a hard crust and a wide-holed crumb. It is also known as French Stick.

BAIN-MARIE — Device for keeping food warm or cooking it very slowly. The bowl or pan containing the food is placed in a pan of hot or gently simmering water, which can be in the oven or over direct heat. It is useful for cooking egg custards and sauces which might curdle if exposed to direct heat. Alchemists found that sea (la mer) water does not evaporate as quickly as fresh water and boils at a higher temperature, so the original bain-marie was invented to aid a chemical experiment. The idea of a water bath was later borrowed by an unknown cook. This explanation of the origin of the bain-marie is the most plausible, though by no means the only one. The name literally means Mary-bath in French and in some legends the Virgin Mary figures in the invention of the utensil.

BAISER — French for kiss, a baiser is two small meringues sandwiched together with cream.

BAKE BLIND — To cook, or partially cook, an empty pastry case. This method is employed when the filling required little or no cooking. To retain the shape of the case it is filled with dried beans or uncooked rice for part of the cooking time; these are removed so that the base can crispen.

BAKED ALASKA — See ALASKA.

BAKEWELL PUDDING/TART — Dessert from Derbyshire, created when the cook at the Rutland Arms in Bakewell forgot to add the flour when making an almond sponge. The mixture of eggs, sugar, butter and ground almonds is cooked over a layer of raspberry jam inside a pastry case.

BAKING — Any method of cooking in which food comes into contact with dry heat. This is usually in the oven, but can also mean on a griddle. Often the term applies to just bread and cakes.

BAKING POWDER — Raising agent used in baking. It is a mixture of alkaline and acid substances, which, when added to liquid, produces carbon dioxide and causes the cake etc. to rise.

BAKING SODA — U.S. for bicarbonate of soda.

BAKLAVA — A pastry from the Middle East composed of at least 19 layers of phyllo pastry, filled with chopped nuts and butter, and drenched in honey syrup. It is baked in a large shallow tray and cut into squares, diamonds or rectangles to serve. It is crispy yet moist: this is achieved by pouring cool syrup over hot pastry or hot syrup over cool pastry.

Ba

BALACHAN/BALACHONG — Condiment made from dried shrimps and prawns, which is used widely in Indonesian and South-East Asian cooking.

BALACHOW/BALICHOW — Strongly-flavoured relish made with prawns, from Southern India.

BALLOTTINE — French for a small bundle. A ballottine is meat, fish, game or poultry which is boned, stuffed and rolled into a bundle. It is usually served hot but can be eaten cold.

BALMORAL LOAF — Bread made in a special mould with a ridged semi- circular cylinder placed on a baking tray to give a flat bottom when turned out. The corrugations are slice-sized. The mould, which is also used for baking cakes, is sometimes called a toast rack tin.

BALONEY — American corruption of Bologna sausage, ie. Mortadella.

BALTI — Indian dish of meat cubes marinated, charcoal grilled then simmered in sauce. The term has recently broadened to describe a stir-fry curry cooked in a balti pan (similar to a wok, but with two small handles) and served with nan bread rather than rice. The popularity of the balti was a restaurant phenomenon of the 1980s and started in Birmingham.

BANBURY CAKE — Traditional English pastry. A flat, oval of puff pastry filled with mixed fruit. In the seventeenth century this was the speciality of a cake shop in Banbury, Oxfordshire.

BANNETON — Small reed basket used for raising bread dough. The basket leaves an attractive pattern on the bread.

BANNOCK — Scottish word for a variety of cakes, but especially for an oval-shaped griddle cake made with oatmeal or barley meal.

BANOFFEE PIE — Dessert comprising a thick layer of toffee-flavoured custard inside a pastry case, topped with sliced bananas and coffee-flavoured whipped cream.

BANQUIERE — A suprême sauce with Madeira, chopped truffles, veal jus, tomato purée and butter added. A la Banquière is a classic garnish for chicken, sweetbreads and vol-au-vent of quenelles, mushrooms, truffles and banquière sauce.

BAP — Soft, floury bread roll from Scotland.

BARA BRITH — A rich, spicy fruit bread, also known as speckled bread, which is a traditional Welsh recipe. Bara means bread and Brith means currants, although a mixture of dried fruit of usually used.

BARAQUILLE — Small triangular pastry, filled with a savoury mixture and served hot as an hors d'oeuvre.

BARANTE, OMELETTE — A luxury omelette filled with lobster meat, mushrooms and cream. The filled omelette is coated with Mornay sauce and browned under a grill before serving, garnished with lobster. Baron de Barante was a famous gourmet in nineteenth century France. This dish was King Edward VII's favourite omelette.

BARBE A PAPA — Candy floss. This spectacular confection of pink spun sugar was first demonstrated at the Paris Exhibition of 1900.

BARBECUE — Barbecuing is cooking food, mostly meat, out-of-doors over an open fire or charcoal grill. A barbecue is also the brazier the food is cooked on and is the open air party at which such food is served. Barbecue sauce is any spicy, tomatoey, sweet and sour sauce served with barbecued meat and often also used as a marinade. The name comes from the French barbe-à-queue, meaning beard to tail, the way a whole pig was impaled on a spit for roasting.

BARD — To cover the breast of poultry or game birds with pork fat or bacon while roasting. A bard is a horse's armoured breast plate.

BARDE — Thinly sliced pork fat sold in a sheet in France.

BARFI — Indian confection made with condensed milk and sugar. It is similar to fudge in texture and is flavoured with cardamom and pistachio nuts or almonds.

BARLEY SUGAR — Traditional English confection made by melting sugar until it caramelizes and forms coarse grains. When it sets it is clear and hard. It was originally made with a barley extract in place of sugar, hence the name.

BARMBRACK — Traditional spicy fruit bread from Ireland, similar to the Welsh Bara Brith in appearance, but made by a different method: the sugar, fat, fruit and spice are added to the risen dough. Scotland has a slightly richer version with the same name, which is flavoured with caraway seeds and black treacle. In gaelic, barm means the froth on fermenting yeast.

BARON — A baron of beef is a double sirloin, ie. both sirloins left uncut along the backbone. A baron of lamb or mutton is a saddle and two legs. The baron of beef is supposed to have been given its title by Henry VIII.

BARQUETTE — Little boat in French, this is a pastry tartlet made in a special boat-shaped mould about 2 inches (5 cm) long. It can be used for a cocktail savoury or petit four, depending on the filling.

BARREL — Cylindrical loaf of bread baked in a ridged tin for convenient round slices.

BARSZCZ — A Polish version of Borscht, with beans, cabbage, apple and tomato added.

BASQUAISE — The Basque country, an area in both France and Spain, has its own style of cooking, with influences from both countries. Mushrooms and red peppers are often found in their local recipes. A la Basquaise is a classic garnish for large cuts of meat, consisting of fried cepes and Anna potatoes cooked in dariole moulds, sprinkled with chopped Bayonne ham.

BASSINE — Deep round copper bowl for whisking egg whites.

BASTE — To keep moist during roasting by spooning hot fat or meat juices over it.

BAT — To flatten fillets of meat, poultry or fish with a flat, heavy, wooden or metal object. The same word is also a French culinary term for the tail of a fish.

BATALIERE, A LA — Garnish for fish of mushrooms, baby onions, fried eggs and crayfish. Also a way of serving fish fillets on tartlets filled with shrimps and mussels in white wine sauce, with chopped herbs and fried gudgeon.

BATARD — French for bastard, this is the name given to a smaller version of the baguette (which is too long for the domestic oven). The bâtard is about two-thirds the length of the baguette.

BATARDE — French sauce which is a mock Hollandaise. It is made with beurre manie and stock, to which an egg yolk, butter, cream and lemon juice are added for flavour.

BATCH — Tall loaf of bread baked without a tin in a batch with others placed so that the sides touch in the oven. Batches have to be split apart after baking. Only the top and bottom have crusts.

BATH BUN — Small yeast cake flavoured with candied peel, with a sugar glaze on top.

BATH CHAP — *See* CHAP.

BATH OLIVER — Crisp water biscuit served with cheese. Invented by Dr. William Oliver of Bath.

BATON/BATONNET — Describes the stick-like shape of the food in question.

BATON DE JACOB — Caramel topped èclair.

BATTENBURG CAKE — Genoese baked in a loaf tin, divided lengthwise. Half the mixture is coloured pink. The cooled cake is cut and reassembled to form a checkerboard effect when sliced. The cake is wrapped in marzipan.

BATTER — A mixture of flour and liquid, which is thin enough to pour. The liquid is usually eggs and milk or water, but proportions vary according to its purpose. Pancakes are made with whole eggs blended with flour and enough milk to produce a thin smooth batter that pours like cream. Batter puddings are heavier, therefore more flour is used. Fritters need to be crisp and light so water or beer replaces the milk and the egg yolks are left out. All batters should be left to rest for an hour or so before cooking to reduce the elasticity of the gluten in the flour.

BATTERIE DE CUISINE — French for cooking utensils.

BATTUTO — A mixture of chopped onion, garlic, parsley, celery leaves, and bacon or ham, which is used as a foundation for soups and stews in Italian cooking.

BAUERNFRUHSTUCK — German for farmer's breakfast. This is an omelette filled with fried potato cubes, fried bread cubes and fried onion. One large omelette is made to feed several people, it is then served flat on the plate and cut into wedges.

BAVAROISE — Also known as Bavarian cream, this is a dessert of egg custard mixed with whipped cream and flavouring, and lightly set with gelatine. It is usually made in a decorative mould and turned out to serve. Bavaroise is also the name for a sauce of Hollandaise flavoured with crayfish, and a garnish of crayfish tails which is used for fish. There is also an alcoholic hot milk drink called Bavaroise.

BAYONNAISE, A LA — A garnish for meat of cooked macaroni in a cream sauce with a julienne of Bayonne ham. As a variation, the macaroni may be made into a croquette, in which case Madeira sauce is also served.

BEACH SALAD — Salad from the United States comprising half a grapefruit, with lettuce leaves arranged between the shell and the grapefruit segments, topped with maraschino cherries and dressed with a mixture of grapefruit juice, oil, salt and pepper.

19

Be

BEAN CURD — Often featured in Chinese cookery, bean curd is made from ground soya beans and water. The mixture sets and is usually sold cut into cubes. It can also be deep-fried and sold as puffed bean curd, or dried and sold in sheets which have to be moistened before use.

BEARNAISE — A version of Hollandaise sauce with shallots, herbs and meat juices, which is served with plainly cooked meat.

BEAR'S PAW — American term for a mixture of ground nuts, sugar, butter and spice which is used to stuff Danish Pastries.

BEAT — To incorporate air into food by mixing it vigorously. This may be done with a wooden spoon, a fork or a mechanical beater.

BEATILLE — French word meaning titbits, used as a culinary term to describe a mixture of sweetbreads, cock's combs, kidneys and mushrooms, bound in a velouté sauce.

BEATRIX — A garnish for large cuts of meat consisting of morels cooked in butter or quartered artichoke bottoms, small carrots and fondant potatoes.

BEAUHARNAIS, A LA — Classic garnish for small cuts of meat, especially tournedos, of artichoke hearts, stuffed mushrooms, little potato balls and béarnaise sauce with a purée of tarragon.

BEAUME SCALE — Density saccharometer for measuring the density of the sugar in sorbet syrup. 30° Beaumé is the usual reading: if it is higher the sorbet will not set, if it is lower it will become icy and heavy.

BEAU SEJOUR — French for beautiful sojourn, this refers to a simple but classic garnish for meat of a clove of garlic and a bayleaf. These are not eaten and only impart a slight flavour.

BEAUVILLIERS — Famous restaurant in Paris before and after the French Revolution, which gave its name to two dishes. One is a garnish for a large piece of braised meat, consisting of spinach kromeskies, tomatoes stuffed with a purée of brains and salsify cooked in butter. The other is an elaborate cake made with ground almonds, egg whites, whole eggs, sugar and flour, baked in a trois frères mould and iced with kirsch icing.

BEC FIN — Familiar French term for a gourmet.

BECHAMEL — Major sauce which is the base for many other sauces. It is a white sauce made with a fat and flour roux, to which milk flavoured with herbs and vegetables is added. This is correctly known a béchamel maigre. A version using meat or poultry stock to replace some of the milk is called a béchamel grasse. The sauce is named after Louis de Béchameil, a financier and politian at the court of Louis XIV, though it was probably invented by one of the royal chefs.

BEESTINGS — Thick milk produced by a cow who has just calved. It clots when heated and is used in milk puddings for extra richness.

BEIGNET — Food dipped in batter and deep fried. The word is French, but is believed to come from the Celtic for swelling.

BELLE HELENE — Garnish for meat joints of grilled mushrooms stuffed with cooked tomato or green peas, carrots and potato croquettes. Pears Belle Hélène is a French dessert of pears poached in a vanilla syrup, then coated with chocolate sauce. Gâteau Belle Hélène is a later invention, consisting of a chocolate sponge cake filled and/or decorated with dessert pears and vanilla-flavoured whipped cream. Named after Offenbach's operetta *La Belle Hélène* (1864).

BELLY — Fatty pork joint, which is often salted and boiled.

BENEDICT — Eggs Benedict is simply poached eggs with spinach, coated with Hollandaise sauce. It was created in 1760 for Pope Benedict XIII by an unknown Vatican chef. Today it is a popular brunch dish in the United States, where it was first served to Diamond Jim Brady, the railroad tycoon and notorious glutton.

BENEDICTINE — A la benedictine is a garnish for fish and eggs consisting of a brandade of cod and truffles. It is named after the Benedictine order of monks. A benedictine is also a rich cake flavoured with almonds and Benedictine liqueur.

BERCHOUX — Sauce Allemande with herb butter and cream. Also a game consommé garnished with cubed quail, sliced mushrooms and truffles and chestnut royale. Joseph Berchoux was a French gastronome.

BERCY — Sauce made with a base of either velouté or brown sauce, to which white wine and shallots are added. It is named after the wine depots on the eastern side of Paris.

BERNER PLATTE — Swiss dish from Berne of beef, pig's trotter, bacon, sausage and onion, served in a casserole together.

BERNY — Tiny balls of potato and truffle, coated in chopped almonds and deep-fried. Also a garnish for game of Berny potatoes and tartlets filled with chestnut and lentil purée. Also beef consommé garnished with pommes dauphine, chopped almonds and truffle.

BERRICHONNE, A LA — Garnish for joints of meat, particularly mutton, consisting of braised cabbage, baby onions, chestnuts and streaky bacon rashers. Also a way of cooking potatoes cut into olive shapes, with onion and bacon.

BESAN FLOUR — *See* GRAM FLOUR.

BEST END OF NECK — Cut of lamb or veal from the lower end of the neck. It can be roasted whole or cut into cutlets, and is also used to make Crown roast and Guard of honour.

BEURRE MANIE — Butter and flour kneaded together in proportions of two (butter) to one (flour), which is added in tiny pieces, off the heat, to a sauce to thicken it.

BEURRE NOIR — Also known by its English name, black butter, this is a sauce for eggs, fish and vegetables. Butter is heated until it burns dark brown, then vinegar and seasoning are added and it is cooked until reduced by half.

BEURRE POMMADE — Softened butter.

BHOONA/BHUNA — Indian cookery term meaning the process of cooking a spice paste in hot oil. A bhoona curry is usually dry and cooked with coconut.

BIARROTTE — Garnish for small cuts of meat, composed of potato galettes topped with cepes.

BICARBONATE OF SODA — Also known as baking soda or sodium bicarbonate. It gives off carbon dioxide when mixed with an acid (lemon juice, vinegar, sour milk, cream of tartar etc) and is used as a raising agent in baking.

BIERWURST — German for beer sausage as it was originally made with ham which had been marinated in beer. Today it is a coarse-textured, smoked sausage made of minced pork, flavoured with garlic and mustard seeds.

BIGARADE — Espagnole sauce flavoured with bitter orange. Often served with roast duck to counteract the richness.

BIGOS — Polish dish using cooked meat, sauerkraut, apples and onions baked together.

BILLI BI — Rich cream of mussel soup from the South of France.

BILTONG — Strips of dried beef which are considered a great delcacy in South Africa. Ostrich meat may also be treated in the same way.

BIND — To moisten a mixture in order to hold it together. This may be done with a thick sauce or with beaten egg.

BIRD'S NEST SOUP — Speciality of China. It is a soup made with the liquor from cooking a dried bird's nest. Saliva from a species of swallow cements the nest and gives the soup its characteristic taste. Chopped meat or poultry is often added to the soup.

BIRNBROT — Swiss fruit bread. An egg-enriched yeast dough is rolled around a filling of chopped prunes, pears, raisins and walnuts like a Swiss roll.

BIRYANI/BYRIANI — Indian dish of baked saffron rice with spiced meat and/or vegetables. Variations are endless. To be correct, it should be garnished with edible silver foil.

BISCUIT — Small crisp cake, also known as a cookie, which comes in very many varieties – bar cookies, drop cookies, shaped cookies, rolled cookies, piped cookies, refrigerator biscuits, sweet and savoury types. The word comes from the French bis cuit, meaning twice cooked. The biscuit was developed from the small hard cakes known as hard tack, which were taken on board ship for long voyages: they were cooked before the journey began to prevent them going mouldy, then cooked again as required to freshen them up. Biscuit is also a term used in French pâtisserie to describe a basic cake mixture made with the same ingredients and proportions as genoise, but the eggs are separated so the beaten egg whites make it drier and lighter than a genoise. It is used for sponge fingers. In the United States a biscuit describes a type of scone, which is eaten with savoury foods to mop up the sauce.

BISMARCK — This is the correct name for a doughnut which has been filled with jam before frying. A Bismarck herring has been soaked in vinegar overnight, then filleted and arranged in a deep dish with a little onion and seasoning. It is left for 24 hours before eating. A Bismarck schnitzel is coated in egg and breadcrumbs, fried and garnished with plover's eggs, mushrooms, truffles and tomato sauce. These dishes are named after the German statesman.

BISQUE — Very rich shellfish soup made with wine, brandy and cream. Lobster is the most usual ingredient.

Bi

BISTAYLA/BISTEEYA — Moroccan pigeon or chicken pie, made with very thin pastry. Traditionally, it is never less than 20 inches (50 cm) in diameter and is fried on a special griddle (although it can be baked). The filling is arranged in three layers: spicy meat, then an egg, lemon and onion mixture, then toasted, sweetened almonds. The top crust is decorated with a criss-cross pattern and is dusted with cinnamon and sugar.

BITOK — Russian meatball. It is small, slightly flattened, fried and served with a piquant sour cream sauce.

BLACK BOTTOM PIE — Rich chocolate pie from Mississippi. It is named after the bottom lands in the Mississippi delta. A ginger biscuit crust contains a layers of chocolate custard, a layer of bourbon-flavoured custard and a layer of whipped cream, which is decorated with chocolate caraque.

BLACK BUN — Traditional Scottish cake, consisting of a dark, spicy cake mixture enclosed in shortcrust pastry. The cake is flavoured with treacle and whisky, and is eaten at the stroke of midnight on New Year's Eve with a glass of whisky.

BLACK PUDDING — Cooked sausage made with chopped pork fat and blood, mixed with cereal, onion and spices. It may be eaten cold or hot (fried in slices). It developed in the Middle Ages when pigs were slaughtered every autumn and every part was used to make something edible that would keep for the winter.

BLADE — Pork joint cut from the top neck. It is often boned, and is best either slow roasted or braised.

BLANC — The French name for water with salt, lemon juice and flour added to it. Food which discolours is prevented from so doing by preliminary cooking in this liquid. Au blanc may mean cooked in the above liquid or served in a white sauce.

BLANCH — To immerse food in boiling water for a very short time. This may be done for one of several reasons: to remove salt or another strong flavour; to loosen the skin of fruit or nuts; to firm sweetbreads or brains; to set the bright colour of green vegetables.

BLANCHIR — French term meaning to whisk egg yolks and sugar until foamy.

BLANCMANGE — French for something white to eat, the present-day moulded cold dessert made with cornflour, flavouring and milk, bears little relation to the original – a sweetened concoction of pounded chicken and almonds. Somewhere between the two is the classic blancmange, a Bavaroise made with almond milk, gelatine and whipped cream.

BLANQUETTE — White ragoût of veal, chicken or lamb, bound with a liaison of cream and egg yolk, garnished with whole baby onions and mushrooms.

BLAZE — U.S. for flamber.

BLEU, AU — Method of cooking freshly caught fish, especially trout, in water to which vinegar is added: the fish's skin then becomes slightly blue, hence the name.

BLIMPY — Alternative New York name for a hero.

BLINI — Small, thick pancake from Russia, made with buckwheat flour and yeast. Blinis are served stacked inside a cloth with various cold accompaniments such as smoked salmon, herrings, sardines, hard-boiled eggs and sour cream, which are spread on the hot pancake.

BLINTZE — Jewish pancakes made with matzo flour, which are filled after cooking by folding the pancake over the filling like a parcel, and then fried again. The most common filling is a rich sweet curd cheese filling.

BLITZTORTE — German cake. Meringue is spread over uncooked cake mixture in sandwich tins, almonds are sprinkled on, then the cakes are baked. The two halves are sandwiched together, meringue side out, with whipped cream and a sharp fruit such as redcurrants or pineapple.

BLOATER — Smoked herring, which has not been gutted before drying and light smoking, and therefore has a strong taste and does not keep long. It is a speciality of the east coast fishing town of Great Yarmouth, where it has been made since the seventeenth century.

BLONDIR — French culinary term meaning to shallow fry to a light colour.

BLOOMER — Crusty loaf of bread, which has several diagonal slashes on the top for maximum crustiness.

BLOQUE — French term meaning the point at which melted chocolate becomes too solid to spread.

B.L.T. — Bacon, lettuce and tomato sandwich. The bread is usually toasted and mayonnaise is spread over the lettuce. Always referred to by its initials, a B.L.T. is a popular American snack.

BLUTWURST — German black pudding.

BOBOTIE — South African dish of minced beef baked in a casserole with curry powder, raisins and nuts.

BOCADILLO — Spanish word or a snack, often a sandwich.

Bo

BOCCONCINO — Italian for delicious little piece of veal. It is a small slice of veal, a slice of raw ham and a slice of gruyère cheese, rolled and tied up with string, coated in egg and breadcrumbs and deep-fried. The cheese is slightly melted by the time the meats are cooked. The string is removed after cooking and the bocconcino is served on a croûte.

BOHEMIENNE — The name given to a dish of chicken sautéed with paprika, peppers, tomatoes, garlic, onion and fennel; also a garnish of rice, tomatoes and onion rings; baked potatoes stuffed with sausage meat; and mayonnaise with cream and tarragon vinegar added.

BOILED DRESSING — Salad dressing made with egg, milk, sugar, flour, vinegar and mustard. The ingredients are cooked in a double boiler until thick. It is served cold.

BOILING — Simple method of cooking, whereby food is immersed and cooked in water which is at boiling point. This is a popular method of cooking vegetables. Many foods described as boiled, eg. boiled chicken, are really simmered after they have been brought to the boil.

BOISTELLE — Name given to chicken breasts which are stuffed with chicken forcemeat, fried and served with mushrooms.

BOLLITO MISTO — Mixed boiled meats. This Italian dish is usually served with a green sauce.

BOLOGNA — Sausage made with lightly seasoned, smoked pork, beef and veal, which is named after the Italian town where it was first made. A corruption of the word, Baloney, is often used instead.

BOLOGNESE — Famous meat sauce usually served with pasta.

BOMBAY DUCK — Dried fish used for flavouring curries.

BOMBE — Iced pudding made in a special mould – though a conical mould often replaces the original sphere. This mould was designed to be easily buried in a bucket of ice and salt – then the only method of freezing. A bombe consists of two layers, a lining and a filling. It is turned out to serve.

BONAPARTE — Chicken consommé with chicken quennelles.

BONDIOLA — Cured shoulder of pork from Parma, Italy.

BONING — Removing the bones from a joint of meat, poultry or fish without damaging the flesh.

BONNE BOUCHE — French term for a savoury mouthful, such as a cocktail snack or hors d'oeuvre.

26

BONNE FEMME — French for good wife. This expression is applied to dishes cooked in a homely, unpretentious way, often including potatoes.

BONNEFOY — A way of cooking fish in the oven with onions, mushrooms, claret and bonnefoy sauce. The sauce is a demi-glace flavoured with shallots, beef marrow and white wine. It is served with meat or grilled fish.

BONVALET — Another name for Beauvilliers gâteau.

BOOKMAKER'S SANDWICH — Steak, spread with mustard, inside a buttered French loaf or roll. The bread is pressed onto the meat so that the juices penetrate the bread.

BORD-DE-PLAT — Device such as a ruff of paper for protecting the border of a dish on which food in a sauce is being served.

BORDELAISE — A la Bordelaise describes four different ways of preparing food: a garnish of artichokes and potatoes; the prescence of cèpes in the dish; the addition of a mirepoix; served with sauce Bordelaise. The sauce is a demi-glace with red wine and bone marrow added. A simplified version is sometimes made with just thickened, reduced red wine and meat glaze.

BORDURE — Plain ring mould with a flat top. It is used for savoury creams and jellies. Meat or fish are usually arranged on top.

BOREK — Turkish savoury pastry made with phyllo pastry and filled with a cheese or meat mixture. It may be small and round or cylindrical, in which case it is fried, or large, round and baked in the oven. Variations are found all over the Middle East.

BORGHESE, CONSOMMÉ — Clear chicken soup with strips of chicken and asparagus tips.

BORGIA, OEUF — Poached egg on a baked tomato half, covered with béchamel sauce.

BORTSCH/BORSCH — Beetroot soup from the Ukraine. The word means beetroot in Ukrainian. It is served with a dollop of sour cream in the middle of each dish. There are many variations on the basic bortsch in Russia and Poland.

BOSAIOLA, ALLA — Way of serving pasta with tomato sauce, slices of aubergine and mushrooms.

Bo

BOSTON BAKED BEANS — Haricot beans cooked in a deep earthenware pot, with salt pork, molasses, onions, mustard and sugar for many hours until the sauce is a rich, dark brown and the beans are tender. This dish was useful for early Bostonian puritans who were forbidden to cook on the Sabbath, as the beans could stay in a low oven almost indefinitely. Those who did not have an oven, took the bean pot to the baker's on Saturday and when it was ready the next day, they were given Boston Brown Bread to eat with it. This is still the traditional accompaniment.

BOSTON BROWN BREAD — Early American bread made with white flour, wholemeal flour, cornmeal, raisins and molasses. It is steamed in earthenware pots.

BOSTON CREAM PIE — Sponge cake filled with vanilla custard and topped with chocolate glacé icing, from New England.

BOTTLING — To preserve food by heating it in a container such as a glass bottle or jar. The heat kills the organisms which would otherwise spoil the food and creates a vacuum which seals the bottle and keeps out bacteria. The temperature required varies according to the acidity of the food: fruit, which tends to be high in acid, can be sterilized at 100°C (212°F), but meat and fish require a much higher temperature which alters the taste and appearance of the food.

BOUCHEE — French for mouthful, this is a tiny cocktail version of a vol-au-vent, usually only 1-1½ inches (3 cm) in diameter. An inbetween size, about 2½ inches (6 cm) can be served as an individual entrée and is still called a bouchée, although more than a mouthful. Queen Marie Lesczynska of France loved vol-au-vents and wanted to eat them all the time, so her chefs prepared special individual ones which they called Bouchée à la Reine (Queen's mouthful).

BOUDIN — French black pudding.

BOUDIN BLANC — French for white pudding. This is made with minced pork and chicken, milk or cream and eggs. It has a delicate flavour and is grilled whole.

BOUILLABAISSE — Rich fish soup from the South of France. It contains a variety of local fish, including the racasse, which are unobtainable elsewhere. It is strongly flavoured with garlic and saffron. The bouillabaisse is served in two dishes: the liquor is strained into a deep dish which is lined with slices of French bread to partially absorb the liquid. The pieces of fish are arranged in another dish.

28

BOUILLANT — Small savoury pastry served as a hot hors d'oeuvre. It is made with puff pastry and filled with a chicken mixture.

BOUILLON — French for stock or broth.

BOULA — Green turtle soup mixed with a purée of green peas and spiked with dry sherry.

BOULANGERE — French for baker's style. The term is used to describe a method of cooking sliced potatoes and onions in a roasting tin under a joint of meat. Lamb Boulangère is probably the best known example of this style. The name refers to the time when few people had their own oven and so they used the local baker's oven for the Sunday joint. This method conveniently provided meat and vegetables all cooked together in one dish. Boulangère potatoes can be made on their own in a baking dish with a little dripping.

BOULETTE — French for small ball, in cookery it means specifically a small ball of leftover meat, poultry or fish, dipped in egg and breadcrumbs and deep-fried, or brushed with fat and baked.

BOUQUET GARNI — A bunch of herbs, usually a bay leaf, a sprig of parsley and a sprig of thyme, used in cooking but removed before serving. The bouquet is often sewn into a muslin bag to prevent the herbs from disintegrating during cooking.

BOUQUETIERE, A LA — Garnish for meat of various vegetables arranged in bouquets.

BOURDAINE, LA — Speciality of the Anjou region of France, this is an apple stuffed with quince or plum jam, enclosed in pastry and baked.

BOURDALOUE — The name of a street in Paris where there was a famous pastry shop. Its specialities carry the name à la Bourdaloue.

BOURGEOISE, A LA — Garnish for meat of diced bacon, baby onions and carrot balls. It is the name of beef consommé when garnished with diced root vegetables and chervil.

BOURGUIGNONNE, A LA — Cooked with red wine, mushrooms and baby onions.

BOURRIDE — Fish dish from Provence. A variety of fish is cooked in stock and seasoning, then drained: a slice of toasted bread is dipped in the fish stock, then spread with aioli and the fish is arranged on top.

BOURRIOL — Thick but light buckwheat yeast pancake from central France.

29

BOUTARGUE — Dried, pressed mullet roe, which is served as an appetizer in Provence.

BOXTY — Irish potato bread traditionally eaten at Hallowe'en. It can be cooked in the oven in four quarters or mixed with milk to make a pancake and cooked on the griddle.

BRABANCONNE, A LA — Garnish for meat consisting of chicory and potato croquettes, sometimes with hop shoots cooked in butter and cream. There is also a more recent garnish specifically for steak of brussel sprouts with cheese sauce and sautéed potato balls, which has the same name.

BRACE — Two game birds, one male and one female. Alla brace is an Italian expression meaning grilled over charcoal.

BRADENHAM HAM — English ham with deep red meat and black skin. It is cured with molasses, which gives it a strong sweet flavour, and it needs to be soaked for several days if bought uncooked.

BRAGANCE, A LA — A garnish for small cuts of meat consisting of tomatoes stuffed with béarnaise sauce and potato croquettes. It is also a beef consommé with sago, cucumber balls and vegetable royale.

BRAISIERE — Deep, heavy pan with a lid and two handles, which is used for braising.

BRAISING — Method of cooking food, usually meat or poultry, slowly in a pan with a well-fitting lid, using very little liquid, in the oven. The word comes from braise, the remains of wood burnt in the oven or live charcoal; early braising pans had indented lids to hold hot coals so that the food inside was cooked from above and below.

BRAN — Fibruous skin of the wheatgerm, which is separated in milling. It is an important source of vitamin B, minerals and roughage.

BRANCAS — The name of a beef consommé garnished with a chiffonade of lettuce and sorrel, vermicelli, a julienne of mushrooms and chervil.

BRANDADE DE MORUE — A dish of salt cod in a fluffy sauce of olive oil and béchamel, which comes from the South of France. Dried salt cod was a standby during Lent, when little fresh fish was available and meat was forbidden by the Church.

BRANDY ALEXANDER PIE — American chiffon pie flavoured with brandy and créme de cacao on a biscuit base. It is based on the flavourings used in Brandy Alexander, a cocktail invented during the prohibition era which looks deceptively like a milk shake.

BRANDY BUTTER — Hard sauce of butter, sugar and brandy. It is served chilled with hot Christmas pudding.

BRANDY SNAP — Wafer flavoured with brown sugar and brandy. It is curled round the handle of a wooden spoon while still hot to obtain the characteristic cylindrical shape. It is filled with whipped cream. Brandy snaps have been popular since the Middle Ages.

BRANTOME — A French writer who has given his name to a sauce for fish. It is a cream sauce with additions of white wine, oyster juice, crayfish butter and cayenne. It is garnished with truffles.

BRATWURST — German pork sausage, seasoned with sage, nutmeg and ginger and served hot, grilled or fried.

BRAWN — A meat jelly made from a pig's head with either pig's trotters or a cowheel to provide the gelatinous liquor which sets when cold. It is served sliced.

BRAZIER — Short-handled metal pot with a thick bottom, used on top of the stove or in the oven for braising. It has small grip handles at the sides and sometimes a lid.

BRAZO DE GITANO — Spanish for gypsy's arm, this is a cake like a Swiss roll, filled and decorated with jam and whipped cream.

BREAD SAUCE — English sauce made of milk flavoured with onion, clove and mace, and thickened with breadcrumbs. It is served hot with roast poultry and game.

BREAST — Cut of lamb or veal, which is usually boned, stuffed, rolled and roasted in a slow oven.

BREAK FLOUR — To stir cold liquid gradually into flour, making a smooth paste.

BRESAOLA — Speciality of the Italian Alps. It is dried beef, matured for about two months until it develops a dark red colour. It is served in thin slices, lightly marinated with olive oil and lemon juice.

BRETONNE — A la Bretonne is a garnish of dried white beans, tomatoes and onions. Bretonne sauce is a velouté sauce with shredded carrots, leeks and celery added.

BREZOLLE — French cut of veal from the leg. It is a thick slice.

BRICK — Clay cooking vessel for cooking food in the oven without additional fat or water. Bricks are often made in the shape of the food they are to contain (mostly chicken or fish), and the lid is almost as deep as the base. It has to be soaked in water for several hours before using, then as the oven heats it the steam condenses on the inside of the lid and bastes the food. The shape is therefore important for maximum effect. This method of oven steaming in the food's own juices produces a very flavoursome result, although the flesh is rather anemic-looking.

BRIDER — French culinary term meaning to truss with a needle and thread.

BRIER — French culinary term meaning to flatten pastry with a rolling pin.

BRIK — Tunisian savoury pastry, made with very thin pastry enclosing minced lamb and an egg which is raw before the pastry is fried. The egg is just cooked by the time the pastry is browned. It is eaten hot and is often sold on the street as a snack.

BRILLAT-SAVARIN — Garnish for lamb noisettes of duchess potato cassolettes filled with foie gras, truffles and asparagus tips. Named after Jean-Anthelme Brillat-Savarin, a French politian and gastronome.

BRINE — Salt solution used to preserve food. Immersing food in brine has been used as a method of preservation since the days of the Roman Empire, and is still very popular in Eastern Europe. Brining is also used as a preliminary to smoking fish.

BRINJAL BHARTHA — Indian dish of aubergines flavoured with ginger, green chilli and tomato.

BRIOCHE — Cake made with a yeast dough enriched with butter and eggs. It usually has a characteristic shape made by placing a small ball of dough on top of a larger ball of dough: this is called a brioche à tête. It may also be made in a fluted mould. Additions of preserved fruit, frangipane or cheese are sometimes found. The word probably comes from two French words, briser (break) and hocher (stir). Faire une brioche is a French slang expression meaning to make a mistake: musicians at the Paris Opera were fined for wrong notes during a performance and the fine money was then spent on brioches for the whole orchestra.

BRIOUAT — Moroccan pancake which is filled with a spicy lamb or chicken mixture, rolled into a cigar shape and fried.

BRISEE, PÂTE — French expression for shortcrust pastry. If an egg is added it is pâte brisée à l'oeuf, if extra fat is used it is pâte brisée fine.

BRISKET — Cut of beef from the chest area of the animal. It requires long, slow cooking to prevent shrinkage and is most often boiled and salted.

BRISLING — Sprat which has been lightly smoked before being canned.

BRITTLE — Confection based on molasses and nuts, which is easily broken into pieces.

BROCHETTE — French version of a kebab, ie. meat, poultry, fish or vegetables threaded onto a skewer then grilled.

BRODETTO — Italian soup from the Adriatic coast which contains local fish, clams, squid and eel. The fish and the broth are served separately.

BRODO — Italian term for stock. In brodo means cooked in stock.

BROGLIE — A demi-glace sauce with mushroom stock, Madeira and butter added, and garnished with fried chopped ham. It is served with meat.

BROIL — American and old English word meaning to grill.

BROILER — American term for the kitchen utensil, the grill. It is also a term used to describe a chicken, however in the United States it refers to a young chicken (ie. one that could be grilled), but in Britain it is used to denote an elderly bird – perhaps used mistakenly where 'boiler' would be more appropriate.

BROSE — Scottish oatmeal porridge or soup thickened with oatmeal. Atholl Brose is a cold dessert made with oatmeal, cream, honey and whiskey.

BROTH — The liquid in which bones, meat or vegetables have been boiled. Unlike consommé it is unclarified. To make a thick and filling broth, the meat and vegetables must be cooked gently and for a long time to extract maximum flavour.

BROUILLES, OEUFS — Scrambled eggs.

BROWN — To cook in an oven, under a grill or in a pan until the food becomes golden brown in colour. This effect is due to the coagulation of the protein.

BROWN BETTY — Hot dessert made with layers of moist fruit (eg. apples, rhubarb etc) alternating with layers of buttered sweetened breadcrumbs, which is then baked.

33

BROWNIE — Small American cake, usually flavoured with chocolate, but always rich and chewy in texture. The mixture is baked in a large shallow tray, then cut into squares to serve. Nuts are often included.

BROWNING, GRAVY — Commercially prepared mixture of caramel and salt, used to colour soups, stews and gravy.

BROYE — Thick savoury porridge made with cornmeal and vegetable stock from the Pyrenees. It is also known as millas.

BRUHWURST — German term for any smoked, scalded sausage sold for immediate consumption, such as Frankfurter or Bratwurst.

BRULE — French for burnt; as a culinary term it is applied to food finished with a caramelized sugar glaze.

BRUN, AU — French term for food cooked or served in a brown sauce.

BRUNCH — Midday meal taken at weeknds with (alcoholic) drinks. The idea comes from the U.S. where it is often a buffet. The name is an amalgam of breakfast and lunch.

BRUNOISE — Mixture of vegetables (carrots, leeks, celery, onion, turnips) cooked in butter. They may be shredded or diced, and may be used as a garnish or as a base for soups, sauces, salpicons etc.

BRUNSWICK STEW — Based on an American Indian squirrel stew, it is now a popular chicken and vegetable casserole from Brunswick county, Virginia.

BRUSH FRY — To fry in a heavy pan very lightly brushed with oil or melted fat. This method is used for pancakes to prevent them sticking to the pan.

BRUXELLOISE, A LA — Garnish for roast lamb of braised chicory, brussel sprouts and sautéed potatoes.

BUBBLE AND SQUEAK — English dish of leftover boiled potatoes and cabbage, which are fried together, sometimes with a little leftover meat. The name is onomatopaeic – the bubble of the boiling water and the squeak of the food meeting the hot fat. Dripping is the ideal fat for this dish.

BUCATINI — Thin macaroni.

BUCKLING — Smoked herring, which has been beheaded, gutted and hot smoked until the skin turns shiny and golden. This method was invented by a Dutchman, Beukels, and the word is a corruption of his name.

BUCK RAREBIT — English savoury – a Welsh rarebit with a poached egg on top.

BUISSON, EN — French for in a bush. This refers to a way of presenting shellfish for the table, grouped together as if there is a bush of shellfish.

BULL'S EYE — Traditional English confection. It is round, black and white striped, peppermint flavoured and long lasting.

BULLY BEEF — Another name for corned beef. The name bully came into used in the First World War, when tins of beef labelled 'bouilé' (boiled) were army rations in the trenches.

BUN — Term applied widely to different kinds of baked goods, but chiefly to a small round, glazed cake, made with a yeast dough. Buns were probably first made in pre-Christian times as part of a religious offering.

BUNDNERFLEISCH — Spiced, salted, air-dried beef, served in very thin slices in vinaigrette dressing. This speciality of the Grisons in Switzerland was developed centuries ago when, as the high altitude meant no grass for the cattle in winter, a convenient means of preserving its flesh was sought. Mutton or goat may also be treated in this way.

BUNDT — German coffee cake like a kugelhopf but denser. It is made in a special mould with distinctive fluting, pointing straight upwards (unlike the diagonal fluting of a kugelhopf) with wide curves separated by sharp pointed promentaries.

BUNUELOS — Spanish fritters – usually a mixture of fillings (shellfish, meat, cheese, vegetables etc) are served. Bunuelos clasicos are a sweet fritter made with a yeast batter.

BUREK — *See* BOREK.

BURRIDA — Italian fish stew made with a wide variey of fish local to the Genoese coastline. To serve, large croûtes are placed in each serving bowl and the stew is spooned over.

BURRITO — Soft tortilla folded to enclose a filling such as cheese and beans or scrambled eggs and chillies. Like other Mexican dishes, burritos are popular snack foods in the United States.

BUSSY, POMMES DE TERRE — Pommes de terre dauphine flavoured with truffles and parsley, and shaped into short tubes by piping short lengths into the hot fat and cutting off the mixture from the piping bag with a knife.

BUTCHER BLOCK — A thick wooden chopping and cutting block on legs.

Bu

BUTCHER KNIFE — Designed for cutting rather than chopping. The shape of the blade may vary, but the handle is enlarged where it meets the blade to act as a cushion for the hand.

BUTCHER'S KNOT — Double knot used for trussing poultry.

BUTIFARRA — Spanish pork sausage, flavoured with white wine, cloves and nutmeg.

BUTTER — Apart from being the name of a dairy product, the word butter is used as a verb in cookery terminology. To butter a pan is to grease it with butter; this may be done by brushing melted butter round it or by using the wrapper of a slab of butter. As a noun, a butter is a sweetened fruit purée, which is spread over bread like jam. It is made from the pulp leftover from making a fruit jelly and resembles butter in texture, hence the name.

BUTTER CREAM — Mixture of butter, icing sugar, flavouring and colouring, which is used as an icing or filling for a cake. It is also known as butter icing.

BUTTERFLY — Way of preparing a leg of lamb by removing all the bones except the shank and flattening the meat with a mallet. The shape resembles a butterfly with the shank serving as a handle. It is grilled or barbecued. A butterfly chop is a double lamb chop taken from the saddle or the neck. A butterfly fillet is two sides of a fish corresponding to two single fillets, held together by uncut flesh and the skin.

BUTTERMILK — That which is left of the milk when butter has been churned. It is low fat, like skimmed milk, but sour because of the length of time it is kept before butter is made. It is used in cooking to react with bicarbonate of soda as a raising agent and it is also popular as a health drink.

BUTTER SAUCE — English sauce made with a roux, but with a large quantity of butter whisked in after the liquid is added. It is served with fish and vegetables.

BUTTERSCOTCH — Cooked mixture of brown sugar and butter which is used as a flavouring for cakes and desserts. In its hard, set state it is eaten as a confection.

BYRON — Sauce for meat, fish or eggs, named after Lord Byron, the poet. It is simply red wine, thickened with arrowroot and butter and garnished with truffles. Pommes Byron are potatoes which have been baked, then mashed, then fried and put into a flan ring, covered with cream and grated cheese, then browned under the grill.

BYRIANI — See BIRYANI.

CABELLO DE ANGEL — *See* ANGEL'S HAIR.

CABINET PUDDING — Traditional English sponge pudding, which is baked in the oven rather than steamed as is usual for sponge puddings. It contains pieces of preserved ginger and glacé cherries, and is flavoured with kirsch. It is made in a decorative mould and turned out like a cake to serve. It is eaten hot.

CACCIATORE — Italian word meaning hunter. Pollo alla cacciatore is a popular chicken casserole with tomatoes, green peppers, mushrooms and garlic.

CACCIATORI, SALAME — Small salami of pork, pork fat, beef, garlic and white wine. Also known as salame Milano.

CACCIUCCO ALLA LIVORNESE — Italian fish stew flavoured with tomatoes, sage and garlic.

CACHOU — An aromatic sweet made of musk, sandalwood, amber, cinnamon and other substances, which is chewed to freshen the breath.

CACIK — Turkish appetizer made with diced cucumber, garlic, mint and yogurt.

CAEN — A town in Normandy, which is famous for the way it cooks tripe. Tripe à la mode de Caen is tripe cooked slowly and for a very long time in Calvados and cider – both local products – with onions and carrots.

CAESAR SALAD — An American salad of shredded lettuce, grated Parmesan cheese, croûtons, anchovy fillets, beaten egg and garlic, which must be eaten as soon as it is mixed. The Caesar who gave his name to the dish was the restaurateur who invented it.

CAFE AU LAIT — French for coffee with milk. A drink of coffee and hot milk, in equal quantities, poured into the cup at the same time.

CAFE BORGIA — A mixture of black coffee and hot chocolate in equal quantities, with a blob of whipped cream and grated orange peel on top.

CAFE BRULOT — Cognac, sugar, cloves, cinnamon and orange peel are heated, flambéed and added to black coffee. It is prepared at the dining table, using a chafing dish.

CAFE DIABLE — Black coffee with lemon and orange peel, sugar cubes, cloves, cinnamon and cognac. It is flambéed before the coffee is added.

CAFE LIEGEOIS — Belgian ice cream dish. Vanilla or coffee ice and sweet black coffee mixed together until thick, then topped with whipped cream.

CAFFE LATTE — Italian milky coffee made with one third espresso, two thirds foamed milk.

CAILETTE/CAYETTE — French flat round sausage or faggot made with chopped chard leaves, pork liver and garlic, and wrapped in caul. It is a speciality of the Ardèche region.

CAKE FLOUR — White, starchy, finely ground flour, milled from low protein wheats and used for cake-making.

CALALOU — Caribbean stew of crab and salt pork, flavoured with the leaves of the taro plant.

CALCIUM — Mineral essential in the diet for strong teeth and bones, which is found in cheese, milk, whitebait, sardines and watercress. It is especially important for babies and pregnant women.

CALDERADA/CALDEIRADA — Spanish/Portuguese fish soup-stew, similar to bouillabaise, but made with local fish.

CALDERETA — General Spanish term for a stew.

CALDO VERDE — A very light Portuguese cabbage soup.

CALORIE — A calorie is the amount needed to heat one kilogram of water by one degree Centigrade. All food contains calories or it would not be food, but some foods contain more than others. Calorie intake should match the body's requirements as the excess is stored.

CALZONE — Half moon shaped pizza stuffed with ham and Mozzarella cheese. A speciality of Naples, the name means trouser leg.

CAMBACERES, A LA — This term indicates that the food in question is stuffed with foie gras. Cambacéres was Napoleon's arch-chancellor.

CAMBRIDGE SAUCE — A sauce for cold meats made by blending hard-boiled egg yolks, anchovies, capers, chives, chervil, tarragon, oil, vinegar and parsley.

CAMERANI — A garnish for poultry and sweetbreads of tartlets filled with foie gras and ox tongue, and macaroni bound in cheese and butter sauce. Also a beef consommé garnished with diced carrots, leeks and celery, pasta and grated Parmesan cheese.

CAMPAGNE — French for country. This word is applied freely to food made with ingredients from the surrounding countryside or in the local style.

CANADIAN PASTRY — Another name for crumble mixture.

CANAPE — Classically, a rectangular slice of crustless bread with a savoury mixture on top. The bread is sometimes toasted or fried and/or cut into fancy shapes. Cocktail biscuits have to some extent replaced bread as a base for canapes. A colourful selection, varying in colour and texture, as well as flavour, is served on a tray with drinks, either as a party food or as an appetizer.

CANARY PUDDING — Traditional English steamed sponge pudding, flavoured with lemon peel. The name refers to the canary yellow colour of the pudding.

CANCALAISE — Garnish for fish of oysters and shrimps in a velouté sauce flavoured with fish stock and mushrooms. Cancale is a small fishing port near the English Channel.

CANDY — As a noun the word is used in America to mean a sweet or confection. As a verb it is a simple, but lengthy method of preserving fruit (and sometimes flowers) in a thick sugar syrup. The syrup is gradually concentrated day by day, so that the fruit becomes impregnated with sugar. It has to be done slowly in stages to give the sugar time to penetrate, as the water in the fruit dilutes it. If it is hurried, the fruit becomes tough and wrinkled. The finished product, which is dry not sticky, is used to decorate cakes and desserts or eaten as a sweet. The word may come from the Latin, candidus, meaning glittering white, or the Sanscrit, khand, meaning sugar cane.

CANELLE KNIFE — Cutting tool with a blade which has a V-shaped tooth within a horizontal slot near the tip. This is used for paring narrow strips of citrus fruit peel, cucumber rind etc. for decorative appearance.

CANNELLONI — Italian for big pipes. Tubular pasta, as the name suggests, about three inches (seven cm) long and one inch (two cm) wide. It has a savoury filling and is baked in tomato sauce.

CANNELON — A French term which refers to a small roll or stick of puff pastry, stuffed with minced meat (often game) or a sweet mixture, then baked or fried. A cannelon of beef is braised, stuffed, rolled beef.

CANNOLI — Sicilian tube-shaped pastry, filled with crème pâtissière or sweetened Ricotta cheese with candied peel and nuts. It is made in a special cylindrical mould and deep-fried, then sprinkled with icing sugar.

CAPILOTADE — A French term for a ragoût made with several different kinds of leftover poultry.

CAPON — Castrated cockeral, or one who has been given female hormones, aged six to nine months. A capon is as large as a small turkey, weighing around three kg. (seven lb).

CAPONATA — Sicilian dish of aubergines cooked in a sweet-sour sauce with capers, olives and anchovies.

CAPPELLETTI — Italian for little peaked hats. Stuffed pasta similar to tortellini, but cut from squares of pasta dough.

CAPPON MAGRO — Elaborate Italian fish salad using a variety of fish and vegetables with a garlic, caper and pickle sauce.

CAPPUCINO — Italian coffee with enough foamed cream or milk added to turn it the colour of a capuchin monk's robe. Powdered chocolate or cinnamon is sprinkled on top.

CAPRICCIOSA — Term used in Italian restaurant which can be roughly translated as whatever filling, or garnish etc. the chef fancies.

CAPUCINE, A LA — Garnish for meat of cabbage leaves or mushrooms stuffed with forcemeat, masked with Madeira sauce. Also a chicken consommé garnished with a chiffonade of spinach and lettuce.

CAQUELON — Earthenware pot with a handle, in which a cheese fondue is traditionally cooked.

CARAMELIZE — To heat sugar and water together until the mixture turns brown, then letting it drop off a spoon into cold water which makes it brittle.

CARAQUE, CHOCOLATE — Long, cylindrical flakes of chocolate, made by melting a bar of chocolate and spreading it thinly on a marble slab. When it is nearly set, the caraque is shaved off the slab with a knife held upright in a sawing movement. It is used to decorate cakes and desserts.

CARBOHYDRATE — Basic food element produced by plants by photosynthesis – a combination of water from the soil, air and sunlight – which is found in sugars and starches. Natural foods high in carbohydrate are usually also high in fibre, vitamins and minerals, but refined sugars and overprocessed starches should be avoided as all they contain is bulk. 43 per cent of a balanced diet is carbohydrate.

CARBONADE — A Flemish stew made with meat (usually beef) and beer. The name originally meant that the dish was grilled or boiled over coals (carbone).

CARBONARA, ALLA — Way of serving pasta, usually spaghetti, with strips of fried bacon. An egg is broken into each plate of hot pasta, the chopped bacon, its cooking oil and grated cheese are stirred in, and the heat of the food cooks the egg. This dish comes from the Abruzzi district where charcoal burners traditionally stay in the woods for long periods, with supplies of spaghetti, ham, eggs, cheese and oil.

CARBORUNDUM STONE — A thick, rectangular block of several abrasives, usually composed of silicon carbide, which is used as a knife-sharpener.

CARCASE/CARCASS — The body of a dead animal, drawn and trimmed.

CARDINAL — A la Cardinal is a garnish for fish of mushrooms, truffles and chopped lobster in cardinal sauce. Cardinal sauce is either a béchamel or mayonnaise, flavoured with lobster coral. The cardinal in question is Cardinal Mazarin, effective ruler of France in the mid-seventeenth century. Bombe Cardinal has raspberry ice outside and vanilla ice cream inside: it is named for its appearance, the red exterior ressembling a cardinal's robes.

CARDINALISER — French culinary term meaning to turn red by plunging into boiling liquid. It applies to shellfish, especially lobster.

CAREME — Garnish for small cuts of meat of olives stuffed with ham forcemeat, Madeira sauce and potato croquettes. Also a garnish for fish of truffles, fleurons and cream sauce. A chicken and veal consommé garnished with carrots, turnips, chiffonade of lettuce and asparagus tips. Named after and created by Marie-Antoine Carême "king of chefs and chef to kings"(Tsar Alexander, the prince Regent, Baron de Rothschild etc), and founder of haute cuisine.

41

Ca

CARMELITE, A LA — Bourguignonne sauce with julienne of ham and button onions. Also a fish consommé garnished with fish forcemeat balls and rice.

CARMEN, GLACE — Apricot ice with a filling of raspberry-flavoured crème chantilly.

CARMINE — Scarlet food dye derived from cochineal.

CARNITAS — Mexican for little meats. Little pieces of browned, shredded pork, eaten as a snack or part of a meal.

CAROLINE — Small version (three inches, seven cm. long) of an éclair. Usually sweet, it may also be stuffed with pâté and coated with chaudfroid to serve as an hors d'oeuvre.

CAROTENE — Orange substance found in certain foods, which is converted into vitamin A in the body. The name comes from carrot, the major source of carotene.

CARPETBAG STEAK — An Australian way of preparing steak, by cutting a pocket in a thick steak and stuffing it with oysters, before sewing it up and frying it in butter. The pan juices are allowed to brown and foam, then poured over the steak to serve.

CARRE — French for the best end of neck joint.

CARRETTIERA, ALLA — The cart-drivers' way of serving spaghetti – with a sauce of tomatoes, garlic and basil.

CARROZZA — Italian for carriage, in cookery terms it means a fried bread case. Mozzarella in Carrozza is a luxury fried cheese sandwich, eaten as a snack or first course.

CARTE, A LA — A menu on which each dish is individually priced and may be ordered separately.

CARTOCCIO — Italian way of cooking fish in paper similar to en papillote.

CARVE — To cut slices of flesh from cooked meat, poultry or game with a sharp knife.

CASA, DELLA — Italian for of the house ie. the house speciality.

CASALINGA — Italian for home-made.

CASEIN — One of the main proteins found in milk.

CASSADOU — A casserole with a lid, a lip and a short handle, which can be used on the hob as well as in the oven.

CASSAREEP — Caribbean condiment made from cassava root, sugar and spices.

CASSATA — An iced pudding from Naples, composed of layers of vanilla and chocolate ice cream, with chopped glacé fruits mixed with whipped cream in the centre. It is made in a bombe mould and turned out to serve. Cassata is also the name of a Sicilian sponge cake filled with cream cheese and candied fruit, and covered with chocolate butter cream. This cake is traditionally served at Easter and Christmas.

CASSEROLE — An ovenproof cooking pot with a lid, which may be made of various materials, but especially cast-iron, copper or terracotta. Some casseroles are also fireproof and may be used on top of the stove. A casserole may be brought to the table and used as a serving dish. The term also has come to mean a recipe cooked in a casserole, ie. a stew of some sort. In classical French cooking, casserole describes a preparation made with rice, which is shaped like a casserole after cooking. In the United States the word also means a dish of two or more parts, one of which is likely to be rice or pasta, the other meat, poultry or fish in a sauce with vegetables: in other words a complete main course cooked in one pot.

CASSOLETTE — A small fireproof dish with or without a lid. It is also the name for duchess potatoes, deep-fried and stuffed with a salpicon.

CASSOULET — A substantial stew of haricot beans with a variety of meats and sausages. The dish comes from the Languedoc region of France, though there are three distinct types: that of Toulouse has breast of pork; that of Castelnaudary has pork, ham and bacon; and that of Carcassone has pork, ham, bacon, mutton and partridge. The name comes from the characteristic pot in which it is cooked, which used to be called a cassolle d'Issel.

CASTAGNACCIO — Italian cake made with chestnut flour, pine kernels, almonds, raisins and candied fruit.

CASTELLANA, ALLA — Italian method of cooking chicken: two chicken breasts are sandwiched with a slice of ham and white truffles in between, the whole is coated in egg and breadcrumbs and deep-fried.

CASTELLANE — Garnish for small cuts of meat of tomatoes cooked in oil, potato croquettes and onion rings. Also snipe consommé garnished with pieces of snipe and a royale of snipe, lentils and hard-boiled egg.

CASTIGLIONE, A LA — Garnish for small cuts of meat, comprising rice-stuffed mushrooms, poached beef marrow and aubergines cooked in butter.

43

CASTLE PUDDING — Traditional English sponge pudding steamed or baked in small dariole moulds and served with jam sauce.

CATALANE, A LA — Garnish for joints of meat and poultry consisting of sautéed aubergines and a pilaf.

CATAPLANA — Hinged pan with handles from the Algarve region of Portugal. It is used for boiling shellfish, especially clams. Because the lid is as deep as the pan it can be turned upside down for even cooking.

CATSUP — Another name for ketchup.

CAUCHOISE — From the Pays de Caux in Normandy. In cookery this usually means cooked with Calvados, cream and apples. Also a beef consommé with diced lamb and bacon and a julienne of braised vegetables.

CAUDEL — Old English sweet oatmeal porridge, flavoured with brandy or sherry.

CAUDLE SAUCE — Hot brandy or rum sauce, flavoured with lemon rind and served as an accompaniment to steamed puddings.

CAUL — Outer membrane covering a pig's intestines, which is used to wrap sausages.

CAVALLEGGERA — Way of cooking spaghetti with eggs, walnuts, cream and Parmesan cheese.

CAVIARE — The roe of the sturgeon, a fish found only in the estuaries of rivers which flow into the Baltic Sea and the river Danube. The roe is lightly preserved in salt and does not keep well. Because of its comparative scarcity it is very much a luxury food. Within the sturgeon family there are several different fish which each produce a different caviar. Beluga caviar is grey and large grained, whereas that of the sterlet is black and so highly esteemed that it was reserved for the Tsar and his family in Imperial Russia. Red caviar is not true caviar, being the roe of the salmon. Caviar is served in a dish in a container of ice, accompanied by lemon wedges and fingers of black bread, as a cocktail snack or appetizer. It may also be served on a canapé or with blinis. However it is served, vodka or champagne should be drunk with it.

CAVOUR, A LA — A garnish for slices of meat of semolina croquettes, timbale of lasagne, and ravioli. Also a garnish for veal escalopes and sweetbreads comprising round cakes of polenta, on which the meat is placed and sprinkled with Parmesan cheese, and mushrooms stuffed with chicken liver purée. In addition there is a chicken consommé with green peas, tiny dumplings and macaroni with the same name.

CAWL — Welsh word meaning a hearty soup or stew of meat, poultry and vegetables.

CAYETTE — *See* CAILETTE.

CELESTINE — Chef to Napoleon III. Poulet Celestine is sautéed chicken with tomatoes, wine, mushrooms and cream.

CENCO — Italian pastry made in the shape of a knot, which is deep-fried and sprinkled with icing sugar.

CENDRILLON — French for Cinderella. Pied de Veau Cendrillon is a calf's foot boned and chopped and mixed with truffles and sausagement, shaped into a cutlet, breadcrumbed and grilled. Poulet Cendrillon is a chicken breast boned, flattened and sandwiched with truffled sausagement, wrapped in sausageskin, grilled and served with perigueaux sauce.

CEREAL — Any grass cultivated for food – wheat, corn, rice, barley, oats, rye etc. The word comes from the Roman goddess of the harvest, Ceres.

CERKES TAVUGU — Strips of boiled chicken in a sauce of ground walnuts, breadcrumbs and paprika. It is usually served cold as a starter. Now considered to be a Turkish speciality, it came originally from the Circassian mountains, brought according to the story, by a captured Circassian girl who joined the Royal Harem.

CERTOSINA, ALLA — The name given to a risotto containing seafood, mushrooms, tomatoes and peas.

CERVELAS — A pork sausage with garlic and pork fat. The name comes from cervelle (French for brain), as pig's brains are traditionally used to make it.

CERVELAT — Large German sausage of smoked, minced pork and beef. It is mild and smooth, and is eaten cold, cut into slices.

CEVAPCICI — Serbian kebab oval balls of minced meat, grilled over charcoal and served with chopped raw onion.

CEVENNES PIE — A two-crust pie with a filling of minced pork, apple and chestnuts from Cevennes in France.

CEVICHE — Raw fish marinated in spicy lime juice and chilli mixture, which "cooks" the fish. It is a traditional Mexican dish, served as an appetizer.

CHA — Chinese cooking term meaning deep-fried.

Ch

CHAFING DISH — This is actually two dishes – a set comprising a large deep frying pan, made of silver plate with a wooden handle, and another silver plate pan without a handle. The frying pan is called a blazer: the second pan is to contain hot water for cooking au bain-marie. The chafing dish is usually operated on a spirit lamp in the dining room. Chafing dish cookery (there is no verb to chafe) evolved at nineteenth century country house parties, where impromptu meals would be concocted in the dining room by the host or the butler – presumably after the kitchen staff had gone to bed. Nowadays it is rarely used except in restaurants, where it is operated on a more powerful gas cylinder and used for dishes which are flambéed at the table (crêpes Suzette, steak Diane etc.).

CHA GIO — Vietnamese omelette stuffed with crab and shrimp.

CHALAZAE — The two membranes which hold the yolk of an egg in the middle of the white.

CHALLAH/CHOLLA — Jewish bread made with an egg-enriched dough and plaited with as many as eight strands.

CHALONAISE, A LA — With a garnish of cock's combs.

CHALUPA — Crisp, fried tortilla, topped with beans, lettuce, guacamole, cheese and tomato. A popular Tex-Mex (rather than authentic Mexican) snack or party food.

CHAMBERTIN, SOLE AU — Sole baked in red wine served on a bed of mushrooms, shallots and parsley.

CHAMBERY — This name is given to a salad, an omelette and a potato dish. The salad is a large tomato filled with lobster, salmon, artichoke bottoms, gherkins, lettuce and mayonnaise. The omelette is filled with diced leeks, bacon, potato and cheese. Pommes de terre Chambéry is boiled, sliced potatoes arranged in layers with butter and cheese, and baked until brown.

CHAMBORD — A la Chambord is an elaborate garnish for a large fish composed of quenelles, roes, truffles, fleurons, mushrooms and crayfish or shrimps. Sauce Chambord is fish stock with a mirepoix, red wine, herbs, anchovy essence and butter.

CHAMONIX, POMMES DE TERRE — A variant on pommes de terre Dauphine, flavoured with gruyère cheese.

CHAMP — Traditional Irish dish of potatoes mashed with chopped spring onion and milk until fluffy. The potato mixture is heaped onto individual plates and served with a spoonful of melted butter on top.

CHAMPIGNON — Wooden pestle used for rubbing purées through a drum sieve. It has a flat head and bears some resemblance to a long-stalked mushroom (champignon means mushroom in French).

CHANTILLY — A slightly sweetened vanilla-flavoured cream, whipped to the consistency of a mousse, sometimes also known as crème Chantilly, which is used mostly in pâtisserie. The royal dairy was at Chantilly, near Paris – hence the name. Chantilly sauce is a mixture of whipped cream and either mayonnaise or hollandaise, which is served cold with salads, cold meat, poultry and fish: a hot Chantilly sauce, made with béchamel and whipped cream, is more often called by its other name, mousseline.

CHAP — A half cheek of an animal, usually a pig. The best known chap is a Bath chap, which is the cured cheek of a pig from the district surrounding the town of Bath, who has been fed on fruit and whose meat, therefore, has a particularly fine flavour. Chaps are rather fatty and are generally eaten cold.

CHAPATI — Unleavened wholemeal bread from India. The dough is flattened by tossing it from one hand to the other, then quickly cooked on each side on a tava (iron hot plate). They are best eaten while still warm, brushed with a little ghee.

CHAPELURE — French culinary term for dry breadcrumbs. These may be used with beaten egg to coat foods for frying, or sprinkled on top of a sauce-covered dish before grilling it au gratin.

CHAPON — A slice of French bread, rubbed with garlic, oil and vinegar, which is put in a salad bowl to flavour the salad. the chapon is not eaten. The idea evolved in the south of France.

CHARCUTERIE — The art of pork butchery. In France a charcuterie is a separate shop from a butcher's and contains a vast selection of sausages, cold meats, pâtés etc. This separation dates from the time when pigs were considered unclean by many ethnic groups.

CHARCUTIER, SAUCE — Demi-glace sauce to which gherkins are added. It is served with grilled or sautéed pork.

CHARENTE, A LA — This term indicates the prescence of truffles or the white wine and brandy apertif, Pineau, in the dish. The region Charente is famous for both.

Ch

CHARLOTTE — A pudding which is encased in sponge cake, biscuits or bread inside a special bucket-shaped mould. There are several types of charlotte. The best known is Charlotte Russe, created by Carême, who called it Charlotte Parisienne before he went to work for the Russian Imperial family. It is a bavarois on a jelly base, lined with sponge fingers; it is unmoulded to serve and a ribbon is tied round the sides. A popular filling for this sort of charlotte is chantilly, lightly set with gelatine as a precaution against collapse on unmoulding. The other dessert called a charlotte is quite different. It is made with a purée of fruit and bread, either in the form of breadcrumbs which are arranged in layers with the fruit or as buttered fingers arranged around the side of the charlotte mould. A fruit charlotte may be served hot as well as cold. There is also a savoury charlotte, usually cheese-flavoured. There is a controversy over the origin of the name. Those who date it from the late eighteenth or early nineteenth century, claim that it is named after either Queen Charlotte, the wife of George III, or her grandaughter Princess Charlotte. Others maintain that it is a much older dish, originally with a custard filling, and that the name comes from the old English charlet, meaning custard.

CHAROLLAISE — Garnish for sliced meat of cooked cauliflower sprigs à la Villeroi and croustades filled with mashed turnips. Also an oxtail consommé garnished with oxtail, julienne of carrot and onion and tiny stuffed cabbage leaves.

CHAROSET — Traditional Jewish sweetmeat eaten during the Passover. It contains chopped apples, nuts, raisins, cinnamon and red wine.

CHARTRES — Garnish for steak of stuffed mushrooms and braised lettuce.

CHARTREUSE — A cold dessert of fruit in a green or yellow jelly, which is made in a decorative mould and turned out to serve. Any fruit can be used and there should be plenty of it in relation to the jelly. The name refers to the colour of the jelly which resembles the liqueur of the same name made by Carthusian monks. It is also the name of a dish of partridge and cabbage cooked together, and a beef consommé garnished with tomato and ravioli stuffed with spinach purée and truffles.

CHASSEUR — French for hunter. A la chasseur is a term applied to meat, poultry or egg dishes cooked with white wine, mushrooms and shallots. Chasseur sauce is a demi-glace to which mushrooms and tomato purée are added: it is particularly good with grilled meat.

48

CHASSE ROYALE — French for royal hunt. This term refers to a way of presenting game: a variety of roasted game is served in a pyramid on one large dish.

CHATCCHOUKA/CHECHOUKA/TETCHOUKA — Tunisian dish of egg shirred with green pepper, tomato and garlic.

CHATEAU — The name given to a sauce, a steak and a potato dish. Château sauce is a blend of meat juices, butter, parsley and cayenne. Château steak is a thin slice cut from the rib of beef, which is usually grilled. Pommes de terre château are tiny oval potatoes cooked in butter: originally these were called pommes de terre Chateaubriand, but the name was abbreviated and a circonflex accent added.

CHATEAUBRIAND — A very thick slice cut from the middle of a beef fillet. It is always grilled – this takes at least 20 minutes as the steak is about two inches (five cm) thick and weighs at least one lb. (450 g) before trimming. It is served with maître d'hôtel butter and pommes de terre château. It is named after the French writer Chateaubriand.

CHATELAINE — Garnish for roast lamb of quartered artichoke hearts, braised celery, whole baked tomatoes and château potatoes: an omelette filled with mashed chestnuts and gravy: a salad dressing of mayonnaise mixed with a little whipped cream: artichoke bottoms filled with onion purée, glazed chestnuts, pommes à la Parisienne and Madeira sauce: chicken consommé garnished with a royale of artichoke and onion, and chicken and chestnut quenelles.

CHATOUILLARD — Name given to potatoes cut into ribbons and deep-fried; also the name of the person who fries them.

CHAUCHAT — Garnish for fish consisting of sliced, boiled potato arranged as a border, coated in Mornay sauce and gratinéed.

CHAUDFROID — French for hot-cold. A chaudfroid is a cold dish of cooked fish, poultry or game coated with a sauce then a layer of aspic. Chaudfroid sauce is either béchamel, velouté or demi-glace with small amount of aspic added: it is allowed to get quite cold before coating the food. The chaudfroid dates from the eighteenth century when the Maréchal of Luxembourg was suddenly called away in the middle of a banquet. When he returned to his meal, the chicken had grown cold in its own sauce, but he ate it anyway and discovered that it was delicious. As a result, it became fashionable to serve a chaudfroid at parties. Nowadays it is often found at formal buffets, decorated with tiny hearts, diamonds, spades and clubs made of truffle and pimiento.

CHAUSSON — Tiny pastry turnover with a savoury filling, served as a cocktail snack. The pastry may be puff or shortcrust, and the shape may be oval, square or circular. Sweet fillings are occasionally found.

CHAWAN-MUSHI — Japanese savoury custard with chicken and prawns.

CHEESE — A fruit cheese is a moulded sweetened fruit purée. To serve it is unmoulded, sliced and eaten either with cold meat or poultry, or as a dessert. The idea was developed by the Victorians to make use of the fruit purée leftover from making a fruit jelly; its dense texture resembles its namesake from the dairy.

CHEESEBURGER — Hamburger served in a bun, with a thin slice of cheese on top of the meat. The cheese is melted by the heat of the meat.

CHEF'S KNIFE — Basic kitchen tool used for chopping. The steel blade is wide at the bolster end, tapering to a point at the tip. The length varies. It is sometimes known as a cook's knife.

CHEF'S SALAD — An American salad of lettuce and tomato with strips of ham and cheese mixed in. Other ingredients such as chicken, turkey, tongue, anchovy or sardine may be added. It is a good way of using up leftovers and it probably originated in restaurants for precisely that purpose.

CHEKCHUKA — North African dish of peppers, aubergines, courgettes, tomatoes, onions and garlic, lightly cooked with beaten eggs in a frying pan. It is like an omelette but the proportion of egg to filling is reversed.

CHELO — Iranian way of cooking rice. It is parboiled then left to continue cooking in its own heat with only melted butter added. The rice forms a crust at the bottom of the pan, whilst the rest is white. Chelo kebab is a complete meal based on chelo rice: a kebab of lamb, which has been pounded until elastic then pinched together into a chunk, is served with raw onion on a bed of chelo rice; butter and a couple of raw egg yolks in their half shells are served with the meal and stirred into the rice at the table.

CHELSEA BUN — Traditional English square-shaped yeast bun, filled with currants and glazed with sugar. The dough is rolled out, sprinkled with currants and rolled up again, then slices are cut and these arranged in a round or oblong tin so that the sides touch. This gives the buns their characteristic shape. They are best eaten warm, split and filled with butter. Originally they were only made in the old Chelsea Bun House in Pimlico Road, London, and were so popular that a quarter of a million were sold in one day.

50

CHEMISE, EN — French for in a shirt. This phrase suggests that the food so described is covered (eg. with cream) or wrapped (eg. with vine leaves).

CHEMISER — French culinary term meaning to coat with aspic. It also means to coat the inside of a mould with a thin layer of a mixture or to line a mould with greaseproof paper.

CH'ENG — Chinese cooking term which means that the food in question has been steamed in an open pan.

CHERBOURG — Name given to a beef consommé flavoured with Madeira, and garnished with mushrooms, truffles, poached egg and ham quenelles. Also a cooking fat from Normandy made with two-thirds beef suet, one-third pure lard, pepper, salt, herbs, onion and garlic. The ingredients are simmered together for an hour, then strained into jars for storage.

CHESS PIE — Sweet custard flan from the southern states of America. Dates and walnuts, and sometimes chocolate are included in the filling, but originally cheese was one of the ingredients and the name is probably a corruption of cheese pie. There are at least two other explanations for the name. According to some it was originally chest pie: in pre-refrigeration days the pies, which contain lots of sugar so would keep for months, were stored in chests. However, when you ask a Southerner what's for dessert, nine out of ten times he will reply "Jes' pie".

CHEUNG FUN — Chinese steamed pancake made of rice-flour filled with meat or prawns.

CHEVALET — A slice of bread and butter or dripping baked with a chicken breast on top.

CHEVREUIL — French for venison. Chevreuil sauce is simply a poivrade sauce with red wine added. It is the classic accompaniment to venison.

CHIBOUST, CREME — Crème pâtissière and Italian meringue mixed in equal quantities. This produces a very light, smooth cream which collapses if overworked and needs a little gelatine if it is to be kept long. It is often flavoured with liqueur. Named after its inventor, a pastry cook who also created Gâteau St. Honoré, which contains crème chiboust.

CHIEN — A sauce from Martinique made of lime juice, oil, onion and hot peppers, which is served with grilled meat, poultry or fish. Also a Chinese cooking term meaning fried without being stirred, therefore crispy.

CHIFFON — A light, foamy mixture of eggs, sugar, liquid (eg. milk) and flavouring, lightly set with gelatine. The eggs are separated so that the stiffly whisked egg whites can be folded into the mixture to create an airy effect. It is used as a pie filling, sometimes topped with whipped cream. Chiffon pies are popular in the United States. Chiffon cake is a sponge made with oil and a greater proportion of egg whites.

CHIFFONADE — French cookery term describing lettuce and/or sorrel and/or spinach, cut into juliennes and cooked in butter. A chiffonade is used as a garnish, mostly for soup. The word is from chiffoner, meaning to rumple. Chiffonade dressing is an American salad dressing of blended and chilled hard-boiled eggs, vinegar, parsley, red pepper and shallots.

CHILAQUILE — Small piece of tortilla fried until crackling crisp. A Mexican snack.

CHILES RELLANOS — Stuffed chillies in a tomato broth. The filling may vary, a favourite being chopped, spiced pork with almonds, candied fruit and tomatoes. From Mexico.

CHILI CON CARNE — Highly spiced mixture of minced beef, kidney beans and tomatoes. Well established Tex-Mex favourite.

CHILL — To cool food without freezing it in the refrigerator.

CHIMAY — Garnish for poached chicken breasts of morels and asparagus tips.

CHINE — The backbone of a carcase. Also a joint of meat containing part of the backbone and its attached flesh: a chine of pork is two undivided loins. To chine a carcase is to sever the ribs from the backbone; this makes carving into chops easier.

CHINESE FIVE SPICES/HEUNG NEW FUN — Important seasoning in Chinese cuisine made with equal amounts of ground star anise, cloves, fennel seed, chinese pepper and cinnamon or cassia. It can be bought ready mixed.

CHINOIS — A conical strainer with a very fine mesh, used for refining soups and sauces. As an adjective chinois (Chinese) describes any dish cooked in what nineteenth century French cooks imagined to be the Chinese style. Nowadays it refers chiefly to desserts flavoured with ginger. It is also the name for a small Chinese orange preserved in brandy.

CHIP— A finger of deep-fried potato, also known as French fried potato. In the United States a chip is what the British call a crisp ie. a wafer-thin slice of potato deep-fried and eaten as a snack.

CHIPOLATA — A small pork sausage. It can be grilled, fried or baked and is often served on a cocktail stick as a party snack. Chipolatas are sometimes served with roast poultry. The name comes from the Italian cipollata, meaning chive; originally it was flavoured with chives. A la chipolata is a garnish of chipolata, diced breast of pork, braised chestnuts and baby onions.

CHIPPED BEEF — An American term for dried beef. It is sold in jars and used as a spread on toast.

CHIQUETER— French culinary term meaning to mark with a knife the small round top of a vol-au-vent case or the edge of a tart. The marks are not purely decorative, they help the dough to rise.

CHIQUIHUITE — Square-shaped basket made of reed grass for serving tortillas. It is lined with a cloth to keep the tortillas hot and soft.

CHITTERLINGS — The small intestines, usually of a pig. They are used in sausage making, and also served in their own right, either stewed, fried or baked, in American soul food cuisine.

CHIVRY, SAUCE — A velouté sauce with white wine, shallots, tarragon, spinach, chives and chervil added. It is a pale green colour and is served with fish, poultry or eggs.

CHLODNIK/KLODNIK — Polish cold soup made with beetroot, sorrel, dill and sour cream. A cube of ice is placed in each bowl.

CHOESELS — A rich Belgian stew of a combination of offal, including the pancreas, in a sauce made with beer or Madeira, herbs and spices.

CHOISY — A garnish for small cuts of meat of braised lettuce and château potatoes. Also an omelette filled with braised lettuce in a cream sauce.

CHOLENT — Slow cooked brisket with butter beans, pearl barley and potatoes. Traditional Jewish sabbath meal.

CHOLLA — *See* CHALLAH.

CHOP — A cut of meat from the loin or ribs, which may be grilled. If it is cut from the chump end of the loin it is a chump chop or loin chop, if it comes from the neck end it is a cutlet. To chop is to cut up into small pieces with a knife using a brisk up and down movement.

CHOP SUEY — A dish invented by Chinese restaurateurs to please western palates, consisting of small pieces of meat cooked quickly with Chinese vegetables such as bean sprouts, bamboo shoots and water chestnuts. Sometimes shrimp is included.

CHORBA — Broth from Turkey and the Balkans, made with either meat, fish or vegetables and thickened with sour cream.

CHORIZO — Spanish smoked pork sausage strongly flavoured with red pepper.

CHORON — Garnish for small cuts of meat consisting of artichoke bottoms, peas, pommes de terre noisettes and sauce Choron. The sauce is béarnaise flavoured with tomato purée, named after its creator who was chef at the famous Voisin restaurant in nineteenth century Paris.

CHOUX — Choux paste is a very light pastry made by beating eggs into a very thick sauce. During baking it trebles in size through the natural lift of air, leaving a hollow surrounded by crisp pastry. It is used mostly in pâtisserie, where the cavity is filled with whipped cream or crème pâtissière, as in éclairs and profiteroles. It can also be flavoured with cheese and used in the making of savoury dishes such as aigrettes and gougère. Because of its light texture, it cannot be rolled out but it can be piped through a forcing bag into decorative shapes. Its name comes from the fact that it puffs up during baking to resemble a cabbage (chou in French) in shape.

CHOW — Chinese cookery term meaning stir-fried.

CHOW-CHOW — Mustard-flavoured mixed vegetable pickle. Also a Chinese preserve of ginger and orange rind in syrup.

CHOWDER — A very thick and filling soup with a milk base. Usually it is made with fish or shellfish such as clams, but corn chowder is a popular exception. The name comes from chaudière, a french cooking pot or cauldron used by farmers and fishermen to cook soups and stews. Chowders are associated with the New England States of America.

CHOW MEIN — A Chinese dish based on hard-fried noodles bathed in a sauce made with small pieces of meat, shellfish and vegetables.

CHUCK — Cut of beef from the top end of the back of the carcase. It is suitable for braising.

CHUDLEIGH — Another name for a Devonshire split.

CHUMP — The tail end of the loin of an animal. A chump chop is usually a lamb chop cut from the tail end.

CHUNK — A small piece of food. It is an imprecise size and shape, suggesting a haphazard approach to the cutting, but chunks of food to be cooked together should be roughly the same size, vaguely cube-shaped and slightly larger than a one-inch (two and a half cm) cube.

CHURRO — Spanish doughnut made in a variety of shapes, using a special press. It is deep-fried and rolled in sugar.

CHURUPAS — A stack of tortillas sandwiched with savoury fillings: from Mexico.

CHUTNEY — An Indian condiment usually made with fruit, vegetables, sugar, vinegar and spices, which is served with curry and also with cold meat or cheese. It may be mild or spicy, sweet or savoury. Originally it was made fresh every day, but nowadays it is usually a preserve. The word comes from the Hindustani, chatni, meaning a strong, sweet relish.

CIABATTA — Long, flat Italian loaf of bread with an open texture, made with olive oil.

CIAMBELLONE — Italian ring-shaped fruit and nut bread.

CICCIOLI — Italian rendered pork fat.

CINGALAISE, SAUCE — Hard-boiled egg yolks mixed with shredded pimiento, tomato, courgette and cucumber, curry powder, salt, oil and lemon juice.

CIOPPINO — Seafood stew, which is a speciality of San Francisco. It is eaten with sourdough bread. The name means a stew of various fishes in an Italian dialect.

CIVET — A stew of furred game, game birds or poultry, to which the blood of the animal is added for a particularly rich flavour. Civet de lièvre is jugged hare in French. Occasionally the word is applied to a stew of squid or octopus, in which case the ink is added to thicken the sauce. The name comes from cive, meaning green onion, which was once an important ingredient.

CLAFOUTIS — A sweet batter pudding containing fruit, especially black cherries, which is baked in the oven and served hot. It is a traditional dish from the Limousin region of France.

CLAMART — Garnish for tournedos of peas arranged on artichoke hearts, served with button mushrooms and a demi-glace sauce. Artichokes Clamart is a dish of globe artichokes cooked with peas and shredded lettuce. The market gardens of Clamart, in the suburbs of Paris, were famous for their peas, hence the name.

CLAPSHOT — Traditional Scottish dish of swede and potato mashed with onion and butter.

CLARIFY — To remove fat and solid particles from stock by adding whisked egg whites, heating, cooling, then straining — Also to remove salt and milk solids from butter by heating, cooling, then scraping the sediment from the bottom. Clarified butter keeps well and is good to use for frying or grilling as it does not burn as easily as unclarified butter.

CLAYON — Wire cooling rack.

CLEAVER — A heavy steel knife with a deep blade, used in the preparation of meat. Its main purpose is to cut through bones and cartilage, although it can be used for general chopping, as in Chinese cuisine. It is important that the blade is heavier than the handle so that the weight alone splits the bone with a clean cut.

CLOCHE — French for bell. As a culinary term it means a cover shaped like a bell, usually made of silver plate, which is used to keep food warm. It is also a glass dome under which certain foods, such as mushrooms, may be cooked and served sous cloche.

CLO-CLO, COUPE — Vanilla ice cream with maraschino-soaked marrons glacés and puréed strawberries.

CLOD — A cut of beef from the neck. It has a good flavour, needs long, slow cooking to tenderize.

CLOTTED CREAM — Very thick cream (55% minimum fat content) from the south west of England. It is made by skimming the cream from scalded milk and warming it. It is not suitable for whipping and is mostly used as a topping for scones.

CLOUD EAR — Delicate Chinese dried mushroom.

CLOUTER — French for to stud. In a cookery context it means to stud meat, poultry, game or fish with truffles, anchovies, ham etc. to give flavour.

CLOUTIE DUMPLING — Traditional Scottish pudding full of dried fruit, which is boiled in a cloth. Sometimes coins are hidden in the dumpling before cooking.

CLUB SANDWICH — Three layers of toasted white bread filled with grilled streaky bacon, cold chicken or turkey, lettuce, tomato and mayonnaise — It is cut into four triangles and each triangle is held together with a cocktail stick — It is a popular lunch or snack dish in the United States.

CLUB STEAK — American name for entrecôte.

CLUNY, OEUFS — Baked eggs with chicken croquettes.

COAT — To cover food with a sauce so that it masks the food completely.

COB — Round loaf with a sprinkling of crushed wheat on top. Usually it is made with wholemeal or granary flour.

COBBLER — A fruit pudding from the United States. The fruit is topped with a scone-like dough, which may be cut into rounds and arranged round the edge of the dish. It is baked in the oven and served hot. The name comes from to cobble up, meaning to put together very quickly.

COBURG — Crusty dome-shaped loaf of bread, with two cuts on the top to form a crown.

COCHINEAL — Bluish-red food dye made from the dried bodies of certain female insects which live on cactus plants on Mexico.

COCIDO — A Spanish term meaning soup or stew, which is also found in South America. Cocido Espanol is a popular dish of chick peas, salt pork, ham, beef, cabbage, potatoes, carrots, chorizo and vermicelli, all cooked together in the same pot: the cooking liquor and the vermicelli are served as soup, followed by the meat and vegetables arranged on a large platter with the chick peas in the centre.

COCKIE LEEKIE — Scottish soup of boiling fowl, leeks and prunes. The liquor is served as soup before the meat, vegetables and fruit. Sometimes beef is included, and the prunes may be omitted.

COCK'S COMB — Fleshy excrescence found on the head of a cock, which is cooked and used as a garnish for entrées in haute cuisine.

COCONUT ICE — English confection made with coconut, sugar and milk. It is usually made in two layers, one pink, the other white.

57

Co

COCOTTE — A non-specific term for a cooking pot with a lid, as well as a particular individual ovenproof dish. Cocotte is a French child's word for chicken: a chicken would just fit inside a cocotte. The phrase en cocotte implies that the food is served in the same dish as it was cooked in. Pommes de terre cocotte are potatoes cut into tiny ovals, parboiled, then cooked in butter.

CODDLE — As a verb, to coddle is to cook slowly in water. It applies particularly to eggs: these are put into water which is brought to the boil and then removed from the heat, while the eggs continue to cook gently in the cooling water. A special container with a tight-fitting lid, called a coddler may be used, in which case the egg is broken into the container before cooking. Coddle is also a traditional Irish supper dish of onions, sausages and bacon cooked together in water and eaten with soda bread and a glass of beer.

COEUR A LA CREME — Simple French dessert made with cream cheese beaten with egg whites and thick cream. It is made in a special individual heart-shaped porcelain mould, which has perforations on the base to allow the whey to drain off. It is unmoulded to serve and sprinkled with sugar. It was invented by Carême and derived from paskha, which he encountered during his spell at the Russian court.

COLANDER — Perforated metal or plastic basket used for draining any fluids from food.

COLBERT — A la Colbert describes a way of preparing fish by dipping it in egg and breadcrumbs, then frying it. Colbert sauce is a béarnaise flavoured with meat glaze. Jean-Baptiste Colbert was chief minister to Louis XIV.

COLCANNON — Irish dish of potatoes mashed with kale. It is traditionally eaten at Hallowe'en, when lucky metal tokens are sometimes hidden in the dish.

COLE SLAW — A salad of raw cabbage, grated carrot and onion. Cole is the generic term for plants of the Brassica family, of which cabbage is a member, and slaw is Danish for salad, but cole slaw is an American invention. The dressing varies but is usually a mixture of oil, cream and vinegar.

COLLAR — Cut of bacon. Prime collar is lower down the neck than end collar. Both are boiling joints.

COLLATION — A collection or a spread of food, for example a cold collation of a selection of cold meats.

58

COLLER — French culinary term meaning to add gelatine to a mixture to give it body.

COLLIOURE, SAUCE — Anchovy-flavoured mayonnaise.

COLLOP — Old fashioned word for a slice, which comes from the same root as the French escalope and the Italian scallopini, although a collop is a much thicker slice than either of these.

COLOMBINE — A croquette coated with semolina and Parmesan cheese. Also a chicken consommé garnished with diced carrot, turnip, julienne of pigeon breast and poached pigeon's egg.

COLONIAL GOOSE — A way of stuffing and roasting a leg of lamb, which was invented in New Zealand.

COLONIAL INNKEEPER'S PIE — Early American dessert from New England. A chocolate and nut cake mixture is baked inside a pastry case.

COLONNE — French apple corer, which is also used to cut root vegetables into the shape of a column.

COLUMBIA, BOMBE — Pear ice with glacé cherries, surrounded by a kirsch-flavoured ice cream

COMAL — Thick cast-iron griddle for making tortillas.

COMFIT — A sugar-coated anise or caraway seed. Comfits were extremely popular as a confection three hundred years ago.

COMMERCY — A town in Lorraine, France, famous for inventing, or at least publicizing, the madeleine.

COMMODORE — Garnish for fish consisting of crayfish or lobster, fish quenelles, mussels à la villeroi and thick crayfish sauce. Also a fish consommé garnished with sliced clams and diced tomatoes.

COMPOTE — Fresh or dried fruit cooked in syrup: what is more prosaically known as stewed fruit. Compotes are usually served cold. The term also applies to a dish of birds cooked slowly and for a long time.

COMTESSE SARAH, BOMBE — Vanilla and kirsch ice enclosing a kummel mousse with crystallized rose leaves.

CONCASSER — French culinary term, meaning to chop roughly.

CONCHIGLIE — Italian for shell. A shell-shaped pasta.

CONDE — A number of dishes have been named after the Prince de Condé. A la Condé implies that rice is an important part of the dish so described. A condé is a creamy rice dessert, set with gelatine and decorated with a fruit purée. It is also an almond-flavoured royal icing and a flaky pastry spread with the above icing.

CONDENSED MILK — Milk which is concentrated by boiling with sugar until reduced by two-thirds.

CONDIMENT — An aromatic substance used to improve the flavour of food. Whereas seasoning is added during cooking, a condiment is added at the table, though otherwise they are much the same. Popular condiments are salt; pepper; acids such as pickles, vinegar, lemon juice; herbs; spices; mustard; horseradish; commercially prepared sauces like Worcestershire sauce, soy sauce, ketchup etc. The word is derived from the Latin condire, to season or pickle.

CONFECTIONARY — The art of sweet-making, also the sweets themselves. All confectionary has sugar as the principal ingredient.

CONFECTIONER'S COMB — A flat piece of plastic with a serrated edge, which can be drawn over melted chocolate on the point of setting to make a wavy line as decoration for cakes and pastries.

CONFECTIONER'S CUSTARD — Another name for crème pâtissière.

CONFECTIONER'S SUGAR — The American name for what the British call icing sugar, ie. powdered sugar.

CONFIT — Rich meat such as goose, duck or pork, cooked in its own fat and preserved in the same fat.

CONFITURE — French word for jam and sweets based on fruit.

CONSERVE — A fruit preserve made with more than one fruit. It is not a mixed fruit jam, but two or three fruits deliberately made into a thick jam because their flavours are complementary. Dried fruit and nuts are sometimes used. A conserve, which may be set or unset, can be used spread on bread like jam, or as a dessert topping, or, if tart or spicy, to accompany roast meat and game.

CONSOMME — French word for meat stock which has been enriched, reduced or clarified. It is served hot as a soup and can also be used in its cold jellied state in place of aspic.

CONTADINA, ALLA — Name given to an Italian dish of chicken braised with ham, tomatoes, rosemary and garlic. Also to stewed, stuffed artichokes.

CONTI — A garnish for sliced meat, of sieved lentils and slices of bacon. Also a lentil soup.

CONTISER — French culinary term meaning to insert truffles (first soaked in egg white to make them stick) into fillets of chicken or fish before cooking.

CONTREFILET — Cut of beef also known as faux filet, which is the part of the sirloin other than the fillet.

CONVENIENCE FOOD — Time-saving food, available frozen, tinned or dried, which requires very little preparation or cooking.

CONVERSATION — French pâtisserie of puff pastry tartlets filled with an almond mixture with royal icing.

COOKIE — American term which covers the small flat cake called a biscuit by the British, as well as a square or oblong cake cut from a thicker, richer mixture, which is baked in one piece in a tray, then cut up to serve.

COPPA — This is the name of three Italian meat preparations as well as the Italian equivalent of the French coupe: a cured shoulder of pork from Parma; a Roman brawn; and a Venetian meat loaf containing ham, tongue and sausage.

COPPER — Mineral necessary for the formation of red blood cells, which is found in shellfish, yeast, liver, gelatine and currants.

COQUILLE, EN — French expression meaning served on a shell.

COQUILLE ST. JACQUES — *See* ST. JACQUES.

CORAL — The ovaries of a female lobster.

CORBEILLE — French for basket, this word implies a basket of fruit on menus.

CORDER — French word meaning to add too much water to pastry resulting in a soggy crust.

CORDON — A border of sauce around a dish.

CORDON BLEU — French for blue ribbon. This expression implies the best French cooking and is also the name of a famous cookery school. The name derives from the eighteenth century when Louis XV enjoyed a particularly good meal at the home of his mistress Madame Dubarry. He sent for the chef in order to pay his compliments and was astonished to find that the chef was a woman – almost unheard of in those days. He created an honour for her on the spot and this was the Cordon Bleu. Veal Cordon Bleu is a veal escalope stuffed with prosciutto and gruyère cheese, coated with egg and breadcrumbs and fried.

CORDON ROUGE — Way of preparing tournedos by larding with Parma ham and stuffing with foie gras, then sautéeing and serving en croûte with a cross of red pepper on top and a port and brandy sauce.

CORNBREAD — American savoury cake, baked in a square tin and cut into squares to serve hot with a main course. The main ingredient is cornmeal.

CORNED — Old English word for cured. Corned beef is usually made with brisket.

CORNELL — Cornell bread is a high protein white bread, containing wheatgerm. The protein is added in the form of soya flour and skimmed milk. Doughnuts, waffles, cookies, even milkshakes are given the Cornell name when reinforced with protein and/or vitamins. The idea was developed in America in the 1940s by Dr. Clive M. McCay of Cornell University.

CORNET — A horn-shaped wafer used as an edible container for ice cream. Also a thin slice of ham or other meat rolled into the shape of a horn.

CORNIOTTE — Triangle of puff pastry with a sweet or savoury cheese filling. The name refers to the cocked hat which it resembles.

CORNISH PASTY — A savoury pastry from Cornwall. A shortcrust pastry circle the size of a saucer or small plate is filled with chopped beef, liver, potato, onion, carrot and turnip, all well seasoned. The pastry is drawn up on two sides to meet in the middle and the edges are sealed before baking. The pasty originated as a convenient way of carrying a complete meal for outdoor workers and miners. In large families each person had his initials marked in pastry at one end of the pasty.

CORN STICK — American cornbread mixture baked in a special mould so that it looks like a corn on the cob sliced vertically in half.

CORNUCOPIA — The horn of plenty. This word is freely applied to food which is shaped like a horn – for example, the pastry also known as a cream horn. It also refers to a slice of ham rolled inside a horn-shaped mould, then filled with a savoury mousse: when the mousse sets the mould is removed, leaving the cornucopia intact. It is served at buffet luncheons or as an appetizer.

CORSER — French term meaning to give body to a dough so that it can be worked until it is firm and elastic.

COSHE — Lithuanian peasant dish of a huge potato and onion pancake, served with a chilled topping which is a mixture of cottage cheese, sour cream and spring onions.

COTECHINO — Large Italian pork sausage, weighing between one and two lbs (up to one kg), which is sold uncooked.

COTELETTE — French for cutlet, this word also describes a chicken suprême which still has the upper part of the wing attached.

COTIGNAC — Dried quince paste from Orléans.

COTOYER — French term meaning to turn a joint of roasting meat so that all sides are evenly cooked.

COTRIADE — A soup of various fishes and potato, which comes from Brittany.

COTTAGE — This name is applied to a loaf of bread, a pie and a pudding. Cottage loaf is two rounds of bread dough one on top of the other, the smaller being on top. It dates back to Roman times, when it was invented to utilize the height of the oven. A knotched cottage has short downward cuts through both sections. Cottage Pie is a British dish of minced beef in gravy, which is topped with mashed potato and browned in the oven. Cottage Pudding is an American term for a sweet sponge pudding served hot with a sauce. It is baked in an oblong tray and cut into squares to serve. There are many variations.

COUCHER — French verb meaning to lay down or put to bed. As a culinary term it can mean two things: either to arrange food on a bed of another food (such as rice); or, to pipe a mixture onto a baking sheet in a round or oval shape.

COUCOU — Popular Trinidad dish of okra cooked in a cornmeal pudding.

COUENNE — French term for thick pork rind. It is used to add flavour and richness to stews.

COULIS — French term meaning a liquid thickened with pieces of vegetables or meat. A tomato coulis is the most usual kind: this is simply several tomatoes, skinned, deseeded and chopped or sliced, then cooked in a covered pan with a little onion and oil until just soft.

COUPE — French for cup. As a culinary term it describes a cold dessert served in a glass – very often it contains ice cream.

COURONNE — French word for crown. This term is applied to food which is arranged in a circle or cooked in a ring mould, so that it resembles a crown.

COURT BOUILLON — Aromatic stock of water, vegetables, herbs, seasoning, lemon juice and olive oil, simmered for about twenty minutes, then used for cooking fish or vegetables.

COUSCOUS — North African dish of steamed semolina, generally served with a tajine of meat or poultry with vegetables. Couscous is very ancient in origin and is cooked in a special pot resembling a double boiler, so that the semolina is steamed over the tajine.

COZIDO — Portuguese term for a boiled dish.

CRACHER — French pâtisserie term meaning to make an incision in puff pastry with a sharp knife. This is done for decoration and to make the dough rise evenly.

CRACK — The stage reached when sugar is boiled to 310°F (152°C).

CRACKER — A dry biscuit. In Britain the term is specifically for a savoury biscuit, which is eaten with cheese. In the United States, it is applied more generally to salted, sweet or plain biscuits.

CRACKLING — The crisp skin of a roasted joint of pork, which has been scored and sprinkled with salt. The crackling is detached from the meat and cut into strips to serve with the meat.

CRACKLING BREAD — U.S. soul food. Cornbread with crackling bread in.

CRACKLING CRUST — A mixture of ground almonds, sugar and beaten egg white made to a stiff paste, which is used to line a flan ring and baked blind.

CRACKNEL — Plain biscuit. The dough is boiled before it is baked and this makes it puff up in the oven.

CRAPAUDINE, A LA — Method of preparing birds, especially pigeons, by splitting them horizontally then grilling them. The name is from crapaud – toad in French – because this is what the bird resembles when cooked in this way.

CREAM CRACKER — Light, puffy, unsweetened biscuit, made from flour, water and very little fat. It is usually eaten with cheese.

CREAMED — This word describes an item of food which has been puréed or at least beaten until smooth, and to which a small amount of cream has been added. It is a popular way of preparing root and leaf vegetables. Poultry and fish are sometimes described as being creamed: this means that small pieces of poultry or fish are coated in a velouté sauce.

CREAM ICE — A type of ice cream made with fruit purée and a strong sugar syrup. Whipped cream is added to the frozen mixture and it is then refrozen.

CREAMING — A method of blending fat, usually butter or margarine, with sugar as part of the preparation of a cake. The fat must be at room temperature so that it is soft, but not melted. It is stirred and rubbed against the side of the bowl with a wooden spoon until smooth. The sugar is added and the creaming continued until the sugar is amalgamated with the fat and the mixture is pale and fluffy in texture. The more thorough the creaming, the finer the texture of the finished cake. Cakes made by this method have a high fat and egg content and do not keep well. Nowadays electric mixers have taken the hard work out of creaming.

CRECY — This term is applied to a number of dishes, all of whom are either made with or garnished with carrots. The town of Crecy in the Seine et Marne district of France (which has nothing to do with the battle of Crécy in 1346) is famous for its carrots.

CREME A LA — This expression describes meat, poultry, fish or vegetables whose pan juices have been mixed with fresh cream to form a simple sauce.

CREME ANGLAISE — French for English cream, this term describes an egg custard made to pouring consistency, which may be served hot or cold with desserts.

CREME BRULEE — French for burnt cream, though, in fact, this famous dessert was created at Trinity College, Cambridge, where it is still served. It is a very rich and solid custard of cream and egg yolks, with a caramel crust on top. It is usually made in individual moulds and served chilled.

CREME FRAICHE — French for fresh cream. It is cream which has been allowed to mature but is not sour – although it has a slightly sharp taste.

CREME PATISSIERE — French for pastry-maker's cream. This is a custard of egg yolks, sugar and cream or milk, which is thickened with flour or cornflour and used when cold as a filling for pastries and cakes. It is normally flavoured with vanilla, but other flavourings may be used.

CREME RENVERSEE — French for upside-down cream. An egg custard which is cooked in a mould and turned out onto a serving dish when cold. Usually there is a sauce, such as caramel at the base of the mould, which becomes a topping when the mould is inverted.

CREMETS — A French dessert made by drawing a mixture of whipped cream and whisked egg whites through muslin. Individual portions, which are referred to in the plural (les cremets), are served with sugar sprinkled over and sometimes with strawberries and raspberries.

CREOLE — A la creole can mean one of several different things; a sweet dish so described is usually flavoured with orange, but a savoury dish à la creole is either based on rice or includes tomatoes and sweet peppers cooked in oil. Creole sauce is a highly seasoned espagnole with mushrooms, onions and peppers added.

CREPE — A very thin pancake.

CREPINETTE — A small square-shaped sausage encased in caul. They are usually coated in breadcrumbs for cooking. Crepinettes may be made of any meat or poultry, but pork is the most popular.

CRESPOLINI — Italian pancakes stuffed with spinach, chicken livers and cream cheese, covered with béchamel and baked in the oven.

CRESSONIERE SAUCE — Vinaigrette with chopped watercress and hard-boiled egg added.

CREVER — French term meaning to overcook rice until it bursts.

CRIMP — This term has two different meanings: either to make deep cuts in a fish and leave it in a vinegar and water solution to marinate; or to decorate a pie by pressing the tines of a fork down on the uncooked pastry edge (this also seals the pastry if there is a top crust).

CRINKLED MUSKET — Another name for a barrel loaf.

CRISP — Commercially prepared game chip.

CRISPBREAD — A cross between biscuit and bread. Thin, flat and made from wholegrain, crispbread originated in Scandinavia.

CROCK POT — Originally a tall, unglazed earthenware cooking pot with a lid, nowadays it refers to an electric slow-cooking pot. A crock pot has a heating element all the way up the sides, so that the food inside cooks evenly on a very low heat. It can be left on all day long comparatively cheaply.

CROISSANT — The French word for crescent. A croissant is a combination of a pastry and a yeast dough, shaped like a crescent before baking. Usually eaten for breakfast, straight from the oven. Croissants were first made in the sixteenth century in Budapest to commemorate the unsuccessful Turkish seige. Some bakers heard the Turks tunnelling their way under the city walls and raised the alarm: their reward was permission to create a special pastry in the form of a crescent, which was the Turkish emblem.

CROQUE AU SEL, A LA — French expression meaning that the food so described is eaten raw with salt.

CROQUE MADAME — Similar to croque monsieur, but with slices of cooked chicken replacing the ham.

CROQUEMBOUCHE — French pâtisserie made particularly for weddings. It is a cone-shaped tower of choux pastry balls on a pâté sucrée base. The height varies and although it is often served plain it can be filled with cream and fruit decorated with spun sugar.

CROQUE MONSIEUR — A popular French snack of a ham and gruyère cheese sandwich, which is toasted or fried after the sandwich has been assembled, so that the cheese melts. The name comes from the French verb croquer, to crunch.

CROQUETTE — A thick, binding sauce containing diced or minced or puréed meat, poultry, game, fish, vegetables, grated cheese or nuts, which is shaped into a cork, a ball or a rectangle, coated in egg and breadcrumbs, then deep-fried and eaten hot. The most usual shape is cylindrical: the size varies. Sweet croquettes may be made of chopped fruit in crème pâtissière.

CROSTATA — Italian fruit flan.

CROSTINO — Italian variety of croûton. Small round of bread which is spread with cheese and grilled or baked until the cheese melts and the bread becomes crisp. Crostini are served with soup.

CROUSTADE — A pastry or fried bread case. Occasionally a croustade may be made with pommes de terre duchesse, pasta or rice. Usually it is filled with a savoury salpicon.

CROUTE — A French term for a slice of bread which has been fried until crisp. Sometimes it is cut into a fancy shape and used as a garnish or as a base for serving food. En croûte means encased in pastry.

CROUTON — A small cube or a flat triangle of dry bread, fried until crisp and used as a garnish, especially for soups.

CROWDIE — Traditional Scottish oatmeal porridge. Confusingly it is also the name of a Scottish cheese, which may be flavoured with nuts or herbs.

CROWN ROAST — Decorative way of serving two best ends of neck of lamb. The joints are bent into semi-circles and assembled to look like a crown, with stuffing or a selection of separately cooked vegetables in the centre.

CRUDITIES — A French word meaning any raw food, but it is usually applied to a selection of raw vegetables served as an appetizer.

CRULLER — A pastry made with a yeast dough, which is rolled out, cut into strips and twisted, then deep-fried, rolled in sugar and served still warm.

CRUMBLE — A verb meaning to reduce to crumbs, but also a mixture of flour, fat and sugar used as a topping for fruit and baked in the oven. The fat is rubbed into the flour and the sugar is stirred in. Porridge oats, wheatgerm, cornflakes, nuts and spices may also be added at this stage. A savoury crumble with cheese replacing the sugar and vegetables in place of fruit is occasionally found.

CRUMPET — Traditional English teacake with a distinctive honeycomb texture. It is a soft, round, flat yeast cake, made with the same ingredients, though more milk, as a muffin, and baked on a griddle. The sudden action of the bottom heat on the yeast and raising agent causes gas bubbles to form quickly: these burst at the surface giving a pitted appearance. To serve, crumpets are toasted, preferably by an open fire, spread generously with butter, then stacked so that the butter melts through. A Scotch crumpet is another name for a Scotch pancake or a griddle cake.

CRUST — The outer edge of an item of baked food. Because it is on the outside and therefore nearer to the source of heat, the crust is more cooked than the inside. A pastry crust refers to a layer of pastry over or underneath food.

CRYSTALLIZE — To preserve fruit or flowers in sugar. Fresh fruit is crystallized by drying it slightly in a warm oven, covering in syrup and leaving it until the syrup hardens, then dredging it in caster sugar. Candied fruit can also be crystallized by blanching and then dipping it in caster sugar. Crystallized flowers (violets, roses, primroses, mimosa) are painted with a sticky glue of gum arabic and flower water. Crystallized fruit and flowers are used as confectionary and as cake decorations.

CU A SICCIA — Way of describing macaroni when served with a sauce of cuttle fish and its ink, plus celery, tomatoes and wine.

CUBAT — Pierre Cubat, chef to Tsar Alexander II of Russia has given his name to many dishes. He was paid according to how many people he fed and consequently became very rich.

CUBE — To cut into small squares.

CUILLER, A LA — French expression applied to beef which is tender enough to cut with a spoon. Boeuf à la mode is sometimes given this name.

CUIRASSE, EN — French for in armour. As a culinary term it means enclosed in pastry and is applied to individual items, such as a lamb chop, which are wrapped in pastry.

CUISINE MINCEUR — A method of cooking based on classic French principles, but avoiding ingredients with high calorie and saturated fat content, such as butter and cream.

CUISSON — A French word which describes the cooking process and also the liquor in which food has been cooked.

CULLEN SKINK — A soup of smoked haddock, milk and potato from Scotland. The name is a mystery as skink is a certain kind of beef in Scotland and Cullen is a town in Banffshire as well as the name of an eighteenth century nutritionist.

CUMBERLAND SAUCE — Redcurrant jelly melted and flavoured with orange, lemon and port. It is served with ham. Cumberland sauce is named after the Duke of Cumberland, son of George III.

CUP — American measuring cup. As a rough guide one cup holds half a pound of butter or sugar but only four and a half ounces of flour.

Cu

CUPCAKE — Small deep individual cake with a flat top, which is usually iced. Its name is due to the fact that the ingredients were measured by the cupful – not because it was baked in a cup.

CURD — The semi-solid part of milk, produced by souring. Lemon curd is a preserve made with lemons, sugar, egg yolks and butter: it has a soft, spreading consistency.

CURDLING — The process of coagulating milk so that it divides into solid curds and liquid whey. Milk is curdled with an acid such as rennet or lemon juice. Also the separation of a mixture resembling milk curds, hence the name, which may happen, for example, to a cake mixture when eggs are added too quickly: a curdled cake will not be as light as it should be.

CURING — Preparing food by drying, salting or smoking in order to preserve.

CURNONSKIY — Garnish for tournedos of grilled tomatoes and beef marrow in a brandy, port and truffle sauce. Ballotine de volaille Curnonskiy is a boned chicken piece with the leg intact, marinated and spread with minced veal, ham and pork, foie gras and truffle, rolled up and wrapped in pork fat, then cooked in wine and vegetables. It is served on a croûte, garnished with artichoke hearts and potatoes.

CURRY — The general name given to food in a savoury sauce flavoured with a mixture of ground spices. The spices are cooked in clarified butter before the main ingredient is added. Although the proportions vary, the principle spices in a curry are: allspice, anise, bay leaves, cumin, curry leaves, dill, fennel, fenugreek, garlic, ginger, mace, mustard, paprika, pepper, poppy seeds, saffron and turmeric. Curry is an Indian invention. Curry powder is a ready made blend of the spices needed for a curry.

CUSSY — A la Cussy is a garnish for small cuts of meat and poultry of mushrooms stuffed with chestnut purée, cock's kidneys and whole truffles cooked in Madeira. Cussy sauce is a demi-glace plus Madeira and jellied poultry stock. Cussy is also the name of a game consommé garnished with cubed chestnut and partridge royale, partridge quenelles and a julienne of truffles.

CUSTARD — A mixture of beaten eggs and milk, usually sweetened, cooked in a bain-marie until it thickens.

CUT IN — A method of adding an ingredient to a mixture which is full of air. A gentle cutting movement with a palette knife blends the mixture without loss of air.

CUTLET — A chop cut from the best end of neck of lamb, mutton, pork or veal. It is usually grilled, fried or braised.

CYRANO — Duck consommé garnished with gratinéed duck quenelles.

CZARINA — Beef consommé flavoured with fennel and garnished with vesiga.

DACQUOISE — A cake of layers of almond-flavoured meringue, which is usually filled with fruit and cream. The meringue mixture is thickened and enriched with cornflour and butter.

DAGWOOD — Giant-size sandwich with many different fillings, named after an American comic-strip character.

DAHI — Indian milk curd like a thin, set yogurt.

DAHL — Indian dish of spicy, mushy lentils.

DAKTYLA — Greek bread made by sticking several rolls of dough together in a long row. It is sprinkled with sesame and nigella seeds.

DALAYRAC — Chicken consommé garnished with julienne of chicken, mushrooms and truffles.

DAME BLANCHE, SOUFFLE — Sweet soufflé made with almonds.

DANISH — Loaf of bread in a rounded rectangular shape. It is open baked and split on the top for crustiness all round, but especially on the top.

DANISH PASTRY — Rich pastry made with a yeast dough in a variety of shapes. It may be decorated or filled with glacé icing, nuts, fruit, spices etc. *See* WIENERBROD.

DANOISE — Wild duck consommé garnished with game and mushroom quenelles, flavoured with Marsala.

DARBLAY, POTAGE — Potato soup with julienne of vegetables added, thickened with egg yolks and cream.

DARIOLE — Small, cylindrical mould used particularly for cakes, sponge puddings and an old English pastry, also called a dariole, consisting of a puff pastry case filled with frangipane, almonds and liqueur. The word, which has been in use since the fourteenth century, comes from doriole, meaning something golden, referring to the golden colour of the cooked pastry.

DARNE — Thick slice of a large fish, often salmon, which can be poached, grilled, braised or sautéed.

D'ARTAGNON, A LA — A garnish for meat and poultry of cepes with bearnaise sauce, stuffed tomatoes and small potato croquettes. D'Artagnon was the hero of several Alexandre Dumas novels.

DARTOIS — French pâtisserie of two layers of puff pastry sandwiched with almond cream and baked with a sugar glaze on top. A savoury version can also be made, filled with any salpicon and served hot as a first course, light main course or cocktail snack, depending on the size. The name comes from d'Artois ie. from Artois.

DASH — Imprecise but small quantity to measure liquid.

DASHI — Japanese fish stock made from dried bonito and dried seaweed, which is the foundation for many Japanese dishes. It tastes more like chicken stock.

DAUB — To make incisions on meat and insert strips of bacon to add flavour and moisture.

DAUBE — Meat cooked slowly and for a long time in a daubière so that the meat is tender enough to eat with a spoon. Sometimes it is described as being en daube. The meat is often larded or marinated, but never seared, and was originally served cold. The word tends to describe an unsophisticated country recipe, and comes from the Italian addobbo, meaning garnish.

DAUBIERE — Heavy casserole with lid and handles at the side, used for braising.

DAUDET — Chicken consommé garnished with a julienne of celeriac, lobster quenelles and chicken and ham royale.

DAUMONT — A la Daumont is a garnish for a large fish of crayfish tails, large whole mushrooms, fish quenelles, soft roes coated in breadcrumbs and fried, and Nantua sauce. Consommé Daumont is a beef consommé garnished with rice, ox palate and mushrooms. Sauce Daumont is a Hollandaise flavoured with oyster juice and lemon juice, and garnished with oysters, mushrooms and truffles.

DAUPHINE — A la Dauphine is a garnish for slices of meat of pommes de terre dauphine in straw potato nests, with demi-glace sauce. It is also a way of preparing fillets of sole: these are poached in Madeira, masked in sauce villeroi and crayfish butter, coated in breadcrumbs and fried, then garnished with a border of mushrooms, fish forcemeat balls, fish quenelles, crayfish and truffles, the garnish coated with velouté sauce and sauce Nantua served separately. Pommes de terre dauphine is smooth, creamed potatoes, beaten with egg yolk, then mixed with choux paste and deep-fried in small balls.

DEAUVILLAISE, A LA — Way of cooking fish, especially sole, au gratin in a sauce of onions, cider or white wine and cream.

DEEP-FRYING — Total immersion of food in a large deep pan of boiling fat. A deep-frying pan has a basket which fits inside it to contain the food and allow it to be lowered into the fat and removed again safely. Food to be deep-fried must be suitable for fast, fierce cooking and is often protected by a layer of batter, egg and breadcrumbs or other coating. The advantage of successful deep-frying is that inside the crisp coating the food retains its juices and is full of flavour. However, if badly cooked, deep-fried food is soggy and indigestible.

DEGLACER — To add wine, water or stock to a pan in which meat has been roasted or sautéed to obtain the juices and particles left behind.

DEGORGER — To soak food in cold water to free it of impurities and strong taste.

DEGRAISSAGE — Removal of fat from stock or a sauce.

DEGRAISSER — French culinary term which means to skim off the excess fat on the surface of a liquid such as stock.

DEGRAISSIS — Fat which has been skimmed from stock.

DELICE — A small piece of food.

DELICATESSEN — Selection of food ready to eat, mostly cold, cooked meats, cheese and made-up salads. It is also the shop were such goods are sold.

DELICIEUSE, BOMBE — A bombe with an outer layer of peach ice and a filling of champagne-flavoured ice.

DELMONICO STEAK — An American term for entrecôte.

DEMI-DEUIL — French for in half-mourning. As a culinary expression it means food dressed with a suprême sauce and garnished with truffles. Chicken demi-deuil is the best-known example: this has truffle arranged under the skin and a veil of sauce over it. A white veil was worn by widows after the period of full mourning was over.

DEMIDOFF — The Russian prince, Anatole Demidoff, a famous gastronome in the nineteenth century, has many extravagent dishes named after him. Sweetbreads Demidoff is braised sweetbreads in a rich sauce, garnished with truffles cut into crescents.

DEMI-GLACE — French for half glazed, this is a major sauce. It is a rich brown sauce, like espagnole, but more stock is added and then the sauce is reduced until it is half glazed. This process takes several hours, and the final result is so refined that it sets like jelly when cold.

DEMI-TASSE — French for half cup. It is a small cup of black coffee served after a meal.

DENERVER — French culinary term meaning to remove gristle, tendons, membranes etc. from meat and poultry.

DENT-DE-LOUP — French for wolf's tooth. This expression describes two types of decorative presentation: either triangles of jelly arranged round a cold dish, or triangles of fried bread arranged round a hot dish.

DENTELLE — Brittany crepe which is very thin and lacy in appearance, hence the name.

DENVER — A Denver sandwich is filled with scrambled egg, ham, green pepper and onion. A Denver omelette is filled with ham, green pepper and onion. Both are from the United States.

DEPOUILLER — French term meaning to skim a sauce, removing impurities and fat, after boiling. It also means to skin a rabbit.

DESOSSER — French for to bone.

DESSECHER — French pâtisserie term meaning to evaporate moisture over a gentle heat.

DESSERT — The last course of a meal ie. sweet dishes, cheese and fruit.

DESSICCATION — Process of drying certain foods, especially coconut, in order to preserve.

DETAILLER — French pâtisserie term meaning to cut out pastry shapes.

DETREMPE, LA — French term for uncooked pastry dough.

DEVIL — To prepare meat, poultry or fish with highly seasoned ingredients for grilling or roasting. Devilled poultry is usually split open along the back. *See* DIABLE.

DEVIL'S FOOD CAKE — American cake named as a counterpoint to Angel Food Cake. It is a light but very rich, dark chocolate cake in three layers, sandwiched together and coated with vanilla frosting.

DEVONSHIRE SPLIT — Also known as Cornish split, this is a light yeast roll, usually served warm, split open and spread with clotted cream.

DHAL — *See* DAHL.

DHANSAK — Spicy dish of chicken with several types of lentils and vegetables. It is a Parsee recipe from the west of India.

DIABLE — French for devil, this word has many meanings and uses in cookery. A diable is a round, single-handled pot with a cover which is the mirror image of the bottom: it is made of unglazed earthenware and is used chiefly for roasting potatoes or chestnuts without any fat. Originally this pot was put into red hot charcoal, hence the name. A la diable means that the food in question has been smeared with mustard or other spicy mixture before grilling or roasting. Au diable refers to a gratin of leftover meat or poultry spread with mustard, cayenne, breadcrumbs and melted butter, then baked. Diable sauce is made of reduced white wine and vinegar with shallots and herbs, added to a demi-glace or espagnole sauce. Bombe Diable Rose has an outer layer of strawberry ice enclosing a kirsch-flavoured ice with glacé cherries in it.

DIABLOTIN — A slice of French bread, covered with cheese sauce, spiked with cayenne pepper, with grated cheese on top, then browned under the grill. Diablotins are served with soup. It is also the name of a chocolate sweet sold in paper cases with a motto.

DIANE — Steak Diane is a famous dish from Australia. A thin steak is quickly fried, chopped shallots are added to the pan with brandy, which is set alight. When the flames die, Worcestershire sauce, tomato sauce and demi-glace sauce are added with parsley and butter. Glace Diane is chestnut mousse flavoured with kirsch and maraschino, surrounded by vanilla ice cream.

DICE — To cut into very small cubes.

75

DIEPPOISE — Classic way of serving fish, with mussels and/or shrimps or crayfish tails, often in a creamy sauce.

DIGESTIVE BISCUIT — Lightly sweetened, crumbly biscuit made with wholemeal flour. The top crust is decorated with tiny holes.

DIJONAISE — This term indicates the prescence of Dijon mustard in the recipe.

DILUTE — To reduce a liquid in strength by adding another liquid, usually water, milk or stock.

DIM SUM — Chinese snack dish of which there are a great many varieties, the most usual being dumplings, buns or croquettes. Literally translated dim sum means lightly brushing the heart. Savoury dim sum are either steamed and served in bamboo baskets or deep-fried. Sweet dim sum may be cake, tart or confection. They are served in Cantonese tea-houses in the afternoon.

DIP — Smooth, soft savoury mixture, usually served as a party food in a bowl surrounded by sticks of raw vegetables, cocktail biscuits etc., which guests use to dip into the mixture. Dips are invariably spicy or tangy to whet the appetite and are served cold. Often they are based on cream cheese, which provides a creamy consistency, but is solid enough not to be a messy party snack.

DIPLOMAT — The name of a pudding made with layers of sponge fingers soaked in liqueur, with crystallized fruit, currants and sultanas. It is also the name of a lobster sauce to serve with fish.

DISSOLVE — To mix a dry ingredient with a liquid until no trace is visible. This may be done with or without heat.

DITALINI — Tubular macaroni slightly less than one cm. in length and diameter. It is used chiefly in soups.

DIVAN — Turkey or chicken strips with broccoli spears in a velouté sauce which is flavoured with sherry and cheese, baked au gratin. Only the breast and thigh meat should be used. It was created at a New York restaurant called the Divan Parisian in the 1920s.

DIVINE — Hollandaise sauce with sherry and whipped cream added. It is served with fish, chicken or eggs.

DIVINITY — Soft, pale-coloured confection with a consistency like a crumbly fudge.

DIZA — Iranian stew of lamb, beans and chick peas. It is served in three separate bowls: the broth is served as soup, the meat and mashed beans are in another bowl, and the chick peas and vegetables are in a third bowl.

DJUVEC — Serbian meat stew with rice, tomatoes, green peppers and carrots. The meat is most often lamb.

DOBOS TORTE — Hungarian gâteau consisting of six thin layers of sponge cake, sandwiched with chocolate butter cream and topped with a layer of hard caramel. It was invented in 1885 by Jozsef Dobos, the owner of a famous restaurant in Budapest.

DODINE — A boned and reshaped bird, braised in wine and served hot with the juices as a sauce.

DOGGY BAG — In the U.S. it is acceptable to ask for a doggy bag to take home leftovers supposedly for the dog. In practice the leftovers are removed from the table and returned discreetly wrapped up ready for reheating at home.

DOLCE TORINESE — Chocolate refrigerator cake flavoured with almonds and rum from Turin in Italy.

DOLMADES/DOLMAS — Turkish dish of vine leaves stuffed with minced lamb and rice. Sometimes the vine leaves are replaced by cabbage leaves, aubergines, peppers, tomatoes or courgettes. With minor variations, this dish is eaten throughout the Middle East and south eastern Europe.

DOMINIQUE, SOLE — Sole stuffed with a mixture of whiting, mushrooms and enriched Mornay sauce, then baked in wine and stock.

DONE — Term used in recipes to mean cooked or ready to serve. For fish, this means opaque, flaky, white fish; meat should be tender and browned; for poultry, the joints must move easily; vegetables are just tender; cakes that are done begin to shrink from the sides of the tin and when a knife is inserted it comes out clean.

DONER KEBAB — This means turning kebab in Turkish. Lamb is cut up and pounded and marinated, then wrapped around a revolving spit. It is smoothed wth lamb fat and placed in front of a charcoal fire. It is carved in layers as it browns and the slices are collected in a tray below. Doner kebab is usually served with salad in pita bread. This dish is not normally made at home.

DOPIAZA — Indian curry in which onions appear twice in the cooking process.

Do

DORIA — A garnish for eggs and fish of cucumbers cut into olives and cooked in butter, with pommes noisettes. Also a chicken consommé with chicken quenelles, olives of cucumber, fried cheese pastry balls and chervil. Salade doria is a julienne of celeriac arranged in a mound, covered with mayonnaise and garnished with julienne of beetroot and asparagus, sieved hard-boiled egg yolk and parsley.

DORER — French pâtisserie term meaning to glaze.

DOSA — Pancake made with a fermented dough of rice flour and lentil flour — It comes from Southern India, where it is sometimes called masala (spiced) dosa and served with a spicy potato mixture.

DOUBLE BOILER — Two saucepans which fit together. The lower pan contains boiling or simmering water, the upper pan contains the food to be cooked by the steam from the lower pan. It is useful for cooking delicate items which must not come into contact with fierce heat, such as egg custards and sauces.

DOUBLE CREAM — Cream with a minimum fat content of 48% which is suitable for whipping and holds its shape well once whipped.

DOUBLER — French word meaning to fold in two or to cover to prevent overcooking.

DOUFEU — Covered casserole distinguished by a depression in the lid in which hot coals were originally put. Nowadays water is used instead to encourage condensation within the pot. Notches on the inside of the lid collect moisture which drops back and bastes the food. It is used on top of the stove so the contents are cooked from above as well as below. The name literally means gentle fire in French: this refers to the open fire over which it was once used.

DOUGH — Mixture of flour and a liquid which is stiff enough to handle.

DOUGHNUT — Small round cake of yeast dough which is deep-fried and sprinkled with sugar. Correctly used the word should only be applied to a ring-shaped doughnut (*see* BISMARCK). This shape was thought up to ensure that the mixture was thoroughly cooked.

DOUGLAS — Beef consommé garnished with sweetbreads, asparagus tips and artichoke bottoms.

DOUILLON,EN — A whole pear wrapped in shortcrust pastry and baked in an upright position. The name comes from douilette, a French word meaning a priest's overcoat. The recipe comes from Normandy.

DOVILLE, MOULE A — Ring-shaped mould.

DRAGEE — French word for a sugar-coated sweet or nut. Usually it means an almond coated with a hard, sweet, pale-coloured icing.

DRAGEMIROFF — Russian dish of flaked chicken in a sauce of sour cream, mushrooms and gherkins.

DRAIN — To remove liquid from food by placing it in a colander or sieve, or to remove fat from food by placing it on absorbent paper.

DRAW — To remove the entrails of a bird.

DRAWN BUTTER — Melted butter, which is sometimes thickened by beating with vinegar or water, and used as a sauce. In the United States the term means clarified butter.

DREDGE — To sprinkle heavily with flour or sugar.

DREDGER — Canister with a perforated lid, which is used for dredging. A flour dredger has smaller holes than a sugar dredger.

DRESS — This word has three meanings as a culinary term. When applied to poultry or game, it means to pluck, clean and truss, ie. to make ready for cooking. To dress a salad is to coat it with a sauce. To dress fish is to gut and trim it.

DRESSING — Something that adds flavouring to a salad in liquid form. In the United States it also means a stuffing.

DRIPPING — The juices (including fat) that drip from roasting meat (not poultry) into the pan. Originally the meat would have been on a spit and a pan would have been placed strategically below to catch the drippings, as the juices were then called. Dripping is used to baste the meat or may be used for frying where a strong flavour is desirable. Cold dripping (which sets firm) is spread on hot toast and eaten as a snack.

DRUMSTICK — The lower part of a chicken or turkey leg.

DRY — To preserve food by drying it, thus ridding it of the moisture which is needed for food-spoilage-organisms to grow. Drying in air is only suitable for small objects which are already naturally low in moisture, such as herbs or chili peppers. Fruit can be dried out in sunshine or in a very low oven. Sausages like salami are dried in a cool constant temperature for a very long time. It is the oldest method of preservation: the ancient Egyptians used to bury figs, dates and grapes in the hot sand.

DRY FRY — Chinese cooking method. Food is stir fried over a low heat until dry and crispy.

DUBARRY — A la Dubarry is a garnish of cauliflower florets coated in Mornay sauce, sprinkled with grated cheese and breadcrumbs, then browned. Crème Dubarry is a cauliflower velouté soup. Both are named after Madame Dubarry, the mistress of Louis XV of France, who was later guillotined. The florets of cauliflower are said to remind one of her head after it had been separated from her body.

DUCHESSE — Pommes de terre duchesse are puréed potatoes, beaten with egg yolk and piped into whirls, croustades or borders. Duchesse is the name given to a chicken consommé thickened with sago and garnished with chiffonade of lettuce and royale, also a cream sauce garnished with tongue and mushroom, and a petit four in the form of a ball, made with chocolate, ground almonds, ground hazelnuts, sugar and egg white.

DUFF — Traditional English thick flour pudding, which is boiled or steamed in a cloth. Sometimes a fruit, such as a plum, is enclosed in the dough before cooking.

DUFFERIN — A mildly curry-flavoured fish consommé, garnished with rice, sole and curried fish quenelles.

DUGLÉRÉ — Adolphe Dugléré was the chef at the famous Café Anglais in nineteenth-century Paris. He created a classic recipe for sole – oven poached and served with a velouté sauce containing pieces of chopped tomato and parsley. This sauce is now used with other fish and shellfish.

DUM — Indian method of cooking. Ingredients are cooked in their own steam under pressure by sealing the lid of the cooking pot with dough.

DUMESNIL — Beef consommé garnished with beef marrow and julienne of mixed vegetables.

DUMPLING — Small balls of steamed or baked dough, usually served with soup or stew. They may also be made of a potato mixture. Sweet dumplings are stuffed with fresh or dried fruit. A whole fruit enclosed in pastry may also be called a dumpling. Dumplings are always served hot.

DUNDEE CAKE — Rich fruit cake with whole almonds arranged in a circular pattern on top.

DUROC — Method of sautéeing chicken with mushrooms and herbs, then garnishing with tomatoes and new potatoes.

DUST — To sprinkle lightly with flour or sugar.

DUTCH OVEN — American term for a large deep pan with a well-fitting lid, which is used on top of the stove to cook a joint of meat.

DUXELLES — Mixture of finely chopped mushrooms, shallots and herbs, cooked in butter and used to flavour sauces, soup and stuffing. Duxelles sauce is a velouté sauce to which the mixture is added. The name comes from the Marquis D'Uxelles, who was the employer of La Varenne, the celebrated chef.

ECALURE — French term for the peel, shell or skin of fruit, nuts, vegetables, eggs and shellfish.

ECARLATE, A L' — This term describes meat pickled in brine and boiled. Salpicon à l'écarlate is chopped pickled tongue bound with a demi-glace sauce. The saltpetre in brine makes the meat pinkish in colour: écarlate is scarlet in French.

ECCLES CAKE — Small, round, flat pastry from Eccles in Lancashire. Made with puff pastry and filled with currants, butter and sugar, it has three diagonal cuts across the top. The original recipe is still a secret, though passable imitations are widely available.

ECHAUDER — French culinary term meaning to plunge (something) into boiling water.

ECLAIR — Fingers of baked choux pastry, filled with cream or crème pâtissière and topped with chocolate or coffee glacé icing.

81

Ec

ECOSSAISE, A L' — Mutton consommé with pearl barley and a brunoise of carrot, celery and leek.

EDINBURGH ROCK — Scottish confection with a powdery texture, which is usually sold as a selection of small pieces of different colours.

EDNA MAY, COUPE — Vanilla ice cream, cherry compote and raspberry-flavoured cream.

EFFEUILLER — French term meaning to remove the leaves from an artichoke or herb.

EGGAH — Arab-style omelette. It is solid in texture and thick in size, and is cut in slices to serve like a cake. It may be plain or filled with almost any savoury filling.

EGGNOG — Thick drink made with eggs, cream, sugar, bourbon and vanilla ice cream, which is served in a large bowl at Christmas time in the United States.

EGGPLANT — American for aubergine.

EGG ROLL — English name for a Cantonese speciality. Julienne of meat or poultry, shellfish and vegetables are wrapped in a rice pancake like a parcel and deep-fried.

EGRUGER — French word meaning to grind in a mill or mortar.

EIGHT JEWEL PUDDING — Elaborate Chinese steamed rice pudding containing eight different types of dried and/or candied fruit or nuts. It is turned out and served with a sugar syrup.

EINTOPF — German one-dish meal (literally one dish) of meat or fish and vegetables. There are many local variations, the most famous being Berliner Eintopf, which contains mixed meats, cabbage, potatoes and beans.

EMINCER — French culinary term meaning to slice finely.

EMINCES — Very thin slices of meat, usually leftovers reheated in a sauce.

EMPANADA — Spanish savoury pie. A yeast dough is rolled out into two circles, one slightly larger than the other. The filling (meat or chicken with chorizo, ham, peppers, tomatoes, onions and garlic) is heaped on the larger circle and the smaller circle goes on top. The edge of the bottom layer is rolled up over the lid to make a seam and the top is decorated with pastry trimmings cut in strips.

EMULSION — Made by mixing two liquids which are not mutually soluble, for example, oil and water. Tiny pellets of one liquid swim around in the other liquid. Sometimes an emulsifying agent such as egg yolk is used to help the process.

ENCHAUD — Rolled stuffed joint of pork cooked by a method which is somewhere between roasting and pot roasting. It is served hot or cold in thick overlapping slices.

ENCHILADA — Fried tortilla rolled around a filling. Among the endless varieties are: enchilada de Acapulco – turkey, olives and almonds; enchilada de Jocoque – cheese, sour cream and spring onions; enchilada roja – ancho chillies, cinnamon and chocolate; enchilada verde – poblano chillies and green tomatoes. The tortilla is dipped in spicy sauce before frying, then after frying and filling it is covered with more sauce and baked in the oven.

ENROBER — French term meaning to cover a cake completely, eg. with icing.

ENTRECOTE — French cut of beef from the wing end of the ribs. The meat is boned and cut into steaks which can be grilled or fried.

ENTRECUISSE — French term for the thigh of poultry or game birds.

ENTREE — The entrée precedes the roast and is brought in at the beginning of the meal ie. after the soup and hors d'oeuvre, but before the main course. Nowadays, however, meals are simpler and entrée is often taken to mean main course.

ENTREMETS — Old fashioned term for the dessert course. Literally it means between dishes in French and originally this indicated an interval after the roast, when lighter dishes, vegetables as well as sweets, were served while entertainments took place.

ENZYME — Organic chemical compound which acts as a catalyst to cause a chemical reaction such as fermentation.

EPIGRAM — A lamb chop with a slice of the breast dipped in egg and breadcrumbs, then fried or grilled. The story as to how the term came to be applied to food is as follows: in eighteenth-century France, a competitive but ignorant hostess overheard one of her guests praising the epigrams at another's dinner party. She ordered her chef to prepare a dish of epigrams on the spot: his creation was served as épigrams of lamb, this was thought very amusing by her guests and the name stuck.

ERWTENSOEP — Dutch pea soup. It is made from dried peas and flavoured with either smoked sausage or bacon.

ESCABAECHE — Fried whole small fish (anchovies, sardines etc.) marinated after cooking in a hot spicy mixture and served as an appetiser in Spain and Portugal.

ESCALOPE — Thin, boneless, fatless, skinless slice of meat, flattened slightly and fried. Veal escalopes are the most popular: these are cut from the fillet, best end of neck, topside or silverside.

ESCOFFIER — Augustine Escoffier was a famous French chef and cookery writer.

ESPAGNOLE — French for Spanish. Classic brown sauce flavoured with bacon, tomatoes, carrot, celery and onion. When the Spanish Infanta married Louis XIV in 1660, she brought her own chefs who created this classic sauce.

ESPERANZA, BOMBE — Orange ice enclosing kirsch and praline ice cream with gooseberries.

ESPRESSO — Coffee made in a machine which forces steam through the powdered coffee. The result is aromatic, flavoursome and comparatively quickly made, hence the name.

ESSENCE — An oily liquid made by distilling vegetable substances in water. It is a concentrated but liquid form of flavouring.

ESTOUFFADE — French term for a very slowly cooked stew. Also a clear brown stock.

ESTOUFFAT — Slowly cooked stew of pork and haricot beans from the Languedoc.

ETOUFFER/ETUVER — Method of cooking food in a utensil with a tightly closed lid, in the oven, with fat but no liquid.

EVAPORATED MILK — Milk which has been evaporated to half its volume, homogenized, canned and sterilized. It is thick with a pronounced flavour and whips well if chilled. Unlike condensed milk it is not sweetened. It can be reconstituted with water and used in cooking as milk.

EVENTAIL — French for fan. In culinary terms it refers to a traditional fanshape arrangement of food, especially fish, on a serving dish.

EVE'S PUDDING — Hot, baked, nursery pudding of sponge cake with a layer of stewed apples underneath. The name is an illusion to Eve eating the apple in the Garden of Eden.

EXTRACT — Product made by evaporating meat juice. In the United States the word is also used to mean essences which have been extracted with a solvent such as water or alcohol.

EXTRA THICK CREAM — Cream with a minimum fat content of 30% which has been homogenized and heat treated in order to thicken it. It is not suitable for whipping.

EYE OF THE ROUND — American name for part of the cut of meat which the British call silverside.

FABADA — Spanish bean-based stew.

FABRIANO, SALAME — Pork and beef salame from Ancona, Italy.

FAGGOT — Mixture of minced offal, pork, breadcrumbs and herbs, usually round, but sometimes loaf-shaped or square. It is wrapped in or covered by caul and baked in the oven. The caul keeps the meat well basted. Faggots, also known as savoury ducks, are a popular way of using up the bits and pieces when a pig is killed. There are regional variations to this traditional dish. The word means a bundle. A faggot of herbs is a bouquet garni.

FAIRE REVENIR — French expression meaning to lightly brown food in fat without cooking.

FAIRY CAKE — Another name for a cupcake.

FAISANDAGE — French word applied to red meat which is high.

FAIT-TOUT — Literally (in French) does everything. All-purpose casserole with a lid.

FAJITAS — Popular Tex-Mex dish: soft flour tortillas are brought to the table and the diner stuffs them with beef, chicken or shrimp cooked with onions, peppers and spices. Guacamole, salsa and sour cream are also added at the table.

FALAFEL — Small, deep-fried balls of spiced, mashed chick peas, from the Middle East. They are served with pitta bread, salad and tahini dressing.

FAR — Breton batter pudding. It may be steamed or baked. Variations include Far Breton, which has prunes in it, and Far Platt, which has raisins.

FARCE — French word for stuffing.

FARFALLE — Italian for butterflies. Pasta shaped like bows or butterflies. Farfalloni are large ones, farfallini are very small and farfallette are quite small.

FARL — Round, flat oatmeal cake, baked on a griddle.

FARMHOUSE — Shorter, fatter version of a split tin loaf of bread.

FAT — Solid substance formed by mixing a fatty acid and alcohol. Most fats come from animal products: these are saturated, keep well, but if eaten in large quantities are thought to be associated with heart disease.

FAT BACK — Salt pork from the upper side of the pig. It is used to give flavour in U.S. soul food cuisine.

FAT RASCAL — Yorkshire teacake flavoured with spices and sultanas. It is served hot, split and spread with butter.

FAUBONNE — Soup of puréed haricot beans.

FAUX FILET — Also known as contrefilet. This is a French cut of meat, the boneless cut of the loin (the undercut is the fillet).

FAVORI, BEIGNET — Fritter made by sandwiching two macaroons with apricot jam, dipping this in a liqueur syrup, coating it in batter and deep frying it.

FAVORITE — This word is applied to a wide variety of dishes. It is a garnish for small cuts of meat of sliced foie gras, truffles and asparagus tips; a garnish for sliced meat of quartered artichoke bottoms, braised celery, pommes Anna or château; a salad of crayfish, asparagus and truffles in vinaigrette; a thickened consommé garnished with a julienne of artichoke bottoms and mushrooms, and small potato balls; coupe favorite is vanilla ice cream flavoured with kirsch and maraschino, enclosing a pineapple ice and strawberry-flavoured whipped cream.

FAVRE, JOSEPH — Nineteenth century chef, cookery writer and founder of the first Academy of Cookery.

FEATHER ICING — Attractive cake decoration using glacé icing. The cake is iced as usual, then coloured icing is piped in straight regular lines across it. A skewer is run across these lines at regular intervals, first in one direction, then in the other. Where the lines meet they make a zigzag pattern. This is the traditional decoration for mille feuilles.

FECAMPOISE, A LA — Garnish for fish, especially sole, which is the same as à la dieppoise, but with shrimp butter in the sauce.

FEDELINI — The faithful in Italian. Very narrow ribbon pasta used in soups.

FEIJAO — Portuguese bean stew, with many local variations.

FEIJOADA — Elaborate Brazilian dish of black beans, a variety of meats including pig's tail and ears, sausage, cassava, rice, hot pepper sauce and sliced oranges.

FELINO, SALAME DI — Delicate salame from Felino near Parma, Italy. It is made from lean pork flavoured with peppercorns, garlic and white wine.

FELL — Very thin tissue on the outside of a leg of lamb.

FERMENTATION — Process of change induced by enzymes. It is used in making bread, cheese and yogurt as well as wine and beer.

FERMIERE, A LA — This term is applied to meat which is pot-roasted with carrots, turnips, celery and onions.

FERMONT, AVOCAT — Half a baked avocado with a poached egg in the cavity, served with béarnaise sauce.

FERRI, AI — Italian for grilled on an iron grid over an open fire.

FERRECAPIENNE — French fish soup, similar to Bouillabaise, but made with only one type of fish instead of a variety.

FETTUCINE — Italian ribbon-shaped pasta. Fetucce is wider, fetucelle is narrower.

FEUILLANTINE — Oblong of puff pastry which has been rolled out and folded into three upon itself at least six times: this results in the flakiest of pastry.

FEUILLETEE, PATE — French for puff pastry.

FEUILLETON — Thin slices of veal or pork layered with savoury stuffing, wrapped in caul and braised.

FICELLE — Long, thin French loaf of bread: it is as long as bâtard, but thinner. A la ficelle is a method of cooking fillet of beef: it is first browned in the oven, then boiled in consommé.

FIDGET PIE — Traditional pie from Shropshire, consisting of bacon, potatoes, apples and onions. It was originally made at harvest time.

FIGARO, SAUCE — Hollandaise with tomato purée, Worcestershire sauce and parsley.

FILE — Powder made from dried sassafras leaves. It is the essential ingredient of gumbo and other Creole dishes.

FILET MIGNON — French cut of beef from the small end of the fillet. It is fried or grilled.

FILLET — As a cut of meat, it refers to the tenderest cut from the hindquarters close to the spine. It may be sold whole or cut into steaks. Fillet of fish is one of the four quarters left after the spine, head and tail have been removed. As a verb, to fillet is to remove the spine of fish.

FILO — See PHYLLO.

FINANCIERE, A LA — Garnish for meat and poultry of cock's combs, cock's kidneys, lamb's sweetbreads, quenelles, mushroom and truffles.

FINANZIERA, RISOTTO ALLA — Rice cooked in beef stock, with chicken livers, onions, wine and cheese.

FINES HERBES — A mixture of fresh herbs such as parsley, chervil, tarragon and chives, all finely chopped.

FINISTE, SAUCE — Tomato coulis with mustard, Worcestershire sauce, lemon juice, butter and cayenne added. It is served with grilled or fried fish or meat.

FINNAN HADDIE — Smoked haddock from Findon, a small fishing village near Aberdeen, where the smoking process originated.

FIORENTINA, SALAME — Large, coarsely chopped lean and fat pork salame from Florence.

FIRE POT — Chinese metal pot set over charcoal for cooking at the table. The pot contains boiling stock and oil. A selection of thinly cut raw ingredients are prepared so that each person can help himself. Beaten egg and various condiments are provided for seasoning. The food is cooked in a precise order, with the noodles last. The broth is then drunk. A Cantonese firepot would include chicken, beef, seafood and local vegetables. A Mongolian firepot is based on lamb cut into paper thin slices. A spicy dip of sesame paste, fermented red bean curd, fish sauce, red wine and soy sauce is the essential accompaniment.

FISH KETTLE — Oval-shaped pan with handles at either end, a lid and a removable grid inside. It is used for steaming a whole fish. The grid enables the fish to be taken out without breaking.

FIVE SPICE POWDER — Liquorice flavoured condiment used in Chinese cooking. It contains star anise, cassia, cloves, fennel with either Szechwan peppercorns or ginger or cardomom.

FLAKE — To separate cooked fish into slivers. Also to grate chocolate or cheese into slivers.

FLAKY PASTRY — A pastry which rises during cooking due to the air trapped in the folding and rolling out process. Proportions are two-thirds fat to flour.

FLAMANDE, A LA — Name given to joints of meat garnished in the Flemish style with diced belly pork, braised cabbage, carrots and potatoes.

FLAMBER — French word meaning to flame food to add flavour. Alcohol, usually brandy or rum, is heated then poured over the food, set alight and allowed to flame until the alcohol is burned out.

FLAMICHE — Leek flan or pie from Burgundy and Picardy. Puff pastry is used, sometimes with a double crust. The filling is rich, containing eggs, cream and cheese as well as leeks. The word means Flemish in French (Burgundy and Picardy, though now in France, were once part of Flanders).

FLAMRIC — Cold pudding of semolina, wine, eggs and sugar. It is baked in a mould and turned out to serve, with a purée of raw, red fruit. The texture is fluffy, yet firm.

FLAN — An open pastry made in a flan ring placed on a baking sheet. It is filled with a savoury mixture, before or after cooking. Flan is also the name of a solid version of crème caramel, which is the national dessert of Spain.

FLANK — Cut of beef or bacon from the belly of the animal. It is suitable for salting.

FLAN RING — Metal ring about two cm deep, varying in diameter, but with vertical sides. It is used to shape pastry or biscuit crust into a neat shape and is removed before serving.

FLAPJACK — A cake baked in a shallow tray and made of oats coated in a mixture of melted butter, brown sugar and golden syrup. It has a chewy texture. In the United States a flapjack is a griddle cake or Scotch pancake.

FLATBREAD — Italian-American bread made with a yeast dough rolled out into a circle and baked. It is usually flavoured with herbs and served warm.

FLENSJES — Thin Dutch pancakes either served hot with jam, sugar or syrup, or frozen layered with custard.

FLEURAGE — Finely ground pasta or cornmeal used to prevent bread dough from sticking to the board when kneading.

FLEURON — Small crescent or oval of puff pastry, used to garnish fish or poultry in rich cream sauces.

FLITCH — A side of bacon.

FLOATING ISLANDS — *See* OEUFS A LA NEIGE.

FLORENTINE — A thin but rich biscuit made with nuts, glacé cherries and other dried fruits, and thickly coated with plain chocolate on one side. As an adjective, Florentine means that the food in question is coated with a spinach and Mornay sauce, and usually baked in the oven. Sometimes it simply means that the food is served with spinach. The fields around Florence were once full of spinach, which was first introduced to France by the chefs of Queen Catherine de Medici, in the sixteenth century.

FLORIAN — Roast lamb garnish of braised lettuce, onions, carrots and sautéed potatoes.

FLUFF — Cold dessert of stiffly beaten egg whites or whipped cream, folded into a sweetened purée of fruit.

FLUTE — Long thin French loaf of bread. As a verb it means to cut vegetables, fruit or pastry so that the edges are serrated.

FOCACCIA — Italian flat bread, flavoured with herbs, garlic or sun-dried tomatoes, and served warm.

FOIE GRAS — French for fat liver. This refers to the liver of specially fattened geese, and sometimes ducks, which is considered to be a great delicacy. It is often made into a pâté. The birds are force fed with such a rich diet that a goose liver can weigh over three lb (1.5 kg).

FOISONNER — French term meaning to beat a mixture to increase its volume.

FOLD — To encorporate a heavy ingredient such as flour into a light, aerated mixture, such as eggs, sugar and butter. This is done with a downward motion, carefully turning over the mixture to prevent air escaping.

FONCER — French word meaning to line with pastry.

FONDANT — French confection made of sugar and lemon juice or other acid. The mixture can also be used as icing.

FONDANTE, POMME DE TERRE — Small new potato cooked in butter in an open pan.

FONDRE — French term meaning to cook vegetables in a lightly covered pan, with little or no liquid or fat, until soft.

FONDUE — This word has several meanings. A cheese fondue is grated cheese melted in white wine and Kirsch. The idea comes from Switzerland, where, according to legend, a shepherd on a mountain, bored with his nightly snack of cheese, bread and wine, heated them all together in a pot and invented the first fondue. It is a popular party dish and is cooked in a fireproof pot over a spirit lamp: cubes of bread held on a long fork are dunked into the fondue, and anyone who loses his cube of bread is expected to buy a round of drinks – women must forfeit one kiss per cube. Fondue Bourguignonne uses the same utensils and party spirit, but cubes of steak are dipped into a pot of boiling oil, and when cooked, dunked into a selection of spicy, cold sauces. Fondue also describes vegetables cooked in a covered pan for a long time until reduced to a pulp.

FONTANGES — Rich pea soup, garnished with a chiffonade of lettuce and chervil.

FOOGATH — Lightly cooked vegetable dish from India.

FOOL — Fruit purée blended with thick custard. Whipped cream may also be swirled in to give a marbled effect. The name comes from the French foule, meaning pulped. Fool is also the staple dish of Egypt, consisting of dried brown beans cooked until soft and served with slices of hard-boiled egg.

FOO YUNG, EGG — Pekinese omelette, which may have almost any filling.

FORCEMEAT — Mixture of minced or chopped and spiced ingredients used to stuff meat, poultry, fish, eggs, game or vegetables. It usually contains meat and is bound with beaten egg. It gives flavour and moisture to the food and makes a small joint of meat go further. It may also be cooked separately and served as an accompaniment to roast meat, poultry or game.

FORCING BAG — Also known as a pastry bag. It is a funnel-shaped bag, which is fitted with nozzles and used to pipe creamy mixtures in decorative designs.

FORE — Part of the pork loin.

FORE HOCK — Bacon cut from the shoulder, which is either boned and rolled or split into three parts.

FORESTIERE — Garnish for small cuts of meat and poultry consisting of morels or mushrooms and diced potatoes fried in butter.

FOUETTER — French for to beat.

Fo

FOUR, AU — French for baked in the oven.

FOYOT, SAUCE — Béarnaise sauce with meat glaze. It is served with eggs.

FRAISAGE — French term meaning pressing a pastry dough with the heel of the hand; this is done to ensure an even blending of fat and flour. The word also means the unkneaded dough.

FRANGIPANE — Cake mixture, strongly flavoured with almonds, which is made like choux paste and widely used in pâtisserie. It was invented by an Italian perfumier called Frangipani, who lived in Paris during the seventeenth century.

FRANKFURTER — Smoked sausage of lean pork, invented in Frankfurt, Germany.

FRAPPE — Fruit juice frozen to a mushy consistency. The word comes from the French frapper, to freeze or chill.

FRASCATI, A LA — Garnish for meat dishes of slices of foie gras, asparagus tips, mushrooms and truffles.

FREEZE — To preserve food by keeping it at or below a temperature of 0°F (18°C). The activity of enzymes and organisms which spoil food is halted at this temperature. Food should be frozen rapidly and never be refrozen once thawed, otherwise it will not be safe to eat. Clarence Birdseye invented the first freezer in 1924, having been inspired by living for several years in Labrador, where it is so cold that fish freeze as soon as they are caught.

FREMIR — French for to shiver. As a culinary term it means to cook very gently, with less heat than is used for simmering. It is used for delicate foods.

FRENCH — American term which describes the removal of meat and fat from the tips of bones of a rib chop or roast.

FRENCH FRY — American term meaning to deep-fry, it also refers to deep-fried sticks of potato, known in Britain as chips.

FRENCH STICK — English name for a long thin baton loaf of bread. It is very crusty with a few diagonal slashes on top.

FRENCH TOAST — A slice of bread which has been dipped into a mixture of beaten egg and milk, then fried on each side. This is sometimes served at breakfast in America, with maple syrup.

FRENEUSE, POTAGE — Thick soup of turnips and potatoes.

FRIAND— Someone who has a refined palate, especially in regard to savoury dishes. The word is French and derives from frire meaning burning with desire. It dates from the Middle Ages. There is also a square shaped game pâté from Paris called a friand.

FRIANDINE— Small patty made with any savoury mixture, rolled in egg and breadcrumbs and fried.

FRIANDISE — French for delicacy. It may refer to a petit four, pâtisserie or sweetbreads.

FRICADELLE — Small ball of minced meat, fried and served with a sauce.

FRICANDEAU — Topside of veal or loin of veal, braised with quenelles, sweetbreads, mushrooms and truffles. Also slices or fillets of fish, especially tuna or sturgeon, braised in stock.

FRICASSEE — White meat or poultry stewed in butter, its gravy thickened with egg yolks and cream. Fricasser is French for to cook in a saucepan.

FRIJOLES REFRITOS — Mexican dish of refried beans. They are fried until almost dry and able to be tipped in one piece from the pan to the plate. They are served with crumbled cheese, lettuce and radishes. Flavours are said to improve with each frying.

FRIKADELLER — Danish meat ball of beef, veal or pork, or a mixture of any of these, which is fried or poached.

FRITES, POMMES — French for fried potatoes or chips.

FRITOT— A French dish of small pieces of food dipped in batter and fried.

FRITTATA — Italian omelette which is baked on a pie plate in the oven, and may be served hot or cold.

FRITTER — Food dipped in batter and deep-fried. A fritter may be sweet or savoury, but usually the food is sliced before cooking.

FRITTO MISTO — Mixed fry in Italian. Food dipped in batter, egg and breadcrumbs, or flour and deep-fried. It contains a variety of offal, with rice croquettes and fried bread. Fritto misto di mare is a selection of seafood treated the same way.

FRITTONS — *See* GRATTONS.

FRITURE — French word used to describe something deep-fried, eg. friture du lac means deep-fried fish from a nearby lake.

FRIVOLITE — Small savoury served at the end of a banquet.

FRIZZLE — To cook in a small amount of fat until the edges curl up and crispen.

FROMAGE DE TETE — French variant on brawn. It is made with pig's head, pork and veal shoulder, pork rind and tongue.

FROST — American term meaning to decorate a cake with icing.

FROSTING — American term for icing. It also describes the process of chilling a glass so that ice crystals form around the edge.

FROTHING — This describes the swelling and bubbling action of yeast when activated. It also refers to a method of treating roasted meat or poultry, by dredging it with flour and salt just before the end of cooking and subjecting it to fierce heat for a short while, so that a crisp frothy case forms around the joint.

FROU-FROU, BOMBE — Vanilla ice surrounding rum-flavoured cream with candied fruit.

FRUCTOSE — Natural sugar found in fruit juice, honey and flower nectar.

FRUMENTY — Old English dessert made with oats, cream, honey and spices – a luxurious version of porridge.

FRY — To cook in hot fat. Fat for frying should be chosen carefully as the flavour of the fat will penetrate the food. Lard and dripping are good where a strong flavour is desirable: butter gives a good flavour but burns easily unless clarified: butter and olive oil is probably the favourite of most professional cooks for shallow frying: oil is best for deep frying. There are two basic types of frying, shallow and deep; this refers to the amount of fat used. Shallow frying is done in a wide, shallow pan or skillet: the fat should cover the base of the pan but no more. Deep frying is done in a strong, deep pan, with a basket to lift the food in and out of the pan: the fat should be deep enough to cover the food completely. Dry frying is a variant of shallow frying, using only the fat which runs from the food. *See* also STIR-FRY and SAUTE.

FUDGE — Creamy confection made with sugar, butter and milk, and flavoured with vanilla, coffee or chocolate. Nuts are often added. It is made in a large tray and cut into squares to serve.

FUL MEDAMES — Egyptian dish of brown beans cooked with garlic until soft, and served with hard-boiled egg, olive oil and lemon juice. The name is sometimes anglicized as fool.

FUMET — Fish, meat or game stock, boiled down rapidly to a syrupy consistency. The concentrated liquid is then used in the accompanying sauce.

FUNERAL PIE — Pennsylvannia Dutch rich raisin tart. Originally it was served at funerals.

FUN KUO — Crescent-shaped fried dumpling filled with prawn and meat. Part of Chinese Dim Sum.

FUNNEL CAKE — Large fritter from New Orleans. A yeast batter is forced through a funnel in a random way until a cake the size and shape of a dinner plate is formed. It is then deep fried and eaten hot dipped in icing sugar, sometimes with fruit.

FUNNY CAKE — Pennsylvannia Dutch recipe. A pie shell is filled with cake batter and a sweet sauce; when it is cooked, the cake is on top, with the sauce between the cake and the pastry.

FUSILLI — Spiral-shaped pasta.

GADO-GADO — Indonesian dish consisting of a selection of vegetables (beansprouts, cabbage, cucumber, potato – all stir-fried) with hard-boiled eggs, which is served with a hot sauce made with peanuts, coconut and tamarind.

GADSKI — Salad of halved cos lettuce with sliced avocado, diced apples, red peppers, white grapes, truffles and a dressing of crushed walnuts and vinaigrette.

GALANTINE — A cold, jellied meat dish. Originally it was a boned, stuffed and pressed chicken (galine is old French for chicken), which was served in its own jelly; but nowadays meat and fish are also made into galantines. The meat may be stuffed or minced, and mixed with other meats and flavourings. The result is similar to a pâté, but the crucial difference is in the cooking – a galantine is always steamed.

GALA PIE — Also known as Veal and Ham Pie. A raised pie with chopped veal and ham surrounding hard-boiled eggs. A layer of jelly separates the dense meat filling from the hot water pastry. It is served in slices so that everyone gets a slice of egg in their portion.

GALATOBOUREKO — Greek pastry made of phyllo pastry with a filling of cream and eggs. A lemon syrup is poured over it after cooking and it is served cold cut into squares.

95

Ga

GALETTE — Flat cake or biscuit made from pastry layers, traditionally baked for Twelfth Night in France. It is also a cake of sliced potatoes.

GALUSKA — Hungarian dumpling made by dropping dough through a special dumpling machine (or spatzle machine or chestnut roaster). It is about half an inch (1.5 cm) long and as thick as a pencil. The dough is made of flour and eggs and is cooked quickly in boiling water.

GAME — Any edible animal which has not been domesticated and is hunted. The word comes from the fact that the animals are killed for sport (ie. a game).

GAME CHIP — Wafer-thin slice of potato, deep-fried and served as the traditional accompaniment to game.

GAMMON — The leg of a pig which is cured while still attached to the side. It has a milder cure than ham. The name comes from the French jambon, meaning ham.

GANACHE — A mixture of whipped cream, chocolate, butter and rum, which is used as a cake filling in French pâtisserie.

GAN-CHAO — Szechuan method of food preparation. Food is fried with a little oil over a high heat for longer than is usual: the result is crispy and deeply-coloured.

GANSELEBERWURST — German goose liver sausage.

GAN-SHAO — Szechuan method of food preparation. Meat or vegetables are cooked in clear broth with wine and spices until the liquid is reduced to a thick, flavoursome sauce.

GARAM MASALA — Indian mixed spices, often sold ready mixed: cinnamon, cloves, cardamoms, black cumin seeds, mace or nutmeg. It means hot, spicy mixture.

GARBURE — Hearty soup from the Basque region of France, containing haricot beans, vegetables in season and various meats and sausage. It is usually served as a main course, with cheese croûtes.

GARGANELLI — Macaroni made by hand from egg pasta.

GARIBALDI — Sweet biscuit with a layer of currants between two layers of dough. It is of Italian origin and named after General Garibaldi.

GARNISH — Trimmings added to a dish or arranged round it. These may be simple or elaborate, but they must always blend with the flavour of the dish which is being garnished, and with one another.

GASTRONOME — Someone who is very knowledgeable about the culinary arts and possesses a very refined palate. Garnish for fish, poultry and sweetbreads, consisting of chestnuts, cock's kidneys, truffles and morels. It is also the name given to demi-glace sauce when champagne, Madeira and cayenne are added to it.

GASTRONOMY — "Reasoned knowledge of everything relating to man and his nourishment" *Brillat-Savarin,* 1825. It derives from the ancient Greek word gaster meaning stomach.

GATEAU — French for cake. Outside France the word is used to imply a cake which is rich and elaborate although in France it may be plain or fancy.

GATINAISE — From Gatinais in France, which is famous for honey: this describes any honey-flavoured dish.

GAUFRE — French waffle.

GAUFRETTE — Lattice round of potato, cut with a mandoline and deep-fried.

GAULOISE — A la Gauloise is a garnish for consommé of cock's combs and kidneys, with a julienne of pancake and chervil or ham royale. It may be enriched with truffles, pickled tongue and a Madeira-flavoured suprême sauce and used to fill vol-au-vents. A gauloise is a small cake made with genoese, topped with apricot jam and chopped almonds.

GAYETTE — Ball-shaped sausage made with offal and tied up in a piece of caul. It comes from southern France.

GAZPACHO — A cold soup from Andalusia in Spain. Raw tomatoes, onions, peppers and cucumber are finely chopped, flavoured with plenty of garlic and diluted with iced water.

GEFILTE FISH — Traditional Jewish dish of stuffed fish. In the United States the fish is made into balls.

GELATINE — Protein substance obtained from bones, which is used to set jellies etc.

GENEVOISE, SAUCE — A sauce of chopped onion and carrot with red wine, anchovy essence, parsley and thyme, which is used with fish.

GENOESE — A basic cake mixture used in French pâtisserie: it is like a sponge cake but with butter added to give a moister, less crumbly texture. Genoese sauce is espagnole with shallots, mushroom ketchup, claret, anchovy essence and a pinch of sugar.

GENOVESE — The name of a spicy beef salame which has some lean and fat pork added. It is also the name of a sauce for pasta made with onion, tomatoes, mushrooms and chopped veal.

GENTLEMAN'S RELISH — Commercially prepared anchovy spread. It should be eaten sparingly as it is very salty.

GEORGES SAND — Fish consommé with fish quenelles, sliced morels, crayfish butter, carp soft roe and croûtons. Named after the nineteenth-century French writer.

GEORGETTE — This term is applied to foods which are stuffed with braised crayfish tails.

GERMINAL — Meat consommé with tarragon, garnished with peas, beans and chervil.

GERMINY — Soup made with sorrel, thickened with cream and egg yolks.

GESIERS — Goose gizzards which have been preserved in fat.

GHEE — Clarified buffalo butter used in northern Indian cooking.

GHIVECI — Rumanian stew based on vegetables such as onions, aubergines, peppers, tomatoes, cabbage, peas and beans: meat or fish may or may not be added.

GIBLETS — The head, neck, heart, pinions, feet, gizzard, liver and kidney of poultry and cock's combs. Giblets are used mostly to make stock, but all the parts are edible in their own right.

GIGOT — French word for a leg of lamb.

GILD — To brush a pastry crust with beaten egg yolk before baking, in order to produce a golden glaze.

GILDERNE — Clear chicken soup eaten on the Jewish sabbath.

GILL — A quarter of a pint, or five fluid ounces.

GINGERBREAD — Moist cake made by melting syrup, sugar and fat, and adding flour, ginger and other spices. The raising agent is bicarbonate of soda. Gingerbread is best kept for several days before eating to allow the flavour to mature. It is said to be the oldest cake in the world, being invented by the Greeks nearly 3000 years BC. In the middle ages it was sometimes coated with gold leaf, hence the expression "taking the gilt off the gingerbread".

GIRARROSTO, AL — Italian for spit roasted.

GIRDLE — See GRIDDLE.

GIZZARD — Part of the digestive canal of a bird, where food is ground up with grit. It is removed before cooking and may be used with the giblets to make stock and gravy.

GLACE — French for iced or glazed. Glacé fruit is fruit dipped in a sugar syrup to which glucose or cream of tartar has been added and which has been boiled to 300°F(150°C). Marron glacé is a chestnut boiled in this same sugar syrup. Meringue glacé is meringue with ice cream. Glacé icing is a simple cake decoration of icing sugar mixed with liquid and flavouring and spread over the cake.

GLADSTONE, BOMBE — Ginger ice cream outside a centre of gin-flavoured whipped cream with diced preserved ginger and angelica.

GLAZE — To cover with a transparent but shiny coat of meat juices, fruit syrup, jam etc.

GLOUCESTER SAUCE — Mayonnaise flavoured with cayenne, chives, lemon juice, Worcester sauce and sour cream. Used with meat salads.

GLUCOSE — Natural sugar found in fruits, sweetcorn and onions.

GLUTEN — Elastic substance found in wheat in varying amounts. Gluten is what makes bread light, by trapping air bubbles in the dough; high gluten flour (strong flour) is best for making bread.

GNOCCHI — Gnocchi is often thought of as pasta, but it is closer to a dumpling. Italian gnocchi (the original) is made with maize meal, French gnocchi is made with flour and eggs, and there is also a potato gnocchi: all are made differently but the end result is very similar. A paste is made, then spread on a tray to harden before being cut into shapes and baked. French gnocchi is made like choux paste, but is poached before being baked in a sauce. Potato gnocchi is little cylinders of creamed potato which are poached.

GODARD — Garnish of chicken or veal and mushroom quenelles, mushroom caps, truffles, cock's combs and kidneys, lamb's sweetbreads and sauce Godard. The sauce is espagnole with champagne, ham, carrot, onion, butter and mushrooms added. Named after Eugéne Godard, who organized the aerial post during the seige of Paris 1870-71.

GODIVEAU — Veal forcemeat.

GOGUETTE — Flat pork spicy sausage from France.

GOLD LEAF — Real gold beaten down until it is wafer-thin. It is occasionally used as a garnish for sweet dishes. Gold was considered the panacea in the Middle Ages, so the wealthy had gold dust sprinkled on their food for health reasons.

GOMASIO — Japanese condiment of crushed, roasted sesame seeds mixed with salt.

GOMOKU-MESHI — Japanese dish which translates as five ingredients and rice. The five ingredients are mushrooms, marrow, peas, carrots and onions.

GORENFLOT — Savarin mixture cooked in a special hexagonal mould. Named after a character in Alexandre Dumas' *La Dame de Monsoreau*.

GOUDALE — Soup from the Béarn district of France. After the bread and vegetables from a bowl of Garbure have been eaten, the diner pours a glass of wine into the broth and drinks the mixture – this is goudale.

GOUGERE — Savoury dish from the Burgundy district of France. It is made of cheese-flavoured choux pastry, which lines a baking dish and is then filled with a meat and vegetable mixture.

GOUJON — Diagonally cut piece of fish.

GOULASCH/GULYAS — Thin meat stew, seasoned with paprika, from Hungary. The meat is usually beef.

GOURMAND — Someone who appreciates fine food and has a hearty appetite. Originally the word meant someone who ate to excess.

GOURMET — Originally a wine expert. Nowadays the term has widened to describe someone who is knowledgeable about food and wine.

GRAHAM — A graham cracker is a wholemeal biscuit invented by the nineteenth century American health food pioneer, Rev. Sylvester Graham. Graham flour is another name for wholemeal flour.

GRAISSE NORMANDE — Special frying fat made in Normandy by rendering down beef and pork fat, simmering it with herbs and vegetables, then straining it.

GRAM FLOUR — Also known as Besan flour. Finely ground chickpeas or lentils used widely in Indian cookery, especially for batters.

GRAMIGNA — Thin, short tubular pasta.

GRANARY — Proprietary meal containing malted flour and pieces of whole grain or coarsely ground flour.

GRAND-DUC — Garnish for fish and poultry of truffles and asparagus tips: crayfish and sauce Mornay may also be included.

GRANDMERE — French for grandmother. When this word is applied to a dish, it implies that it is old-fashioned and home-made.

GRAND VENEUR SAUCE — Poivrade sauce with gooseberry jelly added. Served with game.

GRANITA — Halfway between a water ice and an iced drink, it is a weak sugar syrup, flavoured with fruit juice, tea or coffee, which is then frozen. It is served in a tall glass with whipped cream on top: a long spoon is provided so that the top half can be eaten, although the bottom half is usually drunk.

GRANT LOAF — Coarse wholemeal loaf invented by Doris Grant. Its distinctive feature is that it only needs one rising.

GRAS, AU — French term for food cooked in meat stock or gravy.

GRASSHOPPER PIE — American dessert consisting of a biscuit crust and a light creamy filling of marshmallows, milk, whipped cream, crème de menthe and crème de cacao. Its name is a reference to the cocktail, Grasshopper, made with the same liqueurs.

GRATE — To reduce food to very small pieces by rubbing against a sheet of metal or plastic with shaped perforations stamped in it. The shape and size of the perforations determine the shape and size of the food particles.

GRATICOLA, ALLA — Italian for grilled over charcoal.

GRATIN, AU — French term for food which has been browned on top. Usually the food has been covered in a sauce, grated cheese or breadcrumbs are sprinkled over and the dish is browned under the grill or in the oven.

GRATINER — To form a crust on top of a dish, either under the grill or in the oven.

GRATTONS — The residue of the melted fat of pork, goose or turkey, which is sprinkled with salt and eaten cold as an hors d'oeuvre. Also known as frittons.

GRAVLAX/GRAVAD LAX — Swedish way of preparing salmon by cutting it in half and filling it with dill and salt, then placing a heavy weight on top and leaving it for at least two days. No cooking is required. It is served in thin slices as an appetizer or sometimes with vegetables as a main course.

GRAVY — Sauce to accompany roast meat made from the sediment and juices left in the roasting tin. Stock is added and sometimes flour is included to thicken it. Commercial gravy browning can also be used to thicken, but it lends its own artificial flavour to the gravy. The jug to contain gravy is called a gravy boat.

GREASE — To cover the inside of a cooking utensil with a film of grease to prevent food sticking to the utensil during cooking. This may be done by brushing with oil or melted fat, wiping with a butter wrapper or rubbing with a piece of fat held in the fingers.

GREEK SALAD — Tomato, cucumber, raw onion, black olives and feta cheese cubes.

GREEN BACON — Bacon which has been brine-cured. It is milder in flavour than smoked bacon.

GREEN GODDESS DRESSING — Mayonnaise and thick cream, flavoured with very finely chopped anchovy, parsley, chives, garlic, tarragon vinegar and lemon juice. It is an American salad dressing.

GREQUE, A LA — This expression refers to a method of cooking vegetables in a well-seasoned mixture of oil and water. Such vegetables are usually served lukewarm or cold as an appetizer.

GREMOLATA — Italian garnish of chopped garlic, parsley and lemon rind.

GRENADIN — Small piece of veal resembling a tournedos steak, cut about 2 cm. thick, which is usually taken from the round.

GRESILLER — French term meaning to shrink by heating.

GRIBICHE — A sauce of hard-boiled eggs, oil and mustard, which is served with cold fish and vegetables.

GRIDDLE/GIRDLE — Flat metal surface either built into the top of a stove or portable like a frying pan without sides. It is used for griddle cakes (also known as Scotch pancakes), pancakes etc., and any food which needs fierce heat, as it is able to absorb and retain heat.

GRIESTORTE — Semolina tart in German. In fact it is a very light, short-textured cake, made with semolina in place of flour.

GRIGNON — Dry bread baked hard in the oven. The name comes from the French grignoter, to nibble.

GRILLADE — French for a mixture of grilled food.

GRILLING — Method of cooking using radiant heat from above. Originally grilling was done on a grid or grille (the French) over hot charcoal.

GRIMALDI — Chicken consommé with tomato fumet, garnished with julienne of celeriac and tomato royale.

GRISKIN — The meat left on the spine of a pig after the sides have been removed. The word also means small pieces of pork loin.

GRISSINI — Long (at least a foot) sticks of dry hard-baked bread, which are served with drinks while waiting for a meal. The idea comes from Piedmont.

GRITS — Any grain (corn, oats, barley) which has been coarsely ground. Grits made from cornmeal, either boiled, fried or baked is a staple of U.S. Southern cooking.

GROATS — De-husked grain, usually oats.

GROUND MEAT — American for minced meat.

GRUEL — Thick but liquid mixture of barley, oats and wheat. It is served to invalids, being nutritious but easy to eat and digest.

GRUNT — An American pudding consisting of fruit (usually a berry) with a dumpling on top. It is made in a saucepan and the heat of the fruit juice steams the dumpling.

GRUTZWURSTE — Small pork sausage from Germany, flavoured with lemon peel. They are boiled to reheat for serving.

GUACAMOLE — Mexican speciality consisting of avocado purée flavoured with garlic and chillies, and sometimes other ingredients. It is served as an appetizer or cocktail dip. The name comes from two Nahuatl words, ahuacatl (avocado) and molli (mixture).

GUAI-WEI — Szechuan method of food preparation, using a sauce of peppercorns, sesame seed oil, tahini, garlic, vinegar, shallot, sugar, chilli oil and soy sauce.

GUANCIALE — The cured jaw of a pig from Southern Italy. This is the correct "bacon" to use in spaghetti alla carbonara and all'amatriciana.

GUARD OF HONOUR — Two racks of lamb with the tips bared, arranged so that the ribs interlock. It is roasted and served with a cutlet frill on each rib tip.

GUARD'S PUDDING — English steamed pudding made with suet and breadcrumbs, and flavoured with strawberry or raspberry jam.

GUGELHOPF — See KUGELHOPF.

GULAB JAMUN — Indian sweet of deep-fried balls of milky dough, soaked in a rosewater-flavoured syrup.

GULYAS — Thin stew of beef or other meat, from Hungary.

GUMBO — Creole stew containing filé powder (made from sassafras leaves) which has a distinctive flavour and glutinous quality. The Indian for sassafras is kombo, which became gumbo. Nowadays okra, which has a similar slippery texture, is often used instead.

GUOBA — Chinese dish of rice which has been stuck to the bottom of the pot, carefully removed then slowly roasted.

HACHINETTE — Small, French, wooden bowl with a knife with a crescent-shaped blade, which fits exactly the inside curve of the bowl. It is used for chopping herbs etc.

HACHIS — Mixture of finely chopped vegetables or meat and vegetables.

HACHOIR — French version of a mezzaluna, ie. a crescent-shaped blade with a handle at each end, used for chopping. Sometimes it may have two blades and is used for mincing without squeezing the juices out of meat.

HAGGIS — Scottish dish of minced sheep's heart, liver and lungs, oatmeal, onion and suet, boiled inside a sheep's stomach. It is an economic way of using a sheep's innard so that they keep for a couple of weeks. It is traditionally eaten on Burns Night (January 25) with neeps (turnips) and tatties (potatoes), and whiskey.

HALAL — Food prepared according to the laws of Islam. Livestock must be ritually slaughtered by cutting the throat.

HALF CREAM — Cream with a minimum fat content of 12% which is suitable for adding to coffee and tends to separate when cooked.

HALVA — Middle Eastern confection made from ground sesame seeds.

HAM — Whole hind leg removed from a pig's carcase and cured individually. It has a stronger flavour than gammon. Besides salt and saltpetre, there is usually sugar and sometimes vinegar, molasses, herbs or spices in the cure. It is dried in fresh air or smoked over various woods (eg. hickory, oak) or herbs. The breed of pig used is also a factor in the type of ham produced.

HAMANTASCHEN — Hebrew for Haman's purses. These are three-cornered cakes symbolizing the downfall of Haman who planned the massacre of the Jews in Persia in the fourth century BC. They are stuffed with either a wine and walnut, poppyseed, apple, apricot or prune mixture.

HAMBURGER — Thick ground meat patty, fried or grilled, served inside a split bread roll, with a slice of onion and/or tomato, and accompanied by a selection of relishes. Originally from Hamburg in Germany.

HAND AND SPRING — Pork joint from the shoulder area. It is suitable for roasting and not too expensive as it has a lot of bone.

HANGING — Way of preparing meat for cooking in order to tenderize it and develop flavour. Beef, lamb and game are hung for varying periods. The carcase is suspended in a cool, draughty place where air circulates freely. The bacteria in the flesh break it down and make it tender. If meat is "well hung" it has been hanging, therefore dead, for some time and is rather too close to putrefaction for some tastes.

HANGTOWN FRY — Californian dish of oysters, dipped in flour and beaten egg, and fried.

HANG-YOU — Szechuan method of food preparation, using a sauce of chilli oil, sugar, shallot, ginger, garlic, tahini and soy sauce.

HARD BALL — Term used in confectionary to describe the stage reached when sugar is boiled to 120°C, (245°F).

HARD BOIL — A hard-boiled egg is one which has been immersed in boiling water for ten minutes, until the white is firm and the yolk is pale yellow and powdery solid. It is served shelled.

HARD COOK — American term for hard boil.

HARD CRACK — Term used in confectionary to describe the stage reached when sugar is boiled to 162°C, 325°F.

HARD SAUCE — Mixture of butter and icing sugar creamed until fluffy. It is usually flavoured with vanilla, served chilled and served with sweet steamed puddings.

HARICOT — French term for a mutton stew. The word comes from the old French harigoter, to cut in pieces and has nothing to do with haricot beans.

HARIRA — Moroccan soup of vegetables, meat and spices. There are many variations but tomatoes and lemons are always included.

HARISSA — A sauce made of as many as twenty different spices and chillies, which is the foundation of many North African dishes.

HAROSET — Jewish confection made with a mixture of uncooked dates, figs and other dried and fresh fruit, bound with egg yolk and red wine, and flavoured with spices. It may be mixed with Matzo meal and formed into balls or served as a dessert in a dish with chopped nuts.

HARVEST SHEAF — White bread baked in the shape of a sheaf of corn, which is traditionally made as a church decoration for the Harvest Festival service. It is highly glazed with beaten egg.

HASH — Supper dish made with leftover meat and potatoes: onions and other vegetables may be added. The cooked ingredients are all chopped and mixed thoroughly, before frying in dripping until thoroughly reheated and until the bottom has developed a brown crust. Corned beef is sometimes used. The word is derived from the French hacher, to chop.

HASHED BROWNS — Fried mashed potatoes. Often served for breakfast in America.

HASLET/HARSLET — Mixture of pig innards, minced and spiced, and boiled in a piece of caul. It is eaten cold, cut into slices.

HAUNCH — Refers to the hind quarters of venison.

HAUSFRAUEN ART — German for housewife's style, which means with sour cream and pickles.

HAVRAISE, A LA — Le Havre version of sole à la Dieppoise; garnished with shrimp instead of crayfish.

HEAVY CREAM — American for double cream.

HELDER, A LA — Garnish for tournedos: they are served on croûtes with a ring of béarnaise on top and tomato fondue in the centre of the ring, with pommes parisiennes. Also a garnish for noisettes: these are served with artichoke bottoms filled alternately with asparagus tips, chopped tomatoes and small fried potato balls covered with béarnaise sauce.

HENRI IV — Popular French king who came from Béarn. His name has been given to several dishes: a garnish for tournedos and noisettes of pommes pont neuf and watercress, or artichoke bottoms, pommes noisette and béarnaise sauce; béarnaise sauce with meat glaze; and clear beef broth with strips of chicken breast, carrots and herbs.

HENRIETTE, SAUCE — Hollandaise with tomato purée and chopped parsley.

HERB — Aromatic plant used in cooking for flavour.

HERMIT — Cookie made in a large tray and cut into squares or bars to serve. It is flavoured with dried fruit, nuts and spices.

HERMITAGE, SOLE — Filleted sole stuffed with breadcrumbs, shallots, egg and herbs, in a sauce of stock and cream.

HIMMEL UND ERDE — Heaven and earth in German. This is a peasant dish from the Lower Rhine, made with apples, potatoes, onions and black pudding.

HIND — Part of a pork loin.

HINDLE WAKES — Lancashire dish of medieval origin. A chicken is stuffed with prunes and steamed or boiled, then it is wrapped in bacon rashers and roasted. It is served cold with slices of lemon. The name is a mystery: wakes is a local word for holiday, but there is no town called Hindle in the district.

HOCHEPOT — French term applied to a soup made from various fatty meats and a selection of vegetables, also to a spicy oxtail stew. The name comes from hocher, to shake, as all the ingredients were shaken in the pot to prevent them sticking together. As with many peasant dishes, the liquid becomes a soup and the meat and vegetables are served as the main course.

HODGE PODGE — Yorkshire stew of lamb and a variety of vegetables, especially onions.

HOE CAKE — Primitive corn bread cooked on a griddle. Originally made by slaves in the Deep South of the United States, it is still eaten for breakfast there. It has a sweet and nutty flavour.

HOGGET — Yearling lamb.

107

HOISEN — Chinese condiment made from chilli pods, soy beans, sugar and flour. It is reddish brown in colour, thick in texture and slightly sweet in flavour.

HOKAREPANNA — Swedish hot pot with pork, veal kidneys and sliced potatoes in layers.

HOLLANDAISE — Classic sauce of butter and egg yolks, flavoured with vinegar, mace, bayleaf, salt and pepper. The mixture is stirred in a bain-marie until thickened just enough to hold its shape. Its flavour is sharp yet rich, and it complements fish and vegetables. Béarnaise and mousseline are based on it. The name means Dutch, but it was invented by the French. A la hollandaise describes fish poached in court bouillon with hot melted butter and potatoes, and also a paprika-flavoured consommé garnished with quenelles of calf's liver, bone marrow and chervil.

HOLSTEIN — Garnish for veal escalope or schnitzel of a fried egg, with anchovy fillets placed in a cross on it, and capers. Named after Count Holstein, foreign minister under Bismarck.

HOME FRIES — Sliced or cubed potato fried in bacon fat. Served at breakfast in the U.S.

HOMINY GRITS — Corn kernals soaked in a solution of lye until the husks drop off. Used in the United States for sweet milk puddings, cakes and as a savoury accompaniment to meat and poultry.

HONGROISE — Paprika-flavoured cream sauce.

HOPPING JOHN — Black-eyed peas and rice cooked with ham or bacon. Popular in the Caribbean and the southern United States, it is eaten on New Year's Eve to bring good luck.

HORS D'OEUVRE — French for outside the work. This expression is used to describe an appetizer or light first course. Hors d'oeuvres variés denotes a selection of at least a dozen different dishes served as a first course.

HOSKA — Elaborately plaited bread from Slovakia. It has a sweet, light yeast dough with chopped almonds and dried fruit.

HOTCAKES — American term for thick, small pancakes, served stacked on top of each other with butter and maple syrup.

HOT CROSS BUN — Spicy yeast bun traditionally served for breakfast on Good Friday. It has a cross on the top, to commemorate the crucifixion, made either by cutting with a knife after proving or with pastry or candied peel.

HOT DOG — A Frankfurter sausage inside a long split bun. Usually with mustard and onions. It was first made in St Louis in the 1880s and acquired its name some time later when it appeared in a cartoon as a dachshund.

HOT POT — A stew of meat and vegetables arranged in layers, with a layer of sliced potato on top, cooked in the oven in a little liquid. Lancashire hot pot is the most famous regional variation: it is made with neck of mutton chops standing upright round in the inside of the pot, sheep's kidneys, oysters and root vegetables. In the north of England a hot pot is also a tall earthenware pot.

HOT WATER PASTRY — Pastry made with boiling lard and water added to flour in proportions of one-third fat to flour. It is moulded, while still warm and pliable, from the inside with a clenched fist, like a clay pot. It is then filled and baked, without needing a pie dish. This pastry, which is very crisp, is used to make raised pies, and is normally eaten cold.

HOUSE LAMB — Baby lamb about three or four weeks old, which has been fed only on milk. So called because it is raised in a house or barn. In France it is known as Pauillac lamb. It is lean with little flavour.

HUEVOS RANCHEROS — Mexican country eggs. Fried eggs on a bed of puréed tomatoes, chilies, peppers, onions and garlic.

HUFF — Fruit purée, beaten egg whites and sugar syrup, whisked until in firm peaks. It has to be eaten immediately. Huff paste is a Scottish suet pastry which is used to enclose meat, poultry or fish during baking or boiling so that the juices are not lost, but which is not usually eaten.

HUGUENOTE — French earthenware pan, designed to be large enough for a goose. Oeufs à la Hugenôte are eggs cooked in mutton gravy.

HUILE VIERGE — Virgin oil in French. It is oil made from the first pressing of olives: it has the best flavour and is the most expensive.

HULL — To remove stalks and leaves from strawberries.

HUMMOUS — Middle Eastern dish of puréed chick peas mixed with tahini, lemon juice and garlic. It is served as an appetizer.

HUNDRED YEAR OLD EGG — Chinese appetizer of a duck egg preserved in a casing of ashes, tea, lime and salt inside a dry rice husk and buried for several months (not years). The casing and egg shell are removed and the egg is stuck on a cocktail stick with a slice of fresh ginger. The white will have turned to a dark green jelly and the yolk will be a brown-yellow colour.

HUNDREDS AND THOUSANDS — Cake decoration of tiny multi-coloured sweets.

HUNG-SHAO — Chinese method of cookery also known as Red Braised. It comes from the Shanghai area. Meat, poultry or fish is cooked slowly in a mixture of dark soy sauce and rice wine until the sauce is reduced.

HUSH PUPPIES — Fried pieces of cornmeal mush to accompany fried fish, in the Deep South of the United States. They were originally made to throw to the dogs who were attracted by the smell of frying fish.

HUSSARDE — A la Hussarde is a garnish for meat of tomatoes stuffed with sauce soubise, grated horseradish, mushrooms and duchess potatoes. Hussarde sauce is a demi-glace with ham, white wine, onions, shallots, garlic, tomato purée and horseradish.

HYMETTUS — Name which implies the presence of honey in the dish. From Mount Hymettus in Greece, where a particularly fine honey is made.

ICE — To cover a cake with icing.

ICEBOX CAKE — American term for a cake which is assembled by sandwiching biscuits with butter cream or whipped cream, then refrigerating it until it is firm enough to cut into slices with a knife.

ICE CREAM — A frozen dessert. A simple fruit ice cream is made by freezing a mixture of fruit purée and whipped cream. A richer type of ice cream is a custard made with eggs and cream, which is flavoured with vanilla, nuts, coffee etc. and then frozen. The idea originally came from the East, but was developed in northern Italy. It came to France with Catherine de Medici and did not reach England until the seventeenth century. Ice cream was a luxury food until refrigerators were in common use.

ICING — A sugar coating for cakes.

IDLI — South Indian dumpling made of rice flour and lentil flour and steamed in a special utensil similar to an egg poacher. Idlis are served with a spicy lentil sauce and a mild coconut sauce.

IMAM BAYILDI — Turkish dish of aubergines stuffed with onions, garlic, tomatoes and lots of olive oil. The name means the fainting imam (a sort of priest): it is suggested that he fainted either from the richness or the cost of the dish, due to the amount of olive oil.

IMPERATRICE, A L' — Name given to various dishes and cakes, especially riz à l'impératrice, a rich rice pudding mixed with vanilla custard, cream, crystallized fruits and kirsch. This is the basis of several fruit desserts à l'impératrice.

IMPERIALE, A L' — Garnish for poultry of foie gras, truffles, mushrooms, quenelles, sweetbreads or cock's kidneys and Madeira sauce: sometimes the meat is served in pastry barquettes. Also chicken consommé with chicken forcemeat balls, peas and chervil.

INDIAN BREAD — Rich bread made with white flour and cornmeal, which gives a crunchy texture and interesting flavour. It is an American Indian recipe.

INDIAN PUDDING — Early American dessert made with cornmeal, milk, molasses, raisins and spices. Cornmeal was referred to by the early settlers as "Indian", hence the name.

INDIENNE, A L' — This term, meaning Indian style, is applied to dishes containing curry powder and/or chutney, and served with boiled rice.

INFUSE — To steep food in a liquid in a warm place, so that the liquid takes on the flavour of the food. The liquid is then strained before use and the food is usually discarded.

INVERT SUGAR — Compound of glucose and fructose. It prevents crystallization in syrups and some confectionary.

111

INVOLTINI — Veal escalopes divided into two or three pieces and pounded until very thin, then stuffed with a slice of ham and sage leaves, rolled up, skewered and baked in wine.

IODINE — Mineral found in seafood and seaweed, which is essential to the human body: lack of it causes goitre and other glandular problems.

IRISH STEW — Simple dish of mutton, potatoes, onions, water, salt and pepper cooked slowly for several hours.

IRON — Mineral important for replacing red blood cells, especially for pregnant and menstruating women. Liver, kidney and watercress are very good sources.

ISINGLASS — A setting and clarifying agent made with fish bladders.

ITALIENNE, SAUCE — Demi-glace with mushrooms, ham, wine, onion, tomato purée and parsley.

JACOB'S LADDER — Top ribs of a joint of beef. Its layers of fat and lean meat resemble a ladder, hence the reference to the bible story.

JACQUES, COUPE — Kirsch-soaked macedoine of fruit, topped with strawberry ice cream, lemon water ice and a peeled grape. It is served in a champagne glass.

JAGDWURST — German pork sausage with large chunks of lean and fat in a porous sausagemeat paste.

JAGER ART — German for hunter's style. This generally means with a mushroom and wine sauce.

JAGGER — Old name for a crimped pastry wheel.

JALFREZI — Indian term meaning stir-fried with green peppers.

JALOUSIE — French pastry named after a window shutter with movable louvres which it resembles. A rectangle of puff pastry is spread with puréed apricot jam and covered with a second rectangle which has been slashed widthways at regular intervals. It is cut into slices to serve.

JAM — General name for a fruit preserve. The word jam, which derives from jamming, ie. crushing the fruit, did not appear until the early eighteenth century. Before that the term marmelade was used.

JAMAIQUE, BOMBE — Orange ice inside a pineapple and rum ice.

JAMBALAYA — Creole dish of rice with shellfish, ham, green pepper and tomato. The name probably derives from jambon, meaning ham in French, but there is another explanation: an important man arrived at an inn in New Orleans to find all the supper eaten, so the innkeeper told his cook "Jean, balayez" (John, blend good things together).

JAMBONETTE — Stuffed, boned knuckle end of ham. A speciality of the Ardèche.

JAMBONNEAU — French for a pork foreleg. Jambonneau de volaille is French for a boned, stuffed chicken leg.

JANSSON'S TEMPTATION — Popular Swedish dish of julienne of potato baked with anchovies, onions and cream.

JAPONAIS — Mixture of ground almonds, whisked egg whites and powdered sugar, which is used as a filling or topping in pâtisserie.

JAPONAISE, A LA — Garnish of tartlets filled with Japanese artichoke, with potato croquettes or moulded rice.

JARDINIERE, A LA — Neatly cut, separately cooked vegetables as a garnish.

JARRET — French for knuckle. It is usually a veal knuckle and is added to stews for extra flavour.

JEANETTE, SUPREME DE VOLAILLE — Cold chicken breasts in tarragon chaudfroid, covered in aspic and surrounded by ice. It was created by Escoffier and named after a disastrous polar exploration in 1881, when the ship, La Jeanette, struck ice and all but one crew member died.

JELABIS — Indian sweetmeat flavoured with rosewater and saffron. The thick batter is forced though a funnel into hot fat in the shape of a lover's knot and fried until crisp. It is then soaked in sugar syrup and eaten hot or cold.

JELLIED EELS — Stewed eels in their own jellied stock. This dish is associated with London cockneys: eels were once found in quantity in the river Thames and provided a cheap and nourishing dish for the poor.

JELLO — American term for what the British call jelly.

Je

JELLY — A sweet or savoury gelatinous liquid which sets firm on cooling. Usually it is a fruit-flavoured dessert based on gelatine which is made in a decorative mould. It is also a fruit preserve, which is strained before being allowed to set, and used as a spread on bread, like jam, or to accompany roast meat or game. This last use of jelly is the oldest and is based on the principle of serving the animal with the food on which it lived, eg. redcurrant jelly with lamb.

JELLY BAG — Cloth bag with fine mesh fabric and loops at the top so that it can hang over a bowl. It is used for straining jellies (the preserve).

JERKED BEEF — American term for beef preserved by slicing it into strips and drying it in the sun or over a fire.

JESUS — Small, fat salami from Lyons. Its name derives from the fact that it was originally eaten in December (the pigs having been killed in October-November) and was wrapped in a string netting like the infant Jesus in his swaddling clothes. It is also the name of a smoked, boiling sausage from the Jura region.

JOCONDE, BISCUIT — Delicate sponge mixture relying mostly on a high proportion of beaten egg yolk and whisked egg white for its lightness. It is used in pâtisserie as a base for desserts.

JOHNNYCAKE — A savoury cake of cornmeal from the United States. Originally called journey cake because of its keeping quality, which was useful in the days of wagon trains.

JOINT — To cut poultry or game birds into pieces by severing at the joint of two bones. A joint of meat is a general term for a large cut of meat.

JOINVILLE — Prince de Joinville, the third son of Louis Philippe of France, had many dishes dedicated to him. Sole Joinville, probably the best known, is a fish mousse made in a ring mould and decorated with a velouté sauce, mushrooms and whole, unshelled prawns. Joinville sauce is a white wine sauce flavoured with shrimps or crayfish and truffles, which is served with fish.

JUBILEE — A way of preparing black cherries by heating with spices, cognac and cherry brandy, then igniting. This compote is served with vanilla ice cream.

114

JUDIC — Two famous dishes bear this name, the origins of which are unknown, though it is thought to refer to judicial reform. Sole Judic is paupiettes of sole stuffed with duxelles, wrapped in lettuce leaves and cooked in wine. It is also the name of a garnish of stuffed tomatoes, sautéed potatoes and braised lettuce for roast lamb.

JUG-JUG — Caribbean stew of pork, salt beef, pigeon peas, millet and vegetables. It was invented in the Barbados, a local interpretation of haggis.

JUICE — Liquid squeezed out of fruit, vegetables or cooked meat.

JUIVE, A LA — Jewish way of cooking carp in a sweet and sour sauce with raisins and almonds. It is served cold and the sauce turns to jelly.

JULES VERNE, A LA — Garnish for meat of stuffed potatoes and turnips, braised with mushrooms.

JULIENNE — Garnish of vegetables (usually carrot, turnip, celery and leek) cut into thin strips. It is also applied to strips of cold, cooked meat.

JUMBLES — American cookie. Originally they were shaped into strips and joined at the ends to form rings or knots (the name comes from an old English word gimbal meaning ring). Later they became drop or rolled cookies.

JUNKET — A dessert made from rennet and milk. The rennet is added to warm milk and lightly sets it. It is flavoured with rosewater and sugar. The name comes from jonquet, a Norman French word for a little basket of rushes used for draining cheese. Junket is also known as curds and whey.

JUS, AU — French term for meat served in its natural juices.

JUS LIE — French term for thickened juice or gravy.

KADAIFE ROLO — Greek pastry resembling shredded wheat in honey syrup. A batter of flour and water is poured through a perforated container onto a hot metal plate and this partially cooks into long strands, which are coated in melted butter before baking. It is filled with either a solid ground rice milk pudding or a mixture of nuts and cinnamon, and drenched in orange flower water syrup.

Ka

KAISERFLEISCH — Austrian smoked pork from the loin.

KAISERSCHMARREN — Austrian for Emperor's nonsense, this is a shredded pancake with sultanas and fruit purée, sprinkled with sugar. It was Franz Josef I's favourite dessert.

KAISERSCHNITZEL — Veal schnitzel larded and fried in butter, then braised in stock and cream.

KALBSLEBERWURST — German sausage of calves' liver.

KARTOFFELKLOSSE — German potato and fried bread dumpling.

KASHA — Russian dish of cooked buckwheat to which various other optional ingredients may be added.

KASSELER — German cured pork loin. In Germany it is sold whole and uncooked, but elsewhere it is sold cooked and in slices. It is so popular that pigs with an extra set of ribs have been bred to yield more.

KATENRAUCHWURST — German dried sausage with black skin, which is served cold in slices.

KATSUOBUSHI — Dried fillet of bonito (a fish similar to tuna), which is essential in the preparation of dashi, the basic stock of Japanese cuisine.

KAU — Chinese savoury steamed dumpling, eaten as Dim Sum.

KDRA — Characteristic Moroccan stew flavoured heavily with onions, pepper, saffron, lemon juice and clarified butter.

KEBAB — Turkish name for skewered meat, especially lamb. Kebabs were created in the Caucasus where the people impaled meat on their swords and roasted it over an open fire. To cook in a short time under the grill, the meat must be very tender and is often marinated first then basted with the marinade. The term now applies to any food on a skewer.

KEDGEREE — Anglo-Indian dish of rice, smoked haddock, hard-boiled eggs and cream, which is served at breakfast time. It is based on Khichri, a Hindu dish of rice and lentils.

KEFTETHES — Greek meatballs made with minced lamb, garlic, onion, breadcrumbs, oregano, mint, parsley and vinegar. They are made into ovals, threaded on a skewer and grilled. Tiny balls of the same mixture may also be served as an appetizer.

KENTISH HUFFKINS — Plain white, flat yeast cakes with a depression in the centre.

KENTISH WELL — *See* SUSSEX POND PUDDING.

KETA — Pink salmon roe used as a substitute for caviar.

116

KETCHUP — A commercially prepared condiment which can also be made at home. Tomato ketchup is the best known, but mushroom ketchup is also popular. The word comes from the Chinese ke-tsiap, meaning a fish brine. Also known as catsup.

KEY LIME PIE — Dessert from the Florida Keys, it is a biscuit- crust flan with a lightly set filling of eggs, cream and lime juice.

KHICHRI — Indian rice and lentil dish which was a forerunner of Kedgeree.

KHIR/KHEER — Indian dessert made with rice, milk and nuts, and flavoured with cardamom and rosewater.

KHLODNIK/KOLODNIK — Polish beetroot soup flavoured with herbs and kvass (a Russian alcoholic drink), which is served iced, decorated with slices of hardboiled egg and lemon.

KHORESH — Iranian word for sauce. It has also come to mean a mildly spice meat or poultry stew, often containing fruit.

KHORRMA — *See* KORMA.

KHOSHAF — Middle Eastern compote of dried fruits, nuts and flower water, which is macerated for a minimum of two days.

KHOYA — A stiff paste made by boiling milk in a wide, shallow pan for an hour. It is a basic ingredient for many Indian sweetmeats.

KIBBEH — Finely minced lamb and cracked wheat, pounded together and either fried in balls or baked in a tray. National dish of Syria and Lebanon. It is served only on happy occasions.

KICKSHAW — A small but luxurious or elaborate item of food. The word is derived from the French quelquechose, meaning something.

KIELBASA — Spicy garlic sausage from Poland. The word means any sausage in Polish.

KIEV, CHICKEN — Famous chicken dish in which a supreme is wrapped around chilled herb butter, coated with egg and breadcrumbs, then deep fried. The butter melts during the cooking, but does not escape from inside the chicken.

KIK A'FARZ — Breton boiled dumpling made with buckwheat, which is served with meat.

KING, A LA — Diced cooked chicken in a sauce of red and green peppers, mushrooms, onion, paprika, cream, egg yolks and sherry. It was created at the turn of the century at the Brighton Beach Hotel, Long Island, owned by a Mr King. Others claim that it was first served at Delmonico's, the famous New York restaurant, allegedly from an idea by Jim Keene of the wealthy banking family, and à la Keene soon became à la King.

KIPPER — A herring which has been slit open and cold smoked.

KISHK — Lebanese/Syrian dish made with cracked wheat fermented with milk and yogurt and rubbed to a powder, then cooked with garlic to the consistency of porridge.

KISSEL — Russian dessert made from a purée of various berries, thickened with potato flour. It may be served hot as a sauce or allowed to get cold when it sets like a jelly.

KISSING CRUST — Expression used in bakery to denote the soft pale crust where one loaf has touched another during baking.

KLEPHTI — Greek method of cooking meat and poultry wrapped in paper and baked slowly. Klephti was a Greek mountain brigand and guerilla fighter against the Turks. Originally the meat would have been cooked buried in the earth beside the open fire instead of in a conventional oven.

KLODNIK — See CHLODNIK.

KLOSSE — German for dumpling, of which there are many varieties in German cuisine. It may be based on yeast and flour, breadcrumbs, potato or oatmeal. It may contain meat, poultry, fish, cheese or something sweet.

KNACKWURST — German dried and smoked sausage of pork and beef, seasoned with cumin, garlic and saltpetre. Knackwurst, which is like a fat frankfurter, is usually sold tied in pairs.

KNEAD — To work a dough, especially a bread dough, with the palm of the hand to mix the ingredients and develop the elasticity of the gluten in the flour.

KNEADED BUTTER — Butter and flour worked together in proportions of two (butter) to one (flour), to make a paste which is added in small pieces to thicken liquid.

KNICKERBOCKER GLORY — An ice cream sundae served in a tall, conical shaped glass. It comprises chopped red jelly, ice cream in several flavours and fruit salad, and is topped with a whirl of whipped cream and a glacé cherry.

KNISH — Mashed potato dumpling, with a filling of cheese, onions and/or meat, which is deep-fried. It is Eastern European in origin, but it is now popular in the United States.

KNOBLAUCHWURSTE — German garlic pork sausage which is served cold in slices.

KNOCK DOWN — To knead lightly a yeast mixture after it has risen and before it is shaped.

KNOCK UP — To decorate and seal the edges of a pie by pressing the forefinger of one hand on the pastry rim, then using the back of a knife held in the other hand to make small horizontal cuts where the top and bottom layers of pastry meet. This is repeated all round the pie. The cutting with the knife also encourages the pastry to rise during baking.

KNUCKLE — The lower leg of veal is used to flavour stews and to make stock as it is full of marrow and therefore very gelatinous. Pork knuckle is roasted.

KOCHWURST — Generic term for boiled sausage containing offal, eg. liver sausage, brawn etc.

KOCHWURSTEL — German pork sausage seasoned with saltpetre and poached to serve.

KOFTA — Spicy meatball served, with local variations, all over the Middle East and India. Occasionally the word is used to mean a ball shape, eg. alu kofta is simply a potato ball.

KOLACKY/KOLACHY/KOLACHEN — Czech sweet bread made as small round or square buns filled with fruit, almond paste, curd cheese or poppy seeds.

KOMBO — Japanese seaweed with a sweet flavour which comes in long, flat strips.

KONIGSWURSTE — Large sausage of chicken and partridge meat, mushrooms and truffles from Germany. It is served cold in slices.

KORMA/KHORMA/QUORMAH — Muslim or Moglai way of preparing meat or poultry by marinating and cooking it in mildly spiced yogurt, cream and nuts.

KOSHER — Means fit in Hebrew and describes food prepared according to orthodox Jewish food laws. Kosher meat is killed in a different way from the usual Western method: the animal's jugular is slit to lose as much blood as possible.

119

Ko

KOULIBAC/KOULIBIAKA — A Russian pie made with leavened pastry dough and various savoury fillings arranged in layers. A salmon, rice and hard-boiled egg mixture is very popular. To be correct, the bottom layer should be the gelatinous marrow of the sturgeon's backbone or shredded pancake or rice. This soaks up any excess moisture from the main filling (meat, fish or vegetable) and prevents the pastry becoming soggy.

KREPLACH — Jewish triangular dumpling made with thin noodle-type dough and a cheese filling. It is cooked in vegetable stock, which is served as soup with the kreplach.

KROMESKI — A small piece of cooked creamed chicken, veal, or game mixture, wrapped in thin strips of bacon before being dipped in batter and deep fried.

KRUPUK/KROEPOEK — Indonesian prawn wafer, fried briefly in oil which causes it to puff up.

KUCHEN — Basic German term for cake.

KUGEL — Any baked Jewish pudding of noodles or potato.

KUGELHOPF/GUGELHOPF — A cake made with a yeast dough in a special mould with diagonally fluted sides and a crater in the middle. The Sultan's turban shape is said to have been invented to commemorate the defeat of the Turkish armies which beseiged Vienna in 1683, but the cake is probably of older origin. It is eaten all over eastern Europe.

KULFI — Indian ice cream flavoured with cardamom and pistachios. It is made by heating milk until it is reduced by two-thirds.

KULICH — Russian yeast cake made in a special cylindrical mould, the shape of an orthodox priest's hat. It is traditionally eaten at Easter with pasha. It is cut into rounds from the top to serve.

KUNG PAO CHICKEN — Szechwan way of preparing chicken. It is spicy, stir fried and contains peanuts and chillies.

KUSHI-YAKI — Japanese method of cooking on a skewer or spit.

LACHSSCHINKEN — German sausage of cured, smoked pork from the loin. It is cut in thin slices and eaten as an hors d'oeuvre. The name, which means salmon ham, refers to its pink colour.

LACQUERED DUCK — Chinese method of spit-roasting duck and painting it frequently with a sauce of cinnamon, ginger, soy sauce, sherry and caster sugar.

LACTOSE — Natural sugar occuring in milk.

LADLE — Large spoon with deep round bowl and long handle, used for serving soups and stews.

LADY BALTIMORE CAKE — Speciality from Charleston, South Carolina. The cake is made with egg whites, sugar, butter and a little flour in layers, which are sandwiched together and covered with an icing made with more egg whites and icing sugar, plus a mixture of dried fruits and nuts macerated in sherry. The original recipe first appeared in a nineteenth century novel called *Lady Baltimore*.

LAFFITTE — French chicken consommé flavoured with Madeira, garnished with cock's combs, truffle, mushrooms, cucumber and chives.

LAGUIPIERE — The man who taught Carême to cook has given his name to a game consommé garnished with game royale and pigeon's eggs, and to two sauces for fish: one a sauce of fish fumet, butter, glaze and lemon juice; the other a velouté sauce flavoured with truffles and Madeira.

LAHMAJOON — Armenian pastry topped with a meat mixture flavoured with meat. It can be served as an appetiser or as a snack.

LAIT, AU — French term for food or drink served or cooked with milk.

LAMB — The meat of a sheep less than one year old.

LAMBALLE — A thick soup of tapioca and peas.

LAMBROTSOMO — Greek bread studded with hard-boiled egg, which is served at Easter. The eggs represent life inside the tomb of Christ.

121

La

LAME — French baker's scalpel for slashing bread dough. It is about four inches long (10 cm) and ¼ inch (less than a cm) wide, with very sharp curved ends. The word can also mean a very thin slice.

LAMINGTON — Small cake from New Zealand. It is an oblong of Victoria Sandwich mixture, coated with chocolate icing and coconut.

LANDAISE — Style of cooking with foie gras and truffles.

LANDELEBERWURST — German sausage of pork liver and fat.

LANDLADY'S LOAF — Another name for barrel loaf.

LANGUE DE CHAT — Cat's tongue in French. A crisp, dry little biscuit that gets its name from its shape.

LANGUEDOCIENNE, A LA — This term may mean a specific garnish for meat of stuffed aubergine, minced cèpes, tomatoes, parsley and château potatoes. More generally, it implies a strong garlic flavour.

LANIERE — French term meaning a slice.

LARD — To insert small strips of bacon fat into a piece of meat which will need moistening during cooking.

LARDING NEEDLE — Implement for larding meat.

LARDOIRE — French for larding needle.

LARDON/LARDOON — Matchstick size strip of bacon fat inserted into lean meat to moisten during cooking or added (when fried) to casseroles for flavour.

LARDY CAKE — Crisp, light little cake made with lard rather than butter. It originated in country districts of England when pigs were killed locally and every part was used for something. Leftover bread dough was spread with lard, sugar and currants, then folded and rolled again several times, then cut into separate squares and baked.

LASAGNE — Pasta in squares or long strips which is boiled and then baked in layers with a meat sauce and a white sauce. Lasagna is the singular, ie. one piece of pasta. Lasagne al forno means lasagne baked in the oven. Lasagne verde means green lasagne; the actual pasta is flavoured with spinach.

LASAGNETTE — Wide, flat pasta with a rippled edge.

LASSI/LHASI — Indian drink made with yogurt and crushed ice. It may be sweet or savoury.

LATKE — Jewish grated potato and onion pancake.

LATTE, AL — Italian for cooked in milk.

LAVALLIERE — A la Lavallière is a garnish for poultry and sweetbreads of truffles, lamb's sweetbreads larded with truffles, and crayfish. Also a garnish for tournedos and noisettes of artichoke bottoms filled with asparagus tips, château potatoes and bordelaise sauce. Lavallière sauce is a madeira sauce flavoured with game extract, garnished with tarragon and truffles, and thickened with cream.

LA VARENNE — Francois Pierre de la Varenne was chef to Louis XIV and the author of the first serious book on cooking.

LAVERBREAD — A mixture of seaweed (laver) and oatmeal made into patties and fried in bacon dripping. Once eaten in all coastal regions of Britain, it is now mostly encountered in Wales and the west of England.

LEAVEN — A paste of soured wheat which when added to flour and water ferments and causes the dough to rise.

LEAVENING — The process of lightening a bread or cake by introducing air bubbles which expand during cooking. Leavening agents which supply the air bubbles are yeast, bicarbonate of soda mixed with an acid, and beaten egg.

LEBERWURST — German liver sausage.

LEBKUCHEN — German spice cookie, traditionally eaten at Christmas time. Originally made in Nurnberg, the centre of the spice trade, they were first made by specialist bakers called Lebkuchner, who vied with each other to produce the most ornate shapes: these were then painted and gilded.

LEG — Cut of meat. Leg of pork or lamb is a prime roasting joint, but leg of beef is a stewing cut.

LEGUME — Plant with seed pods, such as peas and beans. French for vegetable.

LEIPZIGER ALLERLEI — Dish of diced vegetables and crayfish tails in white sauce, with small dumplings. A speciality of Leipzig.

LEKACH — Traditional Jewish honey cake eaten at the Jewish New Year.

LEOPOLD — Meat consommé with julienne of sautéed sorrel and chervil.

LESCO — Hungarian stew of peppers, tomatoes and onions, flavoured with bacon and paprika.

LEVURE — French term for luting paste.

LHASI — *See* LASSI.

Ll

LIAISON — The binding or thickening of a sauce by the addition of egg yolks, cream, beurre manié etc.

LIEGEOISE, A LA — Term applied to various dishes, especially offal, cooked with juniper berries.

LIGHT CREAM — American for single cream.

LIGHTS — Butchery term for the lungs of certain animals. Lights are used for pâtés, faggots and pet food.

LIMOUSIN — When applied to meat dishes this means with foie gras, cream and Madeira sauce. Beef Limousin is the most famous example and is made with a larded fillet of beef.

LIMOUSINE, A LA — A way of cooking red cabbage, or meat or poultry garnished with red cabbage.

LIMPA — Swedish light rye bread, flavoured with caraway, fennel and orange rind.

LINDSTROM, BEEF — Well-known Swedish dish of minced beef mixed with chopped potato, pickled beetroot, capers, onion, egg yolk and cream, shaped into patties and fried.

LINE — To cover the bottom and sides of a tin or mould to protect the food which is to be contained and to prevent it sticking to the container. The lining may be paper or an edible substance such as pastry or strips of bacon.

LING — Chinese cooking term meaning that the food in question has been suspended in a basket over a pan of hot oil and the oil has been ladled over the food.

LINGUINE — Short pieces of oval section spaghetti. The name means small tongues in Italian.

LINZERTORTE — Tart from Linz, in Germany, made with a rich hazelnut pastry filled with raspberry jam, and with a pastry lattice on top.

LITTLETON SAUCE — Sauce for fish made with egg yolk, butter, vinegar and redcurrant jelly.

LOAF — Refers to items cooked in a deep rectangular tin with slightly sloping sides (this is a loaf tin). It may be bread, cake, or a savoury mixture served hot or cold as an entrée.

LODGER'S LOAF — Another name for barrel loaf.

LOIN — Cut of meat between the ribs and the tail. Veal, pork and lamb loin are roasted whole or cut into chops.

LOKSHEN KUGEL — Jewish egg noodle custard pudding.

LOKUM — The Turkish name for Turkish delight, a sweetmeat made with cornflour, sugar, nuts and rosewater. It has a jelly-like consistency and is cut into cubes and rolled in icing sugar.

LONDON BROIL — U.S. way of preparing steak: it is marinated in vinaigrette, grilled, then cut into thin, diagonal slices and served with melted butter.

LONGCHAMP — Name of a soup made with green pea purée, sorrel and vermicelli.

LONGE — The top end of the loin. French butchery term.

LONG ISLAND BUCK — American savoury similar to Welsh Rabbit, but with egg yolks beaten into the cheese mixture.

LONG THREAD/LONG FEATHER — The stage reached when sugar is boiled to 110°C (225°F).

LORETTE — A number of dishes have been given this name: a garnish of chicken croquettes, asparagus tips and truffle; chicken consommé with paprika, asparagus tips, truffle and chervil, with pommes Lorette served separately; corn salad with sticks of celery and beetroot; potatoes like pommes Chamonix but in a crescent shape.

LORRAINE — A garnish for meat of red cabbage and fondant potatoes. Also a chicken, veal and almond soup, thickened with breadcrumbs. Lorraine pie has a filling of chopped pork and veal marinated in Madeira and encased in shortcrust pastry: beaten egg is poured into a hole in the top crust when the pie is almost cooked.

LOUIS — American way of serving cold crab or shrimp in a tangy tomato mayonnaise on a bed of lettuce.

LOUISE, POMMES DE TERRE — Grated raw potatoes mixed with chopped onion, flour, parsley, eggs, salt and pepper, made into a thick patty and fried on both sides in oil.

LOUISIANE, A LA — Garnish for poultry or meat of sweetcorn fritters, rice darioles on sautéed sweet potatoes and rounds of fried bananas.

LOUKOUMADES — Greek for honey puffs. Tiny doughnuts, deep-fried, drenched in honey syrup, then rolled in chopped walnuts.

LOX — Jewish word for smoked salmon.

LUCCHESE, DEL — Sauce of spinach, ricotta cheese, chicken livers, mushrooms, cinnamon and nutmeg, usually used with lasagne.

125

Lu

LUCULLUS, A LA — A garnish for poultry and sweetbreads of whole truffles cooked in Madeira and stuffed with chicken forcemeat and chopped truffles: a chicken and calves' brains velouté soup, garnished with diced cucumber: a beef consommé garnished with diced carrots, turnips, cauliflower sprigs and quenelles.

LUGANEGHE — Italian pork and Parmesan cheese sausage from Romagna. It is extremely long, so it is cut to order and fried.

LUI — Chinese cooking term meaning that the food is poached in oil.

LUKANKA — Bulgarian spicy pork sausage.

LUTETIA, SOLE — Baked sole with truffles and mushrooms in cream.

LUTING PASTE — A mixture of flour and water used to seal the gap between a casserole and its lid.

LYONNAISE — This term is used widely to indicate the predominant flavour of fried onions. Lyonnaise sauce is a brown sauce with onion and white wine added.

MAAJTE — Dutch way of preparing herring fillets by lightly brining them to give a delicate flavour. They are sold at stalls and eaten on the street.

MACAIRE, POMMES — Potatoes which have been baked, then the filling scooped out of the skins, fried in butter then returned to the potato skins to serve.

MACARONI — Italian tubular pasta. There is a story explaining how macaroni got its name: a Neopolitan cardinal, on first seeing this new shape of pasta, exclaimed "Ma caroni" – the little dears. The story is spoilt by the fact that the Italian word for this pasta is maccheroni.

MACAROON — Biscuit made with a mixture of egg white, sugar and ground almonds, which is heaped onto rice paper before baking. The rice paper circle under the macaroon is eaten too.

MACDONALD — Meat consommé garnished with royale of lamb's brains, diced cucumber and ravioli.

126

MACEDOINE — A mixture of fruit or vegetables cut into small cubes. The name refers to the Macedonian Empire of Alexander the Great, which was a jumble of small states.

MACERATE — To soak fruit in alcohol or syrup to soften and absorb the flavour.

MACONNAISE — This term generally means that the accompanying sauce or cooking liquor contains red wine.

MADEIRA CAKE — A rich plain cake decorated with a piece of citron peel on top. It gets its name from the fact that it was always served to visitors with a glass of Madeira wine.

MADELEINE — A small plain cake made in a special shallow fluted oval mould. Of ancient origin, it is generally accepted that they were first made in Commercy, a small town in France, where the secret recipe was sold for a large sum of money. A quite different cake from England is also called a madeleine; this is a sponge mixture baked in a dariole mould, brushed with apricot jam, rolled in desiccated coconut and decorated with a cherry and two pieces of angelica on top. Madeleine is also the name of a garnish of artichoke bottoms filled with onion purée and topped with haricot beans. Also a garnish for fish of crayfish cream sauce, diced celeriac and crayfish tails.

MADERE — Demi-glace sauce with onion, tomato purée, herbs and Madeira. Croûte au madère is an apricot pie flavoured with Madeira.

MADRAS — Restaurant term for a fairly hot curry.

MADRILENE — Term, meaning from Madrid, applied to sauces or soups containing tomato ice and sherry or Madeira.

MA FACON, A — This expression simply means in my way.

MAGISTERE — Concentrated meat and vegetable broth.

MAGNESIUM — Mineral important for the formation and maintenance of bones and teeth, which is found in nuts, whole wheat, soya beans and cocoa.

MAGRET — Duck breast cooked on its own.

MAGRO, RISOTTO DI — Non-meat risotto.

MAHASH — Indian spiced and stuffed vegetable.

MAJADO — Spanish sauce of ground almonds, hazelnuts or pine kernels which is used in many dishes.

MAIDS OF HONOUR — A sweet pastry not unlike a cooked cheesecake. It is a small puff pastry tart filled with a curd cheese or junket and lemon mixture. Said to have been made by Anne Boleyn for Henry VIII at Richmond Palace: the original recipe was sold for £1000 according to the legend.

MAIGRE, AU — French term for food cooked without meat or meat stock. This was significant when eating meat was forbidden by the church on Fridays and during Lent.

MAILLOT — Steak garnish of glazed turnips, carrots and onions, braised lettuce, buttered peas and French beans.

MAINGAUX — French dessert of curds similar to junket.

MAISON — French for house, this term implies the house speciality and can aply to any dish, but pâté maison is always a smooth pork and liver mixture.

MAITRE D'HOTEL BUTTER — Butter to which chopped parsley and a squeeze of lemon juice has been added before forming it into a roll, chilling it and cutting it into slices to serve.

MAJADO — Spanish sauce of ground nuts.

MA-LA — Szechuan method of food preparation using a sauce of peppercorns, red chillies, ginger, shallot, soy sauce and sugar.

MALAKOFF — Charlotte Malakoff has a filling of unsalted butter, sugar, ground almonds and cream surrounded by sponge fingers soaked in Grand Marnier. Malakoff pudding has layers of sponge, apple purée, custard, pear purée, almonds, raisins and orange rind chilled until set and unmoulded to serve. The Malakoffs were a noble family in Tsarist Russia.

MALAYA — Term given to a mild curry with pineapple and other fruit in it.

MALTAGLIATI — Offcuts of pasta used in soup. The word means badly cut in Italian.

MALTAISE — This term can be applied to any dish, sweet or savoury, which is flavoured with blood oranges. Maltaise sauce is Hollandaise flavoured with orange.

MALT BREAD — Tea bread made with ordinary white bread dough, malt extract, black treacle and dried fruit.

MANCHESTER TART — Sometimes known as Manchester pudding. It consists of pastry, jam, a custard flavoured with lemon peel, brandy and thickened with breadcrumbs, then a layer of dense meringue.

128

MANCHET — Small oval white bread, also known as hand bread, which was laid for each diner at medieval feasts. It was prepared from the finest white flour which was considered the best in those days – the peasants got the bran. Cuts were made across the top with a knife to allow the dough to rise well.

MANCHETTE — A paper frill for decorating cutlet bones.

MANCHON — French for muff. Two kinds of cakes are thus described, both being muff-shaped. One is a petit four of almond paste which is baked then filled with praline butter cream, the other is a small cake of flaky pastry.

MANDOLIN — Simple mechanical slicer consisting of a wooden board with two adjustable cutting blades, one plain, one with a serrated edge across the centre so that it resembles the musical instrument of the same name. It is used for vegetables.

MANICOTTI — Italian for little muffs. These are stuffed pasta rounds or rectangles rolled around a filling.

MARAICHERE, A LA — Garnish for large cuts of meat of braised stuffed cucumbers, salsify, artichokes, carrots, whole baby onions and château potatoes.

MARBLE — A marble cake is made of two or more different coloured cake mixtures put at random in the same tin and cooked so that the effect is marbled.

MARBLING — A butchery term which describes the fat intermingling in the lean of meat to give a mottled, streaked appearance. Definitive mark of fine quality meat.

MARCASSIN — French term for young wild boar.

MARCERON, POULET — Boned chicken with legs and wings intact, stuffed with ham, foie gras and brandy and braised with vegetables.

MARCHAND DE VIN, SAUCE — Made like Bercy sauce but with meat stock and red wine.

MARECHALE — A la maréchale is a method of preparing small cuts of meats, especially poultry and veal by dipping in egg and breadcrumbs, frying in butter and serving with asparagus tips and truffles. Bombe Maréchale has three interior layers of pistachio, vanilla and orange inside a shell of strawberry ice.

MARENGO, CHICKEN — A dish invented to celebrate Napoleon's victory over the Austrians at the battle of Marengo in 1800. According to legend, all the chef (Dumand) could find on the battlefield was a small chicken, three eggs, four tomatoes, six crayfish, brandy, garlic and olive oil, and it was with these unlikely ingredients that he created a classic dish. Napoleon liked to eat it after every battle thereafter as he thought it brought him luck. Veal is sometimes cooked Marengo-style.

MARGHERITA, PIZZA — Pizza with a topping of mozzarella cheese, tomatoes, basil and Parmesan cheese.

MARGOT — Often applied to desserts and cakes featuring strawberries.

MARGUERITE — American term for various small cakes: a cracker spread with boiled frosting, topped with nuts, chocolate chips etc. and baked until golden; a cracker baked with a marshmallow on top, which melts during baking; a spongecake batter baked in small shapes.

MARGUERY — Famous Paris restaurant, named after its owner, which flourished in the late nineteenth century. Sole Marguery, which was created there, is fillet of sole baked in a little fumet and served with an egg and butter sauce, mussels and shrimps.

MARIE-JEANNE, A LA — Garnish for noisettes and tournedos of tartlets filled with mushroom purée, topped with a slice of truffle.

MARIE-LOUISE, A LA — Garnish for entrees of artichoke bottoms filled with mushroom purée then gratinéed, and asparagus tips.

MARIE-STUART, A LA — Garnish of tartlets filled with a purée of turnips or onions, with marrow bone fat on top, covered with demi-glace.

MARIGNY — Rich pea soup with rice, beans and lettuce garnish. Also a garnish for meat of artichoke hearts filled with sweetcorn and sauteed potato balls.

MARINADE — A liquid in which food, usually meat or poultry, is left for hours or days in order to tenderize and add flavour. The liquid generally contains wine, oil and vinegar or soy sauce – all of which help to break down the fibres and so tenderize – plus herbs, spices and seasoning.

MARINARA, ALLA — Fresh tomato and basil sauce for fettucine. Or the name of a seafood risotto.

MARINATE — To steep food, usually meat or poultry, in a liquid, called a marinade, prior to cooking, to tenderize or improve flavour.

MARINIERE, A LA — Term applied to fish dishes, especially mussels. It means in the style of the fisherman's wife.

MARITOZZI — Italian yeast bun with raisins, candied peel and pine nuts.

MARJOLAINE — Meringue gâteau made with ground almonds and hazelnuts in four layers, which are sandwiched with different butter creams, one chocolate, one vanilla, one praline and the top is dusted with powdered chocolate and sugar.

MARLBOROUGH PIE — Applesauce custard pie from Boston, Massachusetts, which was once a traditional Thanksgiving dessert.

MARLOW — Frozen dessert from the United States, made with melted marshmallows, cream and a flavouring such as fruit purée.

MARLY — Chicken consommé garnished with a julienne of leek, celery, chicken, shredded lettuce, chervil, croûtons and grated Parmesan.

MARMALADE — Fruit stewed for a long time until it is reduced to a thick purée. Although nowadays the term is applied to any jam or conserve made with citrus fruit, but in the middle ages it was made with quinces, honey and spices. When sugar became readily available, sometime in the sixteenth century, fruit was puréed and boiled with sugar until solid, then eaten in lumps as a sweetmeat and called marmelade: this is the French spelling of the word and it is used to describe any stiff sweetened purée of fruit and is used mostly as a flan filling. Marmalade as we know it today was created in Dundee when Janet Keiller bought a consignment of Spanish oranges which were too bitter to sell for eating: the Keiller preserves factory was established in 1797. In 1859 a finely shredded marmalade was introduced by a Mr Robinson, a grocer from Paisley. Marmalade was considered a Scottish speciality until the 1870s when a Mrs Cooper of Oxford made a dark chunky version for undergraduates' breakfasts. There is a controversy over the origin of the name: one story claims that it is a corruption of " Marie est malade" referring to a pick-me-up made for Mary Queen of Scots during her time as Dauphine or Queen of France. More likely it is a derivation of marmelo, the Portuguese for quince, although the Romans had a preserve called melimelum.

MARMITE — Tall stockpot from France. It may have narrow or bulging sides, but its cylindrical shape ensures minimum evaporation and helps to blend the flavour of the ingredients in it. Petite marmite is a clear savoury broth cooked and served in a marmite.

MARQUER — To put food into a greased container; also to prepare food before cooking.

MARQUIS, LE — Chocolate sponge cake.

MARQUISE — Various cakes are called Marquise; they vary enormously except that they all contain chocolate. Chocolate Marquise is a mixture of chocolate and water with a little oil or butter, which is used as a coating for desserts, cakes and pastries. A bombe marquise has apricot ice outside and a centre of chablis, vanilla and orange or lemon rind ice. A la Marquise describes a garnish for noisettes and tournedos of calf's marrow, asparagus tips, julienne of truffles and Hollandaise sauce with a little caviar stirred into it. Also a beef and celery consommé, garnished with chicken quenelles, beef marrow and chopped hazelnuts.

MARSEILLAISE — Garnish for tournedos and noisettes of stuffed olives and anchovies inside sautéed tomatoes, potato chips and provencale sauce. Marseillaise sauce is either mayonnaise flavoured with sea urchins or very garlicky French dressing.

MARSHMALLOW — A confection made of egg white and sugar, which has a soft, sticky consistency.

MARTINE, SOUFFLE — Orange soufflé with layers of sponge fingers soaked in Grand Marnier.

MARY ANN PAN — American term for a shallow cake tin with a raised circular platform in the middle. The cake or pastry case baked in it is inverted to serve so that it has a shallow depression which can be filled.

MARYLAND — A garnish of sweetcorn and ham or bacon. Chicken Maryland is fried chicken with sweetcorn and fried bananas wrapped in bacon. From the state of Maryland.

MARZIPAN — A paste of eggs, ground almonds and sugar used as a sweetmeat and as a cake covering. From the French word massepain, meaning mass bread, because it is thought to have been invented in a convent. In Britain it used to be called marchpane.

MASA — Spanish for dough. Masa harina is maize flour used for making tortillas and other Mexican specialities.

MASALA — Indian term meaning a mixture of spices.

MASCOTTE — A la mascotte describes a garnish for small cuts of meat and poultry of quartered artichoke hearts, small olive-shaped potatoes, both cooked in butter, and truffles. Also a sauce of white wine, veal gravy and meat juice. A mascotte is a genoese cake filled with a hazelnut mocha butter cream.

MASK — To cover food with a sauce to serve.

MASLIN PAN — Another name for a preserving pan. It has a wide, fairly deep pan with a hinged semi-circular handle across the top, a pouring lip and a small grip handle opposite the lip.

MASQUER — French term meaning to cover a dessert with an even layer of cream using a palette knife before adding the finishing touches.

MASSE — French cookery term meaning a mixture of ingredients which will form the basis of a more elaborate dish.

MASSENA, A LA — Garnish for small cuts of meat, especially tournedos, artichoke hearts filled with béarnaise sauce and strips of poached beef bone-marrow.

MASSENAT, A LA — Garnish for tournedos and noisettes of artichoke bottoms filled with marrow bone fat, beans, pommes Anna and Madeira sauce.

MA TAI KO — Chinese sweet jelly made from water chestnut flour.

MATARELLO — Very long rolling pin, designed for rolling out pasta.

MATELOTE — French fish stew made with red wine. The name can also apply to veal and poultry dishes. A matelote may also be known as a meurette or pochouse.

MATIGNON — Preparation of seasoned minced vegetables spread over or under meat or poultry which is to be pot roasted or braised. Sometimes strips of ham may be added to the mixture. The matignon is served as a garnish. Invented in the Hôtel Matignon in eighteenth century Paris.

MATTAR PANEER — Indian dish of dried peas and cubes of a rubbery white cheese in a spicy sauce.

MATZO — Jewish unleavened bread traditionally eaten at the Passover to commemorate the flight from Egypt when there was no time to wait for the bread dough to rise before baking. Matzo meal is used in a variety of ways in Kosher cooking.

MAYONNAISE — A cold sauce of egg yolks and oil blended into an emulsion. It is probably Spanish in origin, though the origin of the word is in dispute: it may be a corruption of moyeunaise, from moyeu, meaning egg yolk in old French; Carême said that it came from an obscure verb magnonner (to stir and stir and stir); another story is that it is named in honour of the taking of Mahon in Minorca by the Duc de Richelieu in 1756.

MAYONNAISE COLLEE — Mayonnaise into which a mixture of aspic jelly and gelatine is whisked. It is used as a coating for cold poultry and fish.

MAZARIN — Cake made with genoese named after France's Cardinal Mazarin. When the cake is baked a cavity is made in the middle which is filled with crystallized fruit in a purée of apricots and kirsch; the cone removed from the cake is decorated with pink fondant icing and crystallized fruit, then inverted over the cavity.

MEAL — Medium-coarse ground grain.

MEATBALL — Small sphere of ground meat, onion, breadcrumbs, herbs and spices, bound together with beaten egg. Meatballs may be fried or braised in a sauce.

MECHOUI — French term (derived from an Algerian word) for whole lamb barbecued over a fire.

MEDAILLON — Half inch thick veal steak. Also a small round flat cut of meat, fish or pâté.

MEDICIS — A la Médicis is a garnish for tournedos and noisettes of artichoke bottoms filled with cooked green peas, carrots and turnips or noisette potatoes, with sauce choron. Also a sauce of Béarnaise wih tomato purée and red wine, and a beef consommé garnished with carrot royale, sorrel and purée of peas. Bombe Médicis has an interior of raspberry ice surrounded by peach ice flavoured with cognac. Named after Catherine de Médicis, Queen of France.

MEGGYLEVES — Cold Hungarian soup of morello cherries, cream and wine.

MELBA — Dame Nellie Melba, the opera singer, gave her name to a peach dessert, a raspberry sauce and a way of preparing toast. The story concerning the invention of the dessert and sauce is as follows: Melba was staying at the Savoy hotel in 1894 while singing *Lohengrin* at Covent Garden. She gave tickets to the Savoy's chef, Escoffier. Next day he served a swan carved from a block of ice – between the wings were ice cream, poached peaches and raspberry purée. Nowadays the swan is omitted and raspberry syrup often substituted. Melba toast is very thin slices of white bread without crusts, that have been left to dry out in a moderate oven until brown and crisp. It is very good with pâté.

MELT — To turn a solid ingredient into a liquid by applying heat.

MELTING — One of the three standard methods of cake making. The dry ingredients are sieved into a bowl and a well is made in the middle. The fat is melted and poured into the well with any other liquid ingredients. Raising is often achieved by the action of bicarbonate of soda and soured milk. Cakes made by this method tend to be moist but heavy and improve with keeping. eg. gingerbread, parkin.

MELTON MOWBRAY PIE — A famous pork pie from the Midland town of Melton Mowbray. It is made in a deep pan with hot water pastry and a well-flavoured jellied pork filling.

MELTS — The spleen of animals. Usually only sold as pet food.

MENAGERE, A LA — French for housewife or housekeeper's style. It implies something simply made, for example, poulet à la ménagère is roast chicken stuffed with cubes of bread and herbs.

MENTONNAISE, A LA — Garnish for meat or chard stuffed with duxelles, artichoke bottoms filled with sautéed potato balls and meat gravy. Also a garnish for meat of courgettes stuffed with rice and tomato purée, artichokes, small potatoes cooked in butter, with demi-glace sauce. At a more popular level it describes food, especially fish, cooked with black olives, tomatoes and garlic .

MENU — A list of the food and drink available at a restaurant and the prices to be charged. Originally the menu was for the staff so that they would know the order to serve each dish. Not until the nineteenth century did menus become common practice in restaurants. In France the term means a fixed price meal.

MENUDO — Mexican soup made from a cow's stomach. Said to be a cure for hangovers.

MERCEDES — French gâteau consisting of a deep pastry case filled with a mixture of ground almonds, kirsch, candied fruit, egg whites and sugar, and topped with slivered almonds and an apricot glaze. A la Mercedes describes a garnish for meat of grilled tomatoes, mushrooms, braised lettuce, croquette potatoes and Madeira sauce. Also consommé flavoured with sherry and garnished with cock's combs and cock's kidneys cut into star shapes. Soufflé Mercedes is a cream based soufflé flavoured with fruit salpicon soaked in kirsch and marashino.

MERE FILLIOUX, POULARDE A LA — Another name for chicken en demi-deuil, named after the restaurant where the dish was created.

MERE POULARD — Proprietress of a small restaurant on Mont St Michel, who was famous for her remarkably fluffy omelette. The recipe is still secret.

MERINGUE — A cooked mixture of whisked egg whites and sugar. Meringue Suisse is the correct name for what most people simply call meringue. It is baked either in the form of small blobs which can be filled with whipped cream, or as the base or topping for a variety of desserts. It was invented in 1720 in the small town of Mehrinyghen in the German state of Saxe-Coburg-Gotha, by a Swiss pastry cook. Two other forms of meringue exist – meringue cuite (cooked meringue) and meringue Italienne (Italian meringue). The former is egg white and icing or caster sugar beaten over a low heat until thick enough to stand in peaks. The mixture requires no further cooking and is used in pâtisserie for decorative piping and cake fillings. Meringue Italienne is used for the same purpose but is made by pouring a sugar syrup into stiffly whisked egg whites and continuing to whisk until thick; the egg whites are set by the heat of the sugar so the mixture requires no cooking.

MERVEILLE — A sweet fritter with a distinctive shape: a thin strip of dough (which may be flavoured with flower water or cognac) is twisted twice before deep-frying.

MESSINE — Consommé garnished with stuffed cabbage leaves and chipolatas. Also a sauce of chopped tarragon, parsley, chervil and shallot blended with cream, egg yolks, lemon juice, butter, a little flour and French mustard: it is served with fish.

METTWURST — German spreading sausage of smoked spicy pork.

MEUNIERE, A LA — French for "in the style of the Miller's wife". Classicly simple method of cooking fish or steak by dipping in seasoned flour, frying butter, adding lemon juice to the butter in the pan and pouring it over the food before sprinkling it with parsley.

MEURETTE — Fish stew that includes lardons and wine.

MEXICAINE, A LA — Garnish for meat of mushrooms, peppers, tomatoes and aubergines with a sauce of meat gravy and tomato juice. Also mayonnaise with anchovy essence and chopped red and green peppers. Mexicaine style usually means sweetcorn and red or green peppers.

MEZE — Hors d'oeuvre from the Middle East (including Greece). A typical combination would be: olives, cheeses, pickled vegetables, tiny meatballs, stuffed vine leaves, fried octopus or shrimp, phyllo pastries and taramasalata.

MEZZALUNA — Half moon in Italian. A mezzaluna is a sharp knife with a long curved steel blade shaped like a half moon, with a handle above the blade, either in the middle or at each end of the inner curve. The former is used in conjunction with a bowl, the latter is used on a flat board.

MIDDLE NECK — Stewing cut of veal or lamb.

MIE DE PAIN — Fresh white breadcrumbs.

MIGAIN — French term for a custard of eggs and cream.

MIGLIACCIO NAPOLETANO — Italian dish of layers of polenta, mozzarella, sausagemeat and pecorino baked in the oven.

MIGNON, A LA — Garnish for poultry and sweetbreads of artichoke bottoms filled with green peas and truffle quennelles.

MIGNONNETTE — French term which describes a tournedos and also potato chips 8 cm (3 in) long and 5 mm (¼ in) wide.

MIJOTER — French term meaning to cook food gently over a low heat.

MIJOTIN — A small cassadou cooking pot.

MIKADO — Garnish for tournedos and noisettes of fried tomato halves, Chinese artichokes sautéed in butter and provencale sauce. Also small piles of curried rice or tartlets filled with beanshoots with cream: either of these can be served as canapé or a garnish for veal or chicken.

MILANAISE — Milanaise sauce is a popular Italian sauce flavoured with tomato and ham which is usually served with pasta. A la Milanaise describes food dipped in beaten egg, then a mixture of grated Parmesan cheese and breadcrumbs before frying.

MILLE FEUILLES — French for a thousand leaves. This is a famous pastry also known as a cream slice: it consists of several layers of cooked oblong-shaped pieces of puff pastry sandwiched with jam and cream or crème pâtissière, and topped with glacé icing.

MILT — Soft roe.

MIMI — Pea and barley soup with carrot garnish.

MIMOSA — Garnish of sliced green beans and chopped hard-boiled egg yolk arranged like a mimosa flower on salads and soups. Eggs Mimosa are hard-boiled eggs stuffed with a mixture of prawns and mayonnaise and coated with mayonnaise and sieved egg yolk.

MINCEMEAT — A mixture of dried and fresh fruits, spices and suet steeped in brandy, rum or Madeira. Originally cooked minced meat was included (and sometimes still is).

MINESTRONE — Italian for a substantial, thick soup with lots of vegetables and pasta or rice in meat stock. The name derives from the Latin verb ministrare: in the Middle Ages travellers stopped at the monasteries for food and shelter, and the monks had to be ready to minister to them whatever time they arrived so a hearty soup was kept simmering on the stove.

MINUTE STEAK — Steak cut to ½ inch (1 cm) thick and grilled or fried on each side for one minute.

MIRABEAU, A LA — Garnish for grilled meat of anchovy fillets arranged in a lattice on the meat, olives, tarragon leaves and anchovy butter. It is named after the French revolutionary Mirabeau.

MIREILLE — Sauce Mireille is Hollandaise flavoured with tomato purée and basil. It is served with eggs, vegetables and offal. Bombe Mireille has redcurrant ice outside with a filling of strawberry ice flavoured with kirsch and maraschino.

MIREPOIX — A mixture of cooked, diced vegetables, bacon and herbs used as a foundation on which meat, poultry or fish is braised. The vegetables – usually carrot, onion, celery and leek – should be balanced in quantity so that no one flavour dominates. If the contents are very finely diced a mirepoix may be used as a garnish for plainly grilled meat or fish. It is named after the duc de Mirepoix who died in 1757

MIRETTE — Beef consommé garnished with chicken quennelles and julienne of lettuce and chervil. Also diced potatoes cooked in butter, mixed with julienne of truffle, served in timbale with Madeira sauce and gratinéed.

MIROTON — French term for a stew made with cooked beef (ie leftovers) and onions.

MISO — Thick brown paste made from soya beans. It is very concentrated and therefore a small amount added to a vegetarian dish will supply all the necessary protein.

MISTINGUETTE — Cooked with foie gras, herbs and white wine and named after the French cabaret artiste.

MISTRAL — Term applied to poultry dishes meaning that it is cooked or served with aubergines.

MITONNER — French term meaning to steep and allow to boil for a certain period. Also to cook bread in soup slowly and for a long time.

MITTOON — Pork Mittoon is a Yorkshire version of potted pork which can be served hot with gravy or pressed and left to set on cooking. A mittoon is also the dish (a small tureen) in which it is cooked.

MIX — To combine ingredients by stirring.

MIXED GRILL — A complete dish cooked under the grill; it comprises a selection of grilled meats such as steaks, chops, kidneys, sausages and bacon with grilled mushrooms and tomatoes, served with maître d'hôtel butter.

MIXED SPICE — Ready ground and blended mixture of cinnamon, nutmeg, ginger and cloves used in cake making.

MOCHA/MOKA — This word implies a coffee flavour and also describes and combination of coffee and chocolate flavours. The name comes from a variety of coffee bean grown in Mocha in the Yemen.

MOCK TURTLE SOUP — Rich brown soup which was originally made in imitation of Turtle Soup but soon became more popular than its inspiration with the Victorians. The principal ingredient is a calf's head, which is used for the stock and garnish. Other ingredients are salt pork, chicken, veal bones, carrots, celery and onion, plus herbs and spices.

MODE, A LA — French for in the latest fashion. This phrase is applied to large cuts of beef braised in red wine with carrots and onions. In the United States it describes pies served with vanilla ice cream.

MOELLE — French for bone marrow. Sauce moelle is bordelaise with added beef marrow bone fat.

MOHNTORTE — Poppyseed cake from Germany. Four layers of pastry are filled with a mixture of ground poppy seeds, raisins, almonds, candied peel and chocolate. The top is glazed and sprinkled with poppy seeds.

MOHR IN HEMD — Popular Viennese light steamed chocolate pudding decorated with whipped cream.

MOISTEN — To dampen ingredients (eg. with milk, stock, water, beaten egg etc) without allowing them to become saturated.

MOKA — *See* MOCHA.

MOLE — Mexican sauce made with chilies and cooked in fat so as to blend the chilies with the other ingredients. Some moles are an integral part of a dish, others are made and served separately. The word comes from the Nahuatl word for mixture or concoction. The most famous mole is mole poblano, a turkey in a very spicy sauce containing chocolate, ground nuts, seeds, chilies and spices. The dish was create in Puebla de Los Angeles when the Sister Superior tried to blend the ingredients of the old world with those of the new (turkey and chocolate) in honour of a visiting archbishop. Another story claims that the various ingredients fell into a pot in which a turkey was cooking.

MOLINILLO — Little mill in Spanish. A wooden whisk for blending chocolate and milk to make a frothy hot drink.

MOLLET, OEUF — Somewhere between a soft-boiled egg and a hard-boiled egg. It has a runny yolk with the white just set. This is achieved by boiling for five minutes.

MONDER — French pâtisserie term meaning to remove skins from nuts by pouring boiling water over them, then after a few seconds, refreshing them in cold water.

MONEGASQUE, A LA — Garnish of calf's brains, ham, mushrooms and demi-glace, with julienne of mushrooms and truffles. Also fried or poached eggs on fried tomatoes and tarragon, with anchovy fillets on top and tomato sauce around. Also chicken consommé with cheese profiteroles.

MONOSODIUM GLUTAMATE — Crystalline salt occuring naturally in many foods. It is sold commercially prepared and should be used sparingly to bring out the natural flavour of food.

MONSELET, A LA — Implies artichoke hearts, truffles, and sometimes fried potatoes in or with the dish so described.

MONTAGNOLA — ALLA — Italian dish of chicken pieces covered in egg and breadcrumbs and then baked.

MONT BLANC— French dessert consisting of sweetened chestnut purée and whipped cream piled into a glass to resemble a mountain with a cap of snow.

MONTE CARLO— Bombe Monte Carlo is vanilla ice cream outside with strawberry mousse inside. Sole Monte Carlo is paupiettes of sole on a bed of spaghetti with a white wine sauce – a marriage of French and Italian cuisines.

MONTER — To incorporate air by whisking or beating.

MONTGLAS, A LA — Salpicon of foie gras, truffle and mushrooms bound with Madeira and demi-glace sauce.

MONTMORENCY — Generally this term indicates cherries in or accompanying the dish in question. Montmorency is the name of a variety of cherry grown around Paris. It is also the name for a garnish for tournedos or noisettes of artichoke bottoms filled with either carrot and noisette potatoes or asparagus and macédoine of vegetables.

MONTPENSIER — Garnish for small cuts of meat and poultry of green asparagus tips and sliced truffles. Also an almond filled tart.

MONTREUIL — Garnish for fish of tiny potato balls masked in shrimp sauce arranged around the fish.

MOORS AND CHRISTIANS — Cuban spicy rice and black bean dish which is popular all over the Caribbean. The beans represent the Moors and the white rice the christians.

MORCILLA — Spanish sausage made with pig's blood, fat, spices and onion.

MORNAY, SAUCE — Béchamel sauce flavoured with cheese. Named after the Duc de Mornay.

MORTADELLA — Italian sausage of pork or pork and veal. There are several varietes, but the best is from Bologna. It is smooth textured and flavoured with coriander, sold cooked and eaten cold in very thin slices.

MORTAR — Thick bowl used in conjunction with a pestle for grinding and pounding spices and other food into a paste. It must be heavy enough to withstand vigorous pounding and should be of the same material as the pestle to equalize pressure and assure even grinding.

MORTIFIER — French term meaning to tenderize meat either by hitting it hard or keeping it in a cool place for several days before cooking it.

MOSCOVITE — Fruit jelly or bavarois made in a hexagonal mould. Also a sauce based on sauce poivrade with juniper berries, almonds, raisins and Malaga or Marsala.

MOSTACCIOLO — Tubular pasta ¾ inch (1.5 cm) in diameter, 2½ inches (7 cm) long.

MOUCLADE — Mussels cooked in a cream, wine and saffron sauce and served on the half shell.

MOULD — To shape either with hands or in a moulded container, as called a mould, to the form required.

MOULE A MANQUE — A French cake tin with sloping sides said to have been christened when a Paris baker made a cake which was deemed a failure (un manqué) by his employer; the baker disguised the cake and sold it to a customer who came back for more. It was called un manqué and a special mould was designed for it.

MOULI-LEGUMES — French vegetable mill.

MOURTAIROL, LE — Traditional soup of bread, chicken stock and saffron from Portugal.

MOUSQUETAIRE — General term meaning spicy food: this is a reference to the activities of *The Three Musketeers* of Dumas.

MOUSSAKA — Greek dish of minced lamb and vegetables arranged in layers. There are many variations but the classic moussaka would contain aubergines, onions and tomatoes, and would be topped with a savoury cheese custard.

MOUSSE — A mousse can be sweet or savoury, but it is always lightly set and with a smooth, spongy texture. The word means foam or froth in French. A sweet mousse, which is served cold, is made by beating eggs with sugar until thick, then adding flavour in a semi-liquid form (fruit purée, melted chocolate), whipped cream and gelatine. A savoury mousse need not contain egg: the main ingredient is flaked or minced and bound with butter or a sauce, then mixed with whipped cream and gelatine. Mousses can be made in decorative moulds and turned out to serve.

MOUSSELINE — Mayonnaise or Hollandaise to which whisked egg whites are added to make a light and fluffy sauce. Crème Mousseline is crème pâtissière into which butter is beaten as it cools. It can be flavoured, keeps well and is used for filling cakes.

MOZART, A LA — Garnish of artichoke bottoms filled with celery or celeriac purée, fried potato shavings and sauce poivrade.

MOZZARELLA IN CARROZZA — Italian fried cheese sandwich.

MUESLI— Mixture of flakes of raw cereal, nuts and dried fruit often eaten for breakfast with milk added. It was invented by nutritionist Dr. Bircher-Benner.

MUFFIN — A quick bread made with a yeast dough traditionally cooked in a special ring on a griddle. When cooked they are pulled apart and filled with butter. Americans eat them for breakfast and call them English muffins, but the British, who invented them, save them for afternoon tea. In America a muffin is a small cake which may have fruit, nuts or chocolate chips added before baking. Also eaten at breakfast.

MULLERIN ART— German term meaning miller's wife style, which is floured and fried in butter.

MULLIGAN STEW — Made with odds and ends of meat and vegetables. It is an American slang term originating with hobos.

MULLIGATAWNY — A spicy meat soup originally from Southern India. The name means pepper water in Tamil.

MURAT, SOLE — Fried sole with dried artichoke hearts and potatoes.

MUSHIMONO — Japanese style of cooking similar to steaming.

MUSHI-YAKI — Japanese cooking term meaning cooked in a casserole.

MUTTON — The meat of a sheep more than 12 months old and less than 18 months old. It has a stronger flavour and is tougher than lamb, and is usually boiled.

NABEMONO— Japanese style of cooking in a frying pan , usually at the table.

NACHOS— Mexican fried tortilla chips topped with melted cheese.

NAGE, A LA — Way of cooking shellfish especially lobster and crayfish, by simmering in a court bouillon.

NAIL — Device used as a guide when piping icing onto cakes. Miniature flowers are piped onto flat headed nails and transferred to the cake when dry: net nails are used for latticework, basketweave effect etc.

NALESNIKI — Russian deep fried pancake filled with a cream cheese mixture.

NAM PLA — Indonesian sauce of salted, spiced, fermented fish.

NAN — Crusty, leavened flat bread from India. It is cooked in a tandoori oven which gives the bread its distinctive smoky taste. Keema Nan is filled with minced meat. Peshwari Nan has a filling of nuts and raisins.

NANTAISE — The name of a butter, a biscuit and a duckling. Beurre Nantaise is warm butter flavoured with shallots, wine, vinegar and salt and pepper: the result, which is also known as beurre blanc is creamy not oily and it is served with trout. A Nantais is an almond biscuit. A Nantais duckling is famous for its small size and delicate flavour.

NANTUA — A garnish of crayfish tails or a covering of crayfish purée.

NAP — To cover food with a sauce which coats it completely but lightly enough for the outline of the food to be visible.

NAPOLEON — Alternative name for a small mille feuille with feather icing on top. It did not appear until half a century after Napoleon's death and there is a dispute between Denmark and France as to who invented it.

NAPOLETANA — Alla Napoletana describes a sauce for pasta of tomato, garlic, onion and olive oil. Pizza Napoletana has a topping of tomato, mozzarella cheese, anchovy fillets, oregano and capers.

NAPOLETANO, SALAME — Spicy pork and beef salame.

NAPOLITAINE — Demi-glace sauce with Marsala and tomatoes. Also a salad dressing of garlic, lemon juice and olive oil. Alla Napolitaine is a garnish for escalopes or fish or spaghetti, tomato sauce and parmesan cheese.

NAPPER — French for to mask. The term napper la cuillère is often used to describe the required thickness of a sauce – thick enough to coat a spoon. It also means to coat a base with jam.

NARGIS KEBAB — Indian scotch egg with spiced meat instead of sausagemeat round a hard-boiled egg.

NASI GORENG — Indonesian dish, also popular in the Netherlands. It consists of fried rice with pork and spices, topped with a lattice made with strips of omelette.

NATUREL, AU — French term for plainly cooked food.

NAVARIN — French term applied exclusively to a stew of lamb or mutton with root vegetables. It is named after the battle of Navarino 1827, but it is really a much older dish. Potage Navarin is a pea soup garnished with peas and crayfish tails.

NAVARRAISE, A LA — Way of stewing lamb with vinegar, red pepper and chilli.

NEGIMAYAKI — Japanese sliced beef with spring onions.

NEGRESSE EN CHEMISE — Chocolate mousse made in bombe, turned out and served with crème anglaise poured over half of it.

NEIGE, OEUFS A LA — Also known as Snow Eggs and Iles Flottantes, these are poached meringues on custard or fruit puree. This dish was very popular in the seventeenth and eighteenth centuries.

NELUSKO, BOMBE — Chocolate ice cream surrounding vanilla mousse.

NEMOURS, A LA — A garnish of peas, carrots and duchess potatoes: a garnish of mushrooms and small potatoes: a potato, mushroom and milk soup: a tartlet made with flaky pastry filled with plum jam and choux paste piped on top before baking.

NENETTE, SAUCE — Cream, mustard, tomato and basil sauce served with pork or boiled beef.

NEOPOLITAN — Ice cream made of layers of plain ice cream and mousse, which is served cut in slices from a block.

NERONE, ALLA — Italian method of cooking chicken. It is halved, sautéed in oil and flambéed in cognac.

NESSELRODE — Elaborate iced pudding created by the chef of the Comte de Nesselrode. It is made of chestnut purée blended with crème pâtissière, flavoured with crystallized and dried fruits steeped in maraschino. It is frozen in a mould and turned out to serve.

NEWBURG — A dish introduced at Delmonico's restaurant in New York. Originally it was named lobster Wenberg after the man who gave Delmonico's chef the recipe, but Wenberg was later banned from the restaurant after a brawl there and the dish was tactfully renamed. Sliced lobster meat in a rich sauce of brandy, sherry, cream and egg yolks.

NEW ENGLAND BOILED DINNER — An American dish dating back to the days when early settlers only had one pot for cooking a meal. It consists of boiled corned beef, tripe, salt pork, onions, carrots, turnips and potatoes. Sometimes a boiling fowl and/or cabbage is included.

NIACIN — Part of the vitamin B complex, niacin is found in liver, kidneys, oily fish, yeast extract and bran. Deficiency can cause pellagra.

NICOISE — Generally means cooked or served with tomatoes, garlic, anchovy fillets and/or black olives. Salade Nicoise also has tuna fish and hard-boiled egg. Coupé Nicoise is vanilla ice cream with a kirsch-flavoured macédoine of fruit.

NIVERNAISE — A la Nivernaise means a garnish of root vegetables cut into small ovals (there are many variations on this, the best known being glazed turnips served as a garnish for duck; glazed carrots and baby onions are also common). Sauce Nivernaise is a Béarnaise sauce with garlic and parsley, which is served with grilled meat. There is also a soup of root vegetables named Nivernaise.

NOISETTE — This term, meaning small nut, has many uses. Noisette sauce is Hollandaise flavoured with browned butter. Pommes noisettes are potatoes cut into small balls, cooked in butter and sprinkled with fines herbes. A noisette is a cut of lamb made from the best end of neck, which is boned, rolled, tied and cut into slices roughly one inch (2.5 cm) thick: each slice is a noisette. The term also describes any dish flavoured with hazelnuts.

NON PAREIL — French term (meaning without equal) for hundreds and thousands.

NOODLE — Flat, narrow ribbon of pasta, usually made from wheat flour and eggs, which are important in Chinese, Japanese and Austrian cuisine. Vermicelli-like noodles made from rice flour or other starches are less common. The word comes from the German for pasta – nudeln.

NORMANDE — When associated with fish this term implies cider and/or Calvados in the cooking. It can also be used to describe small cuts of meat, poultry or game prepared with cream. A la normande is a garnish of oysters, shrimps, mushrooms, truffles, gudgeon or smelt, crayfish and diamond-shaped croûtes. Normande sauce is a velouté sauce made with fish fumet and mushroom stock. It is served with fish.

NORVÉGIENNE — A la Norvégienne is a way of preparing fish to serve cold: poached, skinned, decorated with prawns, cucumber stuffed with a smoked salmon purée, hard-boiled eggs, tomatoes and Russian mayonnaise. There is also a garnish for meat of noodles and Madeira sauce with this name. Omelette à la Norvégienne is another, older name for Baked Alaska, which was invented by scientist Count Rumford in 1804 during experiments on heat induction. Sauce Norvégienne is made by mashing hard-boiled egg yolk, mustard, vinegar and olive oil; it is served with cold fish. Potage Norvégienne is a thick cabbage and turnip soup garnished with beetroot.

NOUGAT — Confection of nuts (almonds, walnuts, pistachios or hazelnuts), honey or syrup and beaten egg white. It can be hard or soft, white or pink. The name means made of honey and it comes from Montelimar in Provence.

NOUVELLE CUISINE — Expression which came into use in the 1970s to describe a new style of cooking based on simplicity rather than richness, with an eye on cholesterol-counting. A typical accompaniment to, say, a chop would be a vegetable purée rather than a thick, flour-based sauce.

NUOC-NAM — Salty condiment made from dried fish, which is important in the cookery of South-East Asia.

NÜRNBERGERWURSTE — German sausage of pork and bacon flavoured with kirsch.

NUSSPUDDING — Austrian steamed pudding with a very light texture, flavoured with hazelnuts.

OBLATEN — Wafers roughly the size of dinner plates, which are used in assembling elaborate cakes and desserts. They came originally from the Czech Republic.

OBSTTORTEN FORM — German for fruit tart mould. It is a cake tin or flan dish with fluted edges and a raised circle platform in the centre. The cake or flan made in it will have a very shallow depression in the centre which is then filled.

OEIL D'ANCHOIS — Raw egg yolk surrounded by circles of anchovies and minced onion. Served as an appetizer.

OEUFS A LA NEIGE — French dessert consisting of a custard topped with spoonfuls of meringue Italienne. Also known as Snow Eggs or Floating Islands.

OFFAL — Also known as variety meats. All the inner organs and outer extremities of animals: liver, kidneys, heart, brains, tripe, sweetbread, head, tails, trotters and tongue.

OIGNONADE/OGNONNADE — Chopped onion, cooked in butter or white wine. It is also the name of a stew containing a high proportion of onions.

OIL — A substance formed by mixing a fatty acid and alcohol which is liquid at room temperature. Oils are found in some fish and in many plants (corn, sunflower, olive, nut etc.) Most oils are polyunsaturated.

OKONOMI — "As you like it" sushi with topping of choice.

OLADI — Russian pancake, like a blini but smaller, thicker, and served with sweet foods.

OLIVE — Thin slice of meat, rolled around a savoury stuffing and braised.

OLLA PODRIDA — Spanish soup of various meats and vegetables. After cooking the meat and vegetables are placed on a serving dish and the liquid served in a tureen.

OMELETTE — Made by beating eggs with seasonings, pouring the mixture into a heavy greased frying pan and cooking quickly in a little butter until the eggs are set. It is usually folded in half to serve. An omelette may be plain or fancy: almost any mixture can be used as a filling. A soufflé omelette is made in the same way, but the eggs are separated and the whites stiffly whisked before being folded back into the mixture. A Spanish omelette is served flat and cut into wedges if large: traditionally it contains only eggs, garlic and cubes of fried potato. The word omelette comes from lamella, latin for blade.

ONGLET — French cut of beef from the top of the skirt.

ORECCHIIETTE — Means little ears in Italian. Pasta used mostly in soup.

OREILLETTE — French sweet fritter traditionally eaten on Twelfth Night and Shrove Tuesday. The dough is layered like puff pastry so that when fried it curls to look like a little pig's ear. (The name means little ear).

ORGANIC — The cereal, vegetable or fruit in question was grown in organic (ie. non-chemical) soil, with no additives.

ORGAN MEATS — American term for offal.

ORIENTALE — Widely applied term used to indicate a touch of the exotic. Orientale sauce is mayonnaise with tomato fondue, saffron and diced pimiento. Sauce à l'Orientale is sauce Americaine with curry powder and cream added. A l'Orientale is a garnish for meat of tartlets or tomato halves filled with rice à la greque and croquettes of sweet potato: also a method of preparing fish, eggs or vegetables poached in white wine and olive oil, with tomatoes, fennel, bay leaf, garlic, parsley and saffron and served cold: and fish fillets or lobster in Newburg sauce to which curry powder has been added.

ORLEANS — Chicken consommé garnished with three different chicken quenelles – one with spinach or pistachio nuts, one tomato and one cream. Also a beef consommé garnished with chicory royale, diced French beans, flageolets and chervil. Orléans salad contains grapefruit segments, halved white and black grapes, pieces of pineapple, orange, banana and pear, served on lettuce leaves, garnished with lemon juice and seasoned with oil, salt and cayenne pepper.

ORLOFF — Elaborate roast veal dish named after Prince Orloff of Russia. Slices of roast veal arranged overlapping in a dish and served with a velouté sauce flavoured with duxelles and soubise, sprinkled with gruyère cheese and gratinéed.

ORLY — A l'Orly denotes food, especially fish, which is coated with a rich batter and deep-fried, then served with sauce Orly. The sauce is tomato sauce flavoured with onion, garlic and thyme.

ORSAY, D' — Chicken consommé garnished with poached egg yolks, strips of pigeon, pigeon quenelles and chervil.

OSSO BUCO — Means bone with the hole in Italian. Speciality from Northern Italy made with slices of shin of veal, with marrow in the bones, in a rich tomato sauce. A special fork is supplied with this dish to excavate the bone marrow.

OTERO, BOMBE — Apricot ice surrounding blackcurrant ice. Named after La Belle Otero, the opera singer. Salad Otero is red pepper, tomato, anchovy and onions in mustard flavoured vinaigrette.

149

OUBLIE — French conical wafer.

OUILLAT — Traditional soup from the Pyrenees, made with tomatoes, onions, garlic and goose fat and served poured over bread.

OXFORD SAUCE — Sauce of redcurrant jelly, port, orange, lemon, shallot, mustard and ginger, which is served with cold venison.

OXYMEL — Syrup made of one part vinegar to four parts honey.

OYSTER — Cut of bacon from the lower back. Also a small piece of meat in the back of poultry.

PACENO, PLATO — Traditional Bolivian dish of corn on the cob, broad beans and fried curd cheese with chilli sauce.

PAELLA — Spanish rice dish cooked in a special pan on top of the stove. Ingredients vary from region to region: Valencia and Barcelona include a variety of seafood with chicken and vegetables, whereas inland more meat and sausage are used. Saffron is added to the cooking stock for colour and flavour. The pan, which is called a paella pan, is a large, shallow, heavy frying pan with two grip handles instead of one straight one. Paella is served straight from the pan.

PAESANA, ALLA — Spaghetti with diced bacon, mushrooms, butter and Parmesan.

PAGLIA E FIENA — Straw and hay in Italian, this is simply egg (yellow) and spinach (green) noodles in a cream sauce.

PAILLE, POMMES DE TERRE — French for straw potatoes. Very long chips.

PAILLETTE — Savoury pastry sticks used as a garnish for consommé. Also sticks of vegetables such as potato.

PAIN — French term for forcemeat cooked in a loaf tin and served hot or cold as an entrée.

PAIN DE MIE — French for crumb bread. This is a white sandwich-type loaf with a thin soft crust.

PAIN DE SEIGLE — French rye bread. It is lighter than rye bread from Eastern Europe.

PAIN PERDU — Literally lost bread, this is a French nursery pudding made with leftover bread. The bread is dipped in a mixture of cream, honey and spices, then fried in butter. It is served hot with sugar, honey or syrup.

PAKORHA — Savoury vegetable fritter from India. Almost any vegetable may be used, either individually or in a mixture. The batter is made with split pea flour and flavoured with pomegranate seeds and spices. Pakorhas are eaten warm at teatime.

PALACSINTA — Hungarian pancakes which form the basis of many sweet and savoury dishes. They are delicate but firm enough to hold a not too liquid filling.

PALET DE BOEUF — A round of boiled minced beef.

PALETTE KNIFE — A flexible wide-bladed knife used for light mixing and spreading.

PALMIER — French pâtisserie of puff pastry shaped like a palm tree and sprinkled with granulated sugar which caramelizes during baking.

PALMYRE, SOUFFLE — Vanilla soufflé in layers with sponge fingers soaked in kirsch.

PALOISE — A la Paloise is a garnish of sautéed potato balls and French beans in cream, which is used for grilled meat. Paloise sauce is similar to a béarnaise sauce, except that mint replaces the tarragon.

PAN — A mixture of betel nut, lime and spices folded in a betel leaf and secured with a clove. It is chewed, but not swallowed, at the end of an Indian meal to refresh the mouth.

PANADA/PANADE — Thick sauce or paste for binding food. It can be made of flour, bread, potato, rice or frangipane. Also a soup made of bread, stock, milk or water and butter.

PANATA — Bread, eggs, cheese, nutmeg mixed to form a pancake served whole in broth. From Italy.

PAN BROIL — American term for cooking food on top of the stove in its own fat, pouring off the surplus as it melts.

Pa

PANCAKE — A batter of flour, milk and eggs poured into a hot, greased pan and cooked quickly on both sides. It may be served with a sweet or savoury sauce or stuffing, rolled or folded, thick or thin, and the batter may be rich or plain or made with different flours like buckwheat or rye. It is thought that the pancake was the first "made-up" dish ever cooked by man, originally being a mixture of meal and water cooked on a hot stone.

PANCETTA — Italian cured and spiced salt pork cut from the belly. It can be eaten cold, served in slices or cut into cubes and used as a flavouring.

PANDORO DI VERONE — Sweet sponge cake sprinkled with icing sugar eaten at Christmas.

PANE — Coated with breadcrumbs.

PANETIERE — Cooked food is put into a hollowed out round loaf of bread and baked for a short time. Also sautéed chicken served on a round of bread spread with foie gras, garnished with mushrooms cooked in cream.

PANETTONE — Italian yeast cake flavoured with sultanas and candied citron peel, which is eaten for breakfast, especially at Christmas. It originated in Milan in the fifteenth century, when a baker named Tonio made a bread using sultanas, then a novelty, and candied lemon peel: the bread made him rich and was known as pan de Tonio (Tony's bread).

PANFORTE DI SIENA — Hard, rich chocolate cake with nuts, candied peel and spices.

PAN-FRY — American term for to sauté.

PANINI — Hot Italian sandwich made with a split oval of pizza dough, generously filled, then grilled. A popular street snack.

PANIR — Inidian curd cheese, usually cut into cubes and fried.

PANNA MONTATA — Italian term for whipped cream.

PANNEKOEKEN — Heavy Dutch pancake served with syrup and bacon.

PANNEQUET — Wheat flour pancake from Brittany. The pancake is spread with a filling and then rolled or folded in flour and glazed under the grill. Sweet pannequets may be dusted with icing sugar or crushed macaroons before grilling. Possible fillings include fruit purée, cream, jam, crème pâtissière, cream cheese or salpicons.

PANTIN — Crescent shaped mould used for pâtés. Also a pork pâté with truffles made in a rectangular mould.

PANURE — French term meaning the coating of food with breadcrumbs and either beaten egg or melted butter, prior to frying.

PANURETTE — Orange-coloured, seasoned breadcrumbs.

PANZAROTTI — Deep-fried, semi-circular pastries filled with three cheeses and served as antipasto.

PAPER-WRAPPED DEEP-FRYING — Szechuan cooking method. Parcels of marinated meat or fish are deep-fried. The wrapping (greaseproof paper or non-stick parchment) seals the flavour and stops the food absorbing the oil. The food is served still in its wrapper.

PAPILLOTE — Envelope of foil or greaseproof paper in which food is cooked in the oven to retain its juices.

PAPPARDELLE — Pasta from Tuscany often served in a hare sauce. It is broad noodles with a fluted edge.

PAPRIKAS — A Hungarian sauce of paprika, tomatoes and sour cream in which chicken, veal or fish may be cooked.

PARATHA — Unleaven bread from India. The dough is brushed with ghee and folded and rolled many times: when it is cooked on a hot griddle it puffs up.

PARBOIL — To partially cook food by boiling prior to completing the cooking by some other means (such as roasting). It is a way of speeding up the cooking process and preparing the surface to allow fat to penetrate as in roast potatoes.

PARCH — To cook in dry heat until the outside is dry and sometimes slightly browned.

PARE — To remove the outer skin or peel of fruit or vegetables.

PARER — French culinary term meaning to trim meat of skin, fat and sinews.

PARFAIT — An iced pudding with a rich mousse base containing whipped cream. When turned out it should just hold its shape.

PARIS-BREST — French pâtisserie of choux paste in the shape of a large ring, sprinkled with almonds, split open after baking and filled with praline butter cream.

PARISIAN SAUCE — Cream cheese, seasoned with paprika and chervil, beaten with oil and lemon juice. It is served with cold asparagus. Not to be confused with sauce Parisienne.

Pa

PARISIENNE — Parisienne potatoes are tiny balls scooped out of a potato with a ball cutter. They can be sautéed in butter or boiled then tossed in melted butter and sprinkled with parsley. A la Parisienne is a garnish for poached fish of mushrooms, truffles, crayfish and white wine sauce. Also a chicken consommé with macedoine of vegetables, royale and chervil. Parisienne sauce is another name for Allemande sauce.

PARKERHOUSE — An American bread dough made with milk, butter, sugar and eggs as well as flour and yeast. It is often made into fancy shaped rolls and eaten warm. The distinctive appearance is caused by cutting the dough with a biscuit cutter and then cutting a crease across each roll just off centre. The larger half is folded over the smaller half shaping the roll into an oval and the edges are pinched to seal. The tops are brushed with lots of melted butter. Any plain white yeast dough can be treated in this way. Parkerhouse croûtons are made from bread toasted on one side: the other side is spread with a mixture of cheese, egg and butter and baked until golden brown, then cut into cubes. The above originated in the Parker House Hotel in Boston.

PARKIN — Form of gingerbread made with oatmeal partly replacing the flour. It is baked in a shallow baking tray and cut into squares to serve. It is best kept several days, well wrapped, before eating. From Yorkshire.

PARMA HAM — Lightly salted, air-cured raw ham which is served in paper-thin slices.

PARMENTIERE — Term which indicates the presence of potatoes in the dish in question. Named after Antoine-Auguste Parmentier (1737-1817), the economist who popularized the potato in France.

PARMESANE, A LA — Denotes Parmesan cheese in the recipe.

PARMIGIANA — When describing rice alla Parmigiana means cooked in beef stock with chicken livers, sausage, mushroom, bacon, vegetables and herbs. Veal Parmigiana is a popular way of cooking veal escalopes with tomato sauce, mozzarella cheese and Parmesan cheese. Parmigiana di Melazane is a simple Italian dish of layers of aubergine, tomato sauce, mozzarella and Parmesan cheese baked in the oven.

PARSON'S NOSE — Sometimes known as the Pope's nose. The tail stump of poultry.

PARTENOPEA, ALLA — Describes pasta, especially cannelloni, stuffed with ricotta, mozzarella and ham, baked in a tomato sauce flavoured with basil and sprinkled with Parmesan cheese.

154

PASKHA — Russian cheesecake traditionally made in a special wooden perforated box shaped like a flowerpot and eaten at Easter. The word means Easter in Russian. It is decorated with the orthodox cross and the letters XB (Khristos Voskryesye – Christ is risen).

PASSION CAKE — A layer cake made with bananas, nuts and carrots in addition to the usual eggs, sugar, flour and fat. It is filled and covered with cream cheese frosting.

PASTA — Italian flour and water paste cut into many different shapes and sizes and boiled. The Chinese were eating macaroni as early as 5000BC, and Marco Polo is often credited with introducing it to Italy in the thirteenth century, but a pasta-making machine found at Pompeii proves that the Romans ate it. Flour from durum wheat is most often used and the dough is sometimes enriched with egg or coloured green with spinach, pink with tomato purée or black with squid ink. There is a wide variety of pasta and an even wider variety of names, as in different regions of Italy identical pastas are known by different names. Tubular pasta includes spaghetti, spaghettini, and vermicelli: flat ribbon pasta includes lasagne, fettucine and tagliatelle. There are also pastas shaped like butterflies, shells, stars, even letters of the alphabet, and stuffed pasta like ravioli and tortellini. Pasta asciutta means dry pasta, ie. not wet like pasta in soup.

PASTEL — General Spanish term for any pastry dish.

PASTEURIZE — To sterilize milk by heating to 60-82°C (140-180°F) to destroy bacteria. Named after Louis Pasteur who invented the process.

PASTICCIO — Italian for pie, but in practice a baked, layered pasta dish.

PASTILA — Moroccan pastry made with very thin pastry filled with pigeon meat and egg. Served with cinnamon and sugar.

PASTILLAGE — Gum sugar paste used by pâtissiers for decoration.

PASTITSIO — Greek dish of macaroni baked in layers with a cinnamon flavoured meat sauce and a cheese sauce.

PASTRAMI — Beef which has been cured in spices for ten days, then smoked for eight hours and seasoned with black peppercorns. It is eaten hot or cold, usually with rye bread. Originally from Rumania, where other meats are also treated in this way, it is now very popular in the United States.

Pa

PASTRY — General term for various types of flour and fat dough, which are shaped and baked. The most common pastries are: shortcrust, suet crust, pâté sucrée, puff, rough puff, flaky, choux and hot water. The ancient Chinese made a flour and water paste which was steamed or fried. The Ancient Egyptians, 5000 years ago had a supply of pastries in their pyramids for the afterlife. Pastries came to Europe from the Middle East to the ancient Greeks, but the Romans developed the art of pastry-making. Originally pastry was a crude flour and water dough wrapped around meat before roasting to seal in the juices: it was not eaten. By the Middle Ages, pies were an important feature on every menu and local variations had evolved. Flaky and puff pastry did not come into use until the seventeenth century.

PASTRY BAG — U.S. term for forcing/piping bag.

PASTRY BLENDER — Utensil for cutting fat into flour. Usually several stiff wires in the form of a curve attached at each end to a straight handle.

PASTY — Individual pastry enclosing a savoury filling.

PATE — Savoury mixture made mostly from chicken, calves' or pigs' livers, with the addition of other meat, poultry or game. The texture can vary from smooth to coarse, but they are always well seasoned, often with brandy or sherry to improve flavour and keeping quality. A pâté is served cold, either in slices or scooped out from a pot. A moulded pâté is also known as a terrine.

PATE SUCREE — French for sugar pastry. This type of pastry dough is used for sweet flans. It is crisp and short and capable of supporting a wet filling without becoming soggy. Egg yolks and caster sugar are added to the basic flour and butter dough, and hardly any water is used to bind the ingredients. Careful handling is necessary otherwise a sticky dough results and more flour (which spoils the texture) is needed to roll it out.

PATIA — Parsee curry with sweet-sour brown sauce.

PATISSERIE — The name for pastry preparations baked in the oven, also the art of the pastry cook and the shop were the pastries are sold.

PATON — French cookery term meaning a block of pastry dough of the correct size for the recipe in question.

PATTY — A small flat cake of chopped meat which is fried or grilled. Also a small pie for one person.

PAU — Chinese snack served as Dim Sum. It is a savoury stuffing in a soft sweet yeast dough, which is steamed.

PAUCHOUSE — *See* POCHOUSE.

PAUILLAC, AGNEAU DE — Milk-fed lamb only two or three months old. It is a great early spring delicacy and is usually roasted whole.

PAUNCHING — Removing the guts of a rabbit or hare.

PAUPIETTE — Thin slice of meat spread with forcemeat, rolled up and tied with thread to form a cylinder. Always cooked in and served with a sauce.

PAVE — Either a cake made in a square tin or cold savoury dish, such as a mousse, made in a square or rectangular mould, coated with aspic and decorated with truffles. Rice pavés are rectangles of cold, thick rice pudding, sometimes spread with fruit purée, then deep fried.

PAVLOVA — A dessert of meringue shaped in one large round with a depression in the centre. It is filled with whipped cream and chopped fruit – especially passion fruit. It was created in New Zealand (though Australia also claims the honour) for the Russian ballerina Anna Pavlova.

PAYSANNE — A la Paysanne denotes braised meat or poultry accompanied by carrots, turnips, celery, onions, potatoes and bacon. Paysanne cut is to cut food into triangular shapes.

PEASANT GIRL IN A VEIL — (Bondepige med slor). Danish dessert made with rye breadcrumbs and apple purée arranged in layers and topped with whipped cream.

PEASE PUDDING — Traditional British vegetable dish, popular in the North of England. It consists of cooked, dried peas, mashed potatoes and fried onions mixed in a bowl and steamed.

PECTIN — A gumlike substance found in most fruit before it is fully ripe. Citrus fruits, cooking apples, gooseberries and plums have a high pectin content. It is essential in jam-making to get a good set and extra may be needed with some fruits.

PEEL — To remove the skin of fruit or vegetables. Also the thick outer covering on citrus fruit.

157

PEKING DUCK — A very crisp roast duck from China. The duck is marinated then hung up in a draught for several hours to dry the skin completely. To serve, the crispy skin is removed and cut into oblong slices and arranged on a separate serving dish from the meat, which is also cut up. Drumsticks and wings are not skinned or cut up. To eat, each diner dips a spring onion (cut to look like a brush) into a bowl of hoisin sauce or soy bean paste and brushes the sauce onto a mandarin pancake. He puts some slices of cucumber and shredded spring onion onto the pancake, then adds duck meat and duck skin. The pancake is rolled up and eaten, still warm, with the fingers.

PELMENY — Russian crescent-shaped dumpling made with a noodle-like dough and filled with a meat mixture. It is served with melted butter or sour cream.

PELURE — French term for parings which can be used in cookery: mushroom parings, for instance, are used to give flavour to several sauces.

PENUCHE — Confection of brown sugar, milk, butter and nuts.

PEPERATA — Italian sauce of beef marrow, breadcrumbs, Parmesan and black pepper, which is served with boiled meat or poultry.

PEPERONATA — Sweet peppers, onions and tomatoes stewed in oil and garlic and served cold. The dish comes from Italy and is usually served as an appetiser.

PERIGOURDINE — A la Perigourdine refers to a garnish of truffles with or without foie gras. Perigourdine sauce is a demi-glace sauce with slices of truffle.

PERIGUEUX SAUCE — Demi-glace sauce with truffle essence, diced truffles and sometimes Madeira. It is served with small cuts of meat or poultry.

PERNOLLET, SALADE — Chopped crawfish on truffles, coated with mayonnaise and served on a bed of lettuce.

PERSILLADE — Term meaning chopped parsley and garlic sprinkled over the dish.

PERSILLE, JAMBON — Burgundian way of preparing ham in layers with chopped herbs, garlic and shallots, and covered with port and brandy-flavoured jelly. It is served cold and when cut in slices the green of the herbs looks like veins running through it.

PESTLE — Kitchen tool of primitive origin for pounding and crushing food such as spices, nuts etc. It is used in conjunction with a mortar. Marble is the best material for a pestle as it is nonporous, but it may also be made of wood, porcelain or glass.

PESTO — Sauce from Genoa, Italy, made by crushing fresh basil leaves, garlic, salt and pine nuts, and mixing them with grated cheese and olive oil. It is served with pasta and also used to flavour soup. According to tradition it should only be served with trenette (thin noodles) and Parmesan and pecorino cheese.

PETITE MARMITE — Well-flavoured soup made with a chicken plus a piece of beef and a veal knuckle as well as a variety of vegetables. The meat is removed before serving and is eaten as a separate course.

PETIT SALE — French for salt pork. It is also a tiny savoury appetizer served with a drink before a meal. It is spicy and light to wake up the tastebuds not spoil the appetite.

PETITS FOURS — Strictly speaking the term applies only to baked goods, but nowadays marzipan fruits, stuffed dates etc. pass under this title. They are a selection of tiny cakes and sweets, all of the same size but different shape, colour etc. served at the end of a dinner party. The term came into use because the little cakes were baked in a slow oven (petit four) after the large cakes were done and the oven was cooler.

PETITS PIEDS — Literally small feet, but used in France to describe small edible birds such as ortolans and blackbirds.

PETRISAGE — French for kneading.

PETS DE NONNE — Sweet puffy fritters served with hot jam sauce. The name means "nun's farts": the recipe is said to have come from a convent.

PETTICOAT TAILS — Traditional Scottish shortbread made into a thin crisp round cake. The name derives from the French petits gâteaux (little cakes) and dates from the days of the Auld Alliance between France and Scotland.

PETTI DI POLLO — Italian for chicken breasts.

PETTITOES — The feet of sucking pigs.

PFANNKUCHEN — Small Austrian yeast cake filled with apricot purée, which is deep fried and soaked in hot rum syrup.

PFERRERNUSSE — German spice cookie with a topping of uncooked meringue.

159

PHOSPHOROUS — Mineral which works in conjunction with calcium to maintain the balance of body fluid and helps to release energy from food in the body.

PHYLLO/FILO — Paper-thin pastry from the Middle East. It is made with flour and water, and is extremely delicate and difficult to handle so it is rarely made at home: instead it is bought in sheets from specialist shops.

PIACERE, A — Italian for as you like it. If you see this on a menu it is likely to mean a choice between grilled or fried, or with or without sauce. It is up to the diner to specify.

PICCALILLI — Chopped, brined, mixed vegetables in a boiled sauce flavoured with mustard, turmeric and vinegar. In the United States piccalilli is a sweet mustard pickle.

PICCATA — Italian term for small thinly sliced squares of veal.

PICKLE — As a verb, to pickle is to preserve and flavour food in brine, vinegar, lemon juice or alcohol. Pickling is an early method of food preservation, known to the ancient Greeks and Romans. As a noun, a pickle is fruit or vegetables preserved in spiced and herbed vinegar or other acidic liquid. Mixed pickles include a variety of chopped vegetables. Other fruit and vegetables may be pickled whole, eg. onions, walnuts, gherkins.

PICNIC SHOULDER — U.S. term for hand of pork.

PIE — A very loosely applied term generally meaning covered with a lid of pastry. A pie can be sweet or savoury, and several types of pastry are suitable. An English pie is made in a pie dish with a lid of pastry on top. A plate pie has pastry both on top and underneath. However, in the United States a pie has pastry underneath and is made in a deep pie dish. Sometimes a savoury pie has a lid of mashed or sliced potatoes instead of pastry. For a sweet pie, the top crust may be of meringue instead of pastry – as in Lemon Meringue Pie.

PIECE DE RESISTANCE — The largest and most important dish served at the meal.

PIECE MONTEE — Lavish table decoration, usually edible, often made with hard icing or pastry.

PIEMONTAISE, A LA — Garnish for meat and poultry of timbales of rice and truffles.

PIEMONTESE, ALLA — Rice cooked in meat stock with butter, cheese and truffles on top.

PIEROGI — Polish for pockets. These are stuffed turnovers of a flour and egg dough which are poached. They may be sweet or savoury.

PIG'S FRY — Liver and lights.

PIKELET — Alternative name for crumpet, used mainly in the north of England.

PILAF/PILAU — Middle Eastern savoury rice dish, which is drier and flakier than a risotto. Pilafs can be plain to accompany a meat or poultry dish, made into a main course with the addition of chopped cooked meat, poultry etc.

PILCHARD — Adult sardine caught in British waters. It is usually canned.

PINCER — French pâtisserie term meaning to pinch up the edges of a tart with your fingers.

PINCH — Imprecise term used in recipes to denote a small amount of seasoning, which is less than a quarter of a teaspoonful.

PINZIMONIO — Italian salad dressing or dipping sauce for crudités, made with oil, salt and pepper.

PIPERADE — Basque dish of scrambled eggs mixed with onions, garlic, peppers, tomatoes and herbs. Sometimes bayonne ham is included.

PIPING — Way of decorating food by forcing soft food, such as icing or mashed potato, through a nozzle to draw a line or shape with it.

PIQUAGE — Form of larding. Strips of fat are sewn through the meat so that fat is introduced in the interior of the joint.

PIQUANT — Agreeably sharp and stimulating to taste. It is applied only to savoury food.

PIQUANTE SAUCE — Diable sauce with pickles and capers added.

PIQUENCHAGNE — Pie made with nut-flavoured yeast dough (hazelnuts, almonds or walnuts). It is filled with pears, apples or quinces. A hole is cut in the top crust before baking and this is filled with whipped cream for serving. From the Bourbonnais district of France.

PIRI-PIRI — Hot pepper and chilli sauce from Mozambique.

PIROG — Large, oval, savoury hot Russian turnover. It can be made with a yeast dough or pastry, and is filled with a meat or vegetable mixture. Occasionally a pirog is made filled at one end with meat and at the other end with vegetables: to serve a slice is cut from each end for each diner.

161

Pi

PIROSHKI — Little pies in Russian. These are pastries made with a sour cream dough and a variety of fillings.

PISSALADIERE — Famous flan from the South of France. Similar to a pizza, but made with rich shortcrust pastry instead of bread dough, it is filled with black olives, anchovies, onions and tomatoes.

PISTACHE, EN — Garnish for mutton of cloves of garlic.

PISTOL/PISTON — Another name for a barrel loaf of bread.

PISTOLET — Round bread roll with a deep slash across the top.

PISTOU — Italian for basil. This is the name for a soup of vegetables and vermicelli, flavoured with garlic and basil.

PISTOU, AU — French translation of with pesto.

PITHIVIERS — Cake made with layers of puff pastry filled with almond paste and glazed on top. A rosette design is made on the top with the point of a knife. It is named after the French town where it was invented, which is also famous for lark pies and spice bread.

PITT — American term meaning to remove a stone or pip from fruit. It also means a pip.

PITTA — Flat round yeast bread from the Middle East. It puffs up during cooking, leaving a hollow centre which can be filled. It is usually cut in half to serve.

PIZZA — Italian for pie. A pizza is a savoury flan made with a yeast dough. The filling varies, but is based on mozzarella cheese, tomatoes, onions, olives and anchovies. Other additions include sausage, peppers and mushrooms.

PIZZAIOLA — Neopolitan fresh tomato sauce with oregano or basil.

PLAKI — Typical Greek way of cooking fish: baked with onions, garlic, tomatoes, parsley, slices of lemon and white wine.

PLANK, ON THE — Way of preparing and serving meat or fish on a specially made board – usually made of kiln dried oak, with a tree design cut along the middle so that the juices drain into a shallow depression at one end. The presentation often includes an elaborate vegetable garnish with a piped border of mashed potato.

PLASTIC ICING — Thick fondant icing, set with gelatine, which can be rolled like pastry and cut and shaped for decoration. It comes from Australia, and takes its name from the fact that it is kept overnight in the fridge in a plastic bag before use.

PLAT DE COTES — French cut of beef or pork from the forequarter flank.

PLATE — American cut of beef, comprising the rear quarter flank.

PLOMBIERES — Rich almond or chestnut ice cream served with apricot jam. Crème Plombières is a custard filling into which beaten egg white and flavouring (such as fruit) are folded: it is then spooned over sponge cake and chilled.

PLUCHE — Garnish of finely shredded lettuce or sorrel, or leaves of parsley, chervil or tarragon.

PLUCK — Butchery term for heart, liver, spleen and lungs of certain animals. Lamb's pluck is the most commonly used. To pluck means to remove the feathers of a bird.

POACH — To cook gently in liquid not hotter than 190-200°F. Poached food, such as eggs, fish or fruit, is suitable for invalids as it is easily digestible. The word, which comes from the French poche, meaning pocket, was originally only applied to eggs.

PO'BOY — American sandwich made with a French loaf split horizontally and filled with cheese, ham and salad.

POCHOUSE/PAUCHOUSE — Fish stew made with white wine from Burgundy. It contains a mixture of river fish – salmon, eel, pike, carp, trout etc. plus smoked bacon lardons, baby onions and heart-shaped croûtes.

POCK-MA BEAN CURD — Szechwan dish of pork and bean curd in a spicy hot sauce. It is the creation of a pock-marked woman, hence the name.

POELAGE — To brown meat then roast it in a covered casserole.

POELE, A LA — To cook in a shallow pan.

POELON — Small, uncovered earthenware or metal casserole with a short, fat handle and a pouring lip.

POH PIAH — Malaysian rice flour pancake wrapped around a mixture of shrimp, eggs, squid, meat and beansprouts in chilli sauce. Popular as a street snack.

POINTAGE — French term describing the rising and proving stage in breadmaking.

POINTE, A — Cooked to the point of perfection. This French term in practice means slightly rare in the case of meat.

POINTE DE CULOTTE — French cut of beef from the rump.

Po

POIRAT, LE — Double crust pear tart from Normandy. The pastry is flavoured with cinnamon and walnuts, and a circle is cut out in the centre of the top crust to show the halved pears inside: this is filled with whipped cream to serve.

POISSONIER — The chef who prepares the elaborate fish dishes in a large restaurant.

POISSONIERE — The French name for a fish kettle. It was invented by Brillat-Savarin, who used a copper laundry boiler with a wicker tray suspended above it.

POIVRADE — A stew flavoured with peppercorns (poivre), usually made with venison. Poivrade sauce is Espagnole with additions of crushed peppercorns, vinegar and vegetables: it is often used as a marinade for game.

POJARSKI — A Pojarski cutlet is a Russian dish of finely chopped meat or poultry, shaped like a cutlet, coated in egg and breadcrumbs, sautéed and served with mushroom sauce. It is named after an innkeeper in a staging post between Moscow and St Petersburg, who made this as the house speciality. Originally the cutlet would have been made with game.

POLENTA — Savoury cornmeal pudding from the Veneto region of Italy, where maize is the staple crop. A paste of cornmeal and water, flavoured with cheese, is spread on a baking tray to cool, then cut into pieces and fried or grilled, or baked in slices with a savoury filling.

POLNISCHEWURSTE — Spicy smoked blood sausage which is poached to serve.

POLO — Iranian rice dish. Usually contains lamb or chicken with vegetables, fruit, nuts, saffron and thin strips of orange peel.

POLONAISE — A la polonaise is hard-boiled egg yolk and chopped parsley used as a garnish. Polonaise sauce is a velouté-based sauce flavoured with sour cream or yogurt, horseradish, fennel and lemon juice. It goes well with grilled meat.

POLYUNSATURATED — Term applied to fat, meaning that it has more than one unsaturated fatty acid. Unsaturated fatty acids (not saturated with hydrogen) are less stable, have a lower melting point and are thought to be less likely to raise the body's cholesterol level to a point where arteries may become clogged.

POMPONETTE — Small, deep-fried pastry with a savoury filling. It has a pouchlike shape and is served as an hors d'oeuvre.

PONE — Flattened cake of cornmeal and water. It may be baked or fried in bacon grease. Pones were the staple diet of American Indians in Virginia and soon became popular with the early colonists.

PONT NEUF — Pommes de terre Pont Neuf are one cm sticks of potato, about six cm. (2½ in.) long, which are deep fried. They are so called because they were sold on the Pont Neuf, the oldest bridge in Paris. A Pont Neuf is also a tartlet filled with a mixture of choux paste and crème pâtissière, flavoured with orange flower water or rum and decorated with icing sugar and apricot glaze in a chequerboard effect.

POORI — *See* PURI.

POOR KNIGHTS OF WINDSOR — A simple pudding made by soaking slices of bread in liquid (milk, fruit juice etc), frying them in butter until crisp and sprinkling them with sugar and cinnamon. They are named after a military order created in 1348, whose members lived in grace and favour houses at Windsor Castle.

POOR MAN'S SAUCE — An English sauce of onions, parsley, breadcrumbs, vinegar and stock.

POPE'S EYE — Small circle of fat in the middle of a leg of lamb or pork. Also a Scottish name for rump steak.

POPE'S NOSE — *See* PARSON'S NOSE.

POPOVER — Individual batter pudding served with fruit or fruit sauce.

POPPADUM — Very thin Indian pancake made with lentil flour, which is fried until crisp.

PORCHETTA, IN — Roast chicken stuffed with ham, fennel and garlic.

PORKOLT — Hungarian dish of largish chunks of pork or veal, braised in a small amount of stock.

PORRIDGE — Thick mixture of specially treated oatmeal and water eaten for breakfast.

PORTERHOUSE — Old term for a tavern where porter (dark ale) was served. Porterhouse steak (cut from the centre of the short loin) was the speciality of a famous New York porterhouse.

PORTUGAISE — This term signifies the inclusion of tomatoes, rice, ham, sausages, mushrooms and garlic in the dish or its sauce.

Po

POT — To preserve food by putting it in a pot or other container and sealing it with a layer of fat to keep out air and moisture. This is a relatively short term method of preservation as the fat seal does not affect air or moisture already in the food, unless the food is first cooked for a long time.

POTASSIUM — Mineral essential for maintenance of body fluids contained in cells of the muscles and red blood corpuscles.

POT-AU-FEU — French for pot cooked over the fire. A joint of beef is cooked in vegetables and water, then strained and the pot-au-feu becomes a two-course meal of soup followed by boiled beef.

POTEE — Thick hearty soup from France, which is cooked in an earthenware pot. It invariably contains cabbage, pork and potatoes.

POT LIQUOR — American term meaning liquid left in the pot after meat or vegetables have been cooked. In the Southern States it refers specifically to the stock remaining after greens are boiled with salt pork.

POT ROAST — A method of cooking small and/or tougher joints of meat and poultry in a heavy covered pan over a gentle heat (or in a slow oven).

POTTAGE — Halfway between a soup and a stew. It dates from medieval times when the available ingredients were boiled a the same pot, thickened with peas, beans or barley, and flavoured with herbs. Pottage can be served in a bowl with salad and bread as a main course.

POTTED — Potted meats are an old English form of pâté: cooked, finely minced meats preserved in pots or jars. The meat is usually covered with a layer of butter to exclude air and aid preservation.

POULARDE — French for neutered fattened hen weighing between 3½ and 5½ lbs.

POULET — French for spring chicken.

POULETTE — Either a béchamel or velouté sauce flavoured with shallots, mushrooms, egg yolks and cream, usually served with chicken.

POULTRY — Farmyard birds bred for eating.

POUND CAKE — Named because a pound of everything (flour, sugar, butter and eggs) went into it. It is yellow and buttery, with a solid, close texture.

POUNTI, LE — Savoury batter pudding from the Auvergne. It is baked in a flan dish and cut like a pie to serve. It contains meat, especially bacon or ham, with Swiss chard or spinach, and prunes or raisins.

POUPETON — Method of rolling one piece of meat inside another into a meat roll which is then braised. It is served cold.

POUSSE — French bakery term for the rising stage of breadmaking.

POUSSIN — A young chicken, only four to six weeks old.

PRAIRIE OATEN — Irish potato and oatmeal patty fried and eaten for breakfast with bacon.

PRAIRIE OYSTER — A turkey egg in a wine glass with vinegar, salt and pepper, which is sometimes taken as a cure for a hangover. It was invented in the United States, when a member of a hunting party in the prairies fell ill and called for oysters, which were unavailable. The prairie oyster which was substituted cured the patient.

PRALINE — A mixture of almonds and caramelized sugar which is crushed and added to desserts, cakes and sweets as a flavouring. The name comes from the Duc de Choiseul-Praslin, who in the seventeenth century presented a lady friend with a sugar almond (previously unknown). It was such a success that a special shop was opened to sell these praslines.

PRE-SALE — Lamb raised on salt meadows near the sea. It has a particularly delicate flavour.

PRESENTATION PAN — Long handled pan used on top of the stove and brought to the table. Usually oval with a handle at the narrow end. It enables two diners to be served at once and can also be used for flambéeing. It is often copper or silver.

PRESERVE — To treat food so that the natural process of decay and putrefaction is halted. Preservation methods include freezing, salting, bottling, drying, potting, pickling in vinegar or alcohol and using sugar to make jam, jelly etc. A preserve is any food, usually fruit or vegetables, preserved by either bottling, pickling or made into jam, jelly etc.

PRESSURE COOKER — A heavy saucepan with a mechanically tightened seal. It cooks the food inside by compressed steam, which shortens the cooking time. Water is able to reach a higher temperature than 100°C (212°F) which would not otherwise happen.

Pr

PRETZEL — German biscuit in the shape of a loose knot. It is crisp and sprinkled with cumin seeds and salt. Pretzels are made of flour and water, and were eaten in the days of Ancient Rome. The origin of the name is the subject of a controversy: it may be derived from a Latin word meaning little reward or another Latin word meaning prayer – the legend that claims that pretzels were given to children as a reward for saying their prayers combines both stories. According to superstition, the breaking of a pretzel with another person entitles one to a wish, and pretzels were hung on trees and even round people's necks to bring good luck.

PRINCESSE, A LA — Garnish for poultry and fish of asparagus tips and truffles.

PRINTANIERE — A selection of cooked vegetables cut in the shape of little balls, dice or diamonds, used to garnish meat dishes.

PROBAKALBSLEBERWURST — German smoked liver sausage.

PROFITEROLE — French pâtisserie in the form of a choux pastry ball. The balls are usually filled with cream or crème pâtissière, and arranged in a pyramid with chocolate sauce poured over. Savoury profiteroles are used to garnish soup.

PROGRES, LE — Cake of almond and hazelnut meringue layers, filled and decorated with butter cream.

PROSCIUTTO — Raw, cured ham from Parma and San Daniele in Italy. It is pinkish in colour and has a delicate flavour. It is sliced very thinly and served with melon, figs or pears. In Italy prosciutto is also served cooked.

PROTEIN — Substance essential every day for many important bodily functions. It may be obtained either from animal products (meat, fish, egg, milk, cheese) or pulses and nuts.

PROVENCALE — Dishes described as in the style of Provence usually some of the following: garlic, tomatoes, olives, anchovies, peppers and aubergines.

PUCHERO — Spanish soup-stew made with meat or poultry, chick peas, chorizo and dumplings.

PUDDING — This term covers many things. A pudding may be sweet or savoury, made in a pudding bowl, often encased in suet pastry. There are also sweet sponge puddings. It is also an alternative word for dessert and suggests a substantial and wholesome dish.

PUFF PASTRY — Very rich and light pastry which is difficult to make in large quantities. Equal amounts of butter and sugar are used, most of the fat being cut into cubes and wrapped in the dough during the lengthy folding and rolling process. The cooked pastry rises high and has an infinite number of layers.

PUGLIESE — Italian bread which is round and white, with a soft crust.

PULAO — Indian pilau.

PULLED BREAD — Fresh unsliced bread with the crust removed, which is torn into pieces and browned in the oven to serve with soup, stew etc.

PULLET — Young female chicken from the time she starts to lay eggs until the first moult.

PULP — The soft fleshy tissue of fruit or vegetables. To pulp food is to reduce it to a soft mass by crushing or boiling.

PULSES — General term for the seeds of legumes (peas, beans, lentils).

PUMPERNICKEL — German black bread made with potato and rye flour. It is moist with good keeping qualities.

PUNCHER — French pâtisserie term meaning to brush a cake with an alcohol-flavoured syrup (as in Rum Baba).

PUREE — Thick sieved or blended pulp of vegetables or fruit.

PURI/POORI — Very light puffed up bread served with curries. It is deep fried and often flavoured with turmeric.

PUTTANESCA, ALLA — As a prostitute would cook it, ie. fairly basic. It is a sauce for spaghetti of garlic, peppers and olives fried in olive oil.

PYTT I PANNA — Swedish supper dish of chopped cooked meat, diced boiled potatoes and fried onions. It is served with fried eggs on top and garnished with gherkins.

QUADRILLE — Fine lattice.

QUADRUCCI — Italian for little squares. These are pasta for soup.

Qu

QUARK — German word meaning curd or cottage cheese used widely in German and Austrian cuisine.

QUATRE-EPICES — Mixture of four spices (white pepper, cloves, ginger and nutmeg) used in charcuterie.

QUATRE MENDIANTS — Simple French dessert of medieval origin. It is a plate of dried figs, raisins, hazelnuts and almonds: these represent the mendicant orders; the figs are grey friars (Franciscans), the raisins are black friars (Dominicans), the hazelnuts are Augustinians who wear brown, and the blanched almonds are white friars (Carmelites).

QUATRE-QUARTS — French version of pound cake, though lighter in texture. It is made with equal amounts of fat, flour, sugar and eggs. It means four quarters.

QUATTRO FORMAGGIO — Italian for four cheese. This name is given to pizza with a topping of Mozzarella, Parmesan, Pecorino and Ricotta cheese.

QUATTRO STAGIONI — Italian for four seasons. This is another popular pizza topping. There are four quarters to the pizza: the first is topped with seafood, the second with tomato and anchovy, the third with cheese, the fourth with tomato, anchovy, capers and oregano, and a fried egg is placed in the middle.

QUEEN OF PUDDINGS — Popular nursery dessert dating from Victorian times. It is an egg custard thickened with breadcrumbs, topped with jam and meringue and served hot.

QUENELLE — Fish or meat forcemeat bound with beaten egg and poached. It may be many different shapes or sizes and is often used as a garnish. Quenelles de brochet (pike) are the best known.

QUESADILLA — Cheese filled chilli tortilla, which is crescent or tube shaped and deep fried.

QUICHE — Savoury custard flan from Alsace-Lorraine. Quiche Lorraine, the most famous example, has a filling of cream and bacon, and sometimes gruyère cheese.

RABOT — Wooden T-shaped implement used in Brittany to spread crêpe batter on the griddle.

RABOTTE — Dessert from Normandy consisting of an apple enclosed in rich shortcrust pastry.

RACHEL — A garnish for grilled meat of artichoke bottoms under the meat and ox marrow, parsley and red wine sauce on top. This name is also given to fish stuffed with fish forcemeat and sliced truffle, poached in white wine and garnished with asparagus tips. Consommé Rachel is chicken consommé garnished with strips of artichoke bottom, with ox marrow served separately on toast. Rachel was a French actress in the nineteenth century.

RACK — Rack of lamb is one side of the ribs with skin and cartilage removed.

RACLETTE — Simple Swiss dish made by holding a large piece of semi-soft cheese against an upright hot grill and scraping off the melted cheese. The scrapings are served with baked potatoes, gherkins and pickled onions. The idea comes from the Valais canton and the name derives from racler, the French for to scrape.

RAGOUT — Pieces of meat, poultry or fish slowly cooked in spicy liquid, usually with vegetables. Ragoûter is French for to reawaken the taste.

RAGU — Italian thick meat sauce such as Bolognaise sauce.

RAHMSCHNITZEL — Schnitzel floured and fried in butter, and served with a sauce of mustard, paprika, capers and cream.

RAIDIR — To seal or sear in hot fat.

RAISED CRUST — Hot water pastry.

RAISED PIE — A pie made in a special oval, springform mould with deep-ridged sides, so that the cooked pie is tall and impressive looking, with decorated sides. It is a favourite for buffets. Raised pies are made with hot water pastry, which is firm enough to hold its shape. The dense filling (a chopped veal and ham mixture or a variety of game, for example) is separated from the pastry by a thin layer of meat jelly. Raised pies are served cold.

RAISING AGENT — Substances (such as baking powder, bicarbonate of soda and yeast) which react when heated or added to other substances, producing a gas which causes the flour mixture to rise.

RAITA — Cold flavoured yogurt, which may be sweet or savoury, eaten as an accompaniment to an Indian meal.

RAITO — Sauce of onions, tomatoes, garlic, capers, black olives, walnuts, herbs and red wine in which eels or salt cod are cooked. This is traditionally eaten on Christmas Eve in Provence.

RAMEKIN — Small tarts of savoury choux pastry filled with a creamed cheese mixture. Also an individual earthenware or porcelain baking dish.

RANCID — Term used to describe stale fat. Rancidity is caused by glycerol breaking away from the fatty acid.

RANCIN — Pudding from Alsace of cherries and sliced buttered brioche baked in the oven until crisp.

RAPER — To grate or shred.

RARE — Term applied to undercooked meat, especially beef.

RAS EL HANOUT — Ready ground mixture of spices used in North African cuisine. The exact contents varies regionally, but it usually includes cinnamon, ginger, nutmeg, cloves, rose buds, peppers and sometimes the supposedly aphrodisiacal Spanish Fly.

RASHER — A slice of bacon cut on a bacon slicer to a specified thickness.

RASPINGS — Fried dry breadcrumbs to accompany roast game.

RASSOLNIK — Russian kidney soup flavoured with dill pickles.

RATAFIAS — A button-size macaroon strongly flavoured with almonds. It is used mostly in decorated desserts. It is also the name of a liqueur made with the kernels of apricots and peaches.

RATATOUILLE — Mixture of aubergines, onions, tomatoes, courgettes and peppers, flavoured with garlic and cooked slowly in a covered pan in olive oil. It may be eaten hot or cold. The word means stew in a provencal dialect.

RAVIER — Shallow boat-shaped porcelain dish for hors d'oeuvre.

RAVIGOTE SAUCE — A béchamel or velouté sauce flavoured with white wine, onions and herbs. Occasionally vinaigrette can be flavoured in the same way.

RAVIOLI — Little parcels of forcemeat wrapped in pasta, usually served hot in a tomato sauce. The name derives from the fact that the fillngs were made from leftovers and the dish was called rabiole – Italian for something of no value – until the nineteenth century. To be correct, ravioli should only be stuffed with eggs or cheese: otherwise it is called agnoletti.

RAYTE, EN — Provencal way of cooking fish, in a red wine sauce with garlic, herbs and capers.

REAMER — The part of a lemon squeezer which the lemon fits on to.

RECHAUFFE — French for reheated. Its uses implies something more interesting than merely warmed up leftovers.

RECIPE — The formula for making a dish. The word was originally receipt.

RED COOKED — Chinese cooking method used primarily for large cuts of meat and poultry. These are cooked in a sauce of soy sauce, sugar and sherry. The result is reddish brown in colour (hence the name) and rich in flavour.

RED EYE GRAVY — Gravy made with dripping from a baked ham. It has a reddish colour.

RED FLANNEL HASH — An early American dish designed to use up the leftovers of a New England Boiled Dinner. Beetroot was added, contributing its characteristic colour, the meat and vegetables cut up and the mixture was fried in bacon fat.

RED HERRING — Heavily salted and smoked herring which was popular until it was replaced by the less salty kipper at the turn of the century. The salting was necessary for preservation but it meant that the red herring had to be soaked for some hours to be palatable.

REDUCE — To boil liquid rapidly to loose some of its volume in steam.

REFAIRE — French term meaning to turn poultry or game in the bottom of the pan until the flesh swells.

REFOGADO — Thick onion and olive oil purée which forms the basis of many Portuguese dishes. It is sometimes flavoured with garlic and tomato.

REFORM — Lamb chops Reform are coated in egg and breadcrumbs, then fried, garnished with sliced gherkin, egg white, carrot, mushroom and espagnole sauce flavoured with port and redcurrant jelly. This was created by Alexis Soyer, chef at the London Reform Club in the nineteenth century.

REFRESH — To pour cold water over vegetables or meat which has been blanched in order to set the colour, and, in the case of meat, remove any scum.

REGENCE — Garnish for poultry, vol-au-vents and sweetbreads of truffled chicken quennelles, veal quennelles, cock's combs, foie gras, mushrooms and sauce allemande. Also a garnish for fish of oysters, round quennelles of whiting stuffed with crayfish butter, small fluted mushrooms, scallops of soft roe, truffles and sauce normande. Régence sauce is white wine, truffles and mushrooms added to either sauce normande, supreme or demi-glace.

REHRUCKEN — Traditional Austrian cake resembling a saddle of venison (hence the name). It is made with chocolate, ground almonds, eggs and sugar and has a chocolate glaze. It is made in a special semi-cylindrical mould with ribbed sides.

REINE — French for a chicken whose size is between a poulet and a poularde. Reine also means queen and a number of dishes are named à la reine: the majority are named after Marie Leczinska, wife of Louis XV, but potage à la reine refers to Margot, first wife of Henri IV.

REJANE — Garnish for sweetbreads of artichokes, bone marrow and duchess potatoes fried and filled with spinach. Garnish for meat and poultry of tartlets stuffed alternately with foie gras and asparagus tips, covered with Madeira sauce. Garnish for fish of duchess potatoes with a whipped sauce of white wine, demi-glace and crayfish butter. Also a chicken consommé with carrot royale, hazelnut royale and raw beaten egg.

RELACHER — French culinary term meaning to thin a mixture to the desired consistency with liquid.

RELIGIEUSE — French for nun. This is a famous French pastry shaped like the head and shoulders (back view) of a nun and made of choux paste. There are large and small versions. The smaller one is a small ball on a large ball. The large is a cone of éclairs on a circle of pâte sucrée, with a tiny ball on top. Both are filled and iced with chocolate or coffee flavoured cream and icing, and sometimes extra piped whipped cream. The prototype was made at Frascatis in Paris in 1856. Another pastry is also called a religieuse: it is a strip of puff pastry covered with apple and apricot jam and currants, and a pastry lattice.

RELISH — Strongly flavoured pickle, usually consisting of tart fruits, served with food to stimulate the appetite.

REMONTER — To enhance the taste of food such as a sauce by the addition of a condiment.

REMOULADE SAUCE — Mayonnaise flavoured with anchovies, pickles, capers and herbs.

REMOVE — A course in a full banquet between the fish and the entrée.

RENAISSANCE, A LA — Garnish for roasted meat of a selection of new vegetables arranged in small piles around the meat.

RENDANG — Indonesian beef curry. It is dry and extremely hot.

RENDER DOWN — To cut fat in small pieces and cook gently until it melts.

RENNET — Substance extracted from the stomach lining of an unweaned calf. It is used in cheese-making and to prepare junket. It curdles milk by coagulating the milk protein.

REPERE — Paste of flour and egg white which is used as an edible glue in elaborately decorated dishes.

RESTES, LES — French for leftovers.

REVENIR — French cookery term for browning meat in fat or oil to seal in the juices prior to further cooking.

RIB — Cut of beef from the centre back. Fore rib and wing rib are all suitable for roasting or, if cut into steaks, frying and grilling. As a joint ribs are often sold boned and rolled up. Back rib and top rib are better braised.

RIBOLLITA — Soup of white beans, vegetables, breadcrumbs and cheese from Florence, Italy.

RIBBON, TO THE — Phrase used to describe the consistency of eggs and sugar whisked until a ribbon-like trail forms on the surface of the mixture when it is trailed with a whisk. When the mixture is thick and fluffy enough for this to happen, it is ready to receive other ingredients to be folded in.

RIBOFLAVIN — Vitamin B2, which is found in liver, kidneys, yeast extract, egg, milk and cheese, and is necessary for the functioning of the muscles.

RICE PAPER — Edible glossy white paper made from the pith of a tree grown in China. It is used in cooking as an edible base and lining paper for macaroons and other biscuits and cakes.

RICER — A press for ricing potatoes. It has two handles attached to a flat pusher that operates on a potato placed in an aerated bowl-shaped container. By squeezing the handles, the potato is forced through the holes.

Ri

RICHE, A LA — Garnish for meat of foie gras medaillons, truffle, artichoke bottoms filled with asparagus tips, all coated in Madeira sauce. Also a garnish for fish fillets, especially sole, of lobster, truffles and sauce Victoria. Sauce à la Riche is sauce normande with lobster butter, brandy and cayenne. All these recipes were created at the Cafe Riche in nineteenth century Paris.

RICHELIEU — A la Richelieu, an expression in honour of Cardinal Richelieu, applies to several culinary preparations. It is a method of preparing fish by coating in egg and breadcrumbs, cooking in butter and serving with maître d'hôtel butter and truffles. It is also a garnish of roast potatoes, braised lettuce, stuffed tomatoes and mushrooms. A Richelieu is a large light cake flavoured with almonds and maraschino, and decorated with fondant icing and angelica. Richelieu sauce is made with onions, sugar, nutmeg and chervil in a cream sauce.

RIGATONI — Large grooved tube pasta.

RIGODON — Batter pudding from Burgundy. It may be savoury (with ham or bacon) or sweet (with fruit purée), eaten hot or cold and is usually made in large quantities.

RIGO JANCSI — A light chocolate cake filled with chocolate flavoured whipped cream and glazed with a rich chocolate icing. It is made in a swiss roll tin and cut in half to make two oblong layers, then cut into squares to serve. This Hungarian speciality is named after a gypsy violinist who eloped with a married princess at the turn of the century.

RIJSTTAFEL — Dutch for rice table. This is an Indonesian feast of rice with a large selection of accompaniments. It is very popular in Holland.

RILLETTES — Finely chopped pork and pork fat gently cooked in lard then pounded in a mortar. When cooked, rillettes are put into small stone jars and a layer of lard is poured over when they are cold. Rillettes de Tours (the original) are made with pure pork, but rillettes du Mans are made with half pork and half goose, and rillettes d'Orléans are half pork and half rabbit.

RILLONS/RILLAUDS/RILLOTS — Cubes of belly pork cooked slowly in a closed pot until golden brown.

RIND — The skin of pork or bacon. Also the peel of citrus fruit.

RINDFLEISCHKOCHWURSTE — German beef and pork sausage, seasoned with saltpetre and coriander, tied in pairs and dried for 48 hours, before being poached to serve.

RIS DE VEAU — French for sweetbreads.

RISI E BISI — Italian for rice and peas. These are cooked in equal proportions to a soupy consistency and served on the feast of St Mark at the Doge of Venice's banquets.

RISOTTO — Italian rice dish. Thick grain rice is used and plenty of stock is absorbed by the rice during cooking. The result has a creamy consistency and spreads a little on the plate. Various flavourings can be added during cooking.

RISSOLE — Savoury pastry filled with forcemeat and fried in deep fat. Usually made with puff pastry, a rissole may vary in size and shape and is served hot as an appetiser or light entrée. The name goes back to the twelfth century, originally being rousole, meaning reddish, ie. well-coloured by frying. A meat patty made with leftovers is also sometimes called a rissole.

RISSOLEES, POMMES — Château potatoes, but cooked until dark brown.

RISSOLER — To brown in a pan in fat.

RIVIERA — This name is given to a salad and a sauce. The salad consists of tangerine segments, chopped apple, pineapple, strawberry and celeriac on lettuce leaves, with mayonnaise mixed with chopped sweet pepper. Riviera sauce, also known as beurre Montpellier, is green mayonnaise mixed with butter or cream cheese, capers, anchovies and pickles: it is used as a spread for bread.

ROASTING — True roasting is done on a revolving spit over or in front of the source of heat. Nowadays what passes for roasting is baking in the oven, with a little fat where necessary.

ROBERT, SAUCE — Brown sauce flavoured with vinegar, onions and mustard. Robert Vinot was the chef who invented it in the early seventeenth century.

ROCHAMBEAU, A LA — Garnish for meat of braised carrots, stuffed lettuce, boiled cauliflowers, pommes Anna and demi-glace sauce.

ROCHESTER SAUCE — Chili sauce, sherry and brown sugar, served with ham and tongue.

ROCK CAKE — Small plain fruit cake named for its craggy appearance when cooked, not for its texture.

ROCKEFELLER, OYSTERS — Poached oysters with anise-flavoured spinach purée, served in their shells. This is the speciality of Antoine's famous restaurant in New Orleans.

177

Ro

RODGROD— Danish dessert made with a purée of raspberries and redcurrants lightly set with potato flour and served with cream (med flode).

ROE— The reproductive organ of a fish. Soft roe or milt is the testis, hard roe is the ovary. Caviar and taramasalata are made with roe of particular fish. Roe from some white fish can be bought separately, fried and eaten hot.

ROGHAN JOSH/GOSHT — Rich spiced dish of lamb in a reddish sauce. The colour is due to the inclusion of beetroot juice. It is a North Indian Moslem dish.

ROGNURES — French term for pastry trimmings.

ROHWURST — Generic German term for sausages sold cooked and either smoked or air-dried to preserve for several months, eg salami.

ROLL, BREAD — Individual round loaf of bread.

ROLLING OUT — To roll out is to spread and flatten a dough with a rolling pin.

ROLLING PIN — Wooden rod for rolling out. Occasionally other materials – glass, plastic, china – may be used in place of wood.

ROLLMOP — Raw herring fillet rolled round a pickling onion, gherkin and spices, impaled on a long cocktail stick and marinated in vinegar and salt for several days. The marinade "cooks" the fish.

ROLY POLY — Traditional British pudding made with suet pastry spread with jam and rolled up like a Swiss roll. It is wrapped in a cloth and boiled. The same pudding when baked is known as Baked Jam Roll.

ROMAINE — Garnish for large cuts of meat of spinach timbales with anchovies and individual Anna potatoes. Romaine sauce is a demi-glace with sugar, vinegar and sultanas added: it is served with tongue and venison.

ROMANA, ALLA — Roman style generally means tomatoes and onions in a rich sauce, as in chicken alla Romana, which is braised chicken with ham, tomatoes, onion, sweet peppers and rosemary. Gnocchi alla Romana is potato gnocchi with tomato sauce and cheese. Pizza alla Romana, however, has a topping simply of mozzarella and Parmesan cheeses with basil.

ROMANOFF — Strawberries Romanoff is vanilla ice cream, whipped cream, cointreau and whole strawberries mixed together.

ROMANOV, A LA — Garnish for meat of cucumber stuffed with duxelles au gratin and duchess potatoes filled with celeriac and mushroom in a horseradish velouté sauce. Both Romanov and Romanoff refer to the Russian royal family.

ROMESCO — Spicy Spanish sauce of hot red peppers, nuts and garlic, used in very small quantities with meat, poultry or fish or added to other sauces or stews. It is a feature of Catalan cuisine.

ROMPRE — French bakery term for to knock down risen dough to its original volume.

RONDEAU — Wide, fairly shallow pan with two ear-shaped handles and a flat lid. It is used for braising or poaching.

RONDIN — Round casserole with a tight lid and two handles.

ROPING — What happens when gelatine in a mixture goes lumpy. This is due to it setting before it is thoroughly blended with the mixture it is to set.

ROSETTE — Pig's gut, about 50 cm (20in.) long, used to encase sausages. A rosette iron is a Swedish fire iron with a fancy shape at one end, which is used for making fritters or deep-fried cookies. The iron is heated in the hot oil, dipped into a batter and returned to the oil to cook the batter.

ROSSINI — Tournedos Rossini is a classic French dish invented by the composer Rossini. Tournedos are cut from the eye of the fillet of beef. The fried meat is topped with a slice of foie gras with a piece of truffle in the centre and served with a Perigord sauce.

ROSTI — Grated, boiled potatoes packed into a frying pan, then inverted and cooked on the other side. It is served in one piece and cut into slices like a cake. Rosti is a Swiss invention.

ROTHSCHILD, SOUFFLE — Vanilla cream based soufflé flavoured with crystallized fruits soaked in brandy, kirsch or Danziger goldwasser.

Ro

ROTISSERIE — A modern device for roasting meat on a spit. The spit turns automatically so that the meat revolves slowly and each side is in turn directly exposed to the source of heat. The result is that the natural juices are sealed in and the meat cooks evenly.

ROUENNAISE — Canard Rouennaise is distinguished by very dark, rich flavoured meat. This is because the duck is smothered to death so that no blood is lost. The breast meat is served saignant, so the legs have to be cooked separately for longer. The blood is used to make a sauce.

ROUGAIL — Hot spicy sauce used in creole cooking. The ingredients vary but it is usually based on fruit, vegetables or fish. In the Caribbean rougail is mashed and spiced vegetables, fruit or fish served as an hors d'oeuvre or side dish.

ROUGE, AU — French term for food served with a red sauce.

ROUGH PUFF PASTRY — Richer than flaky but less rich than puff pastry. Rough puff is made with three-quarters fat (margarine or lard) to flour. It is best eaten hot.

ROULADE — A soufflé mixture cooked in a Swiss roll tin, spread with an appropriate filling, then rolled up. Also a rolled piece of veal or pork, or a thin slice of meat spread with stuffing and rolled up.

ROUX — A fat and flour liaison, which is the basis of white and brown sauces. The proportions of fat to flour are equal, or slightly more fat than flour. The roux can be white, blond or brown, depending on how long it is cooked. A roux is made after the flour is added by melting fat in a thick pan and stirring in flour off the heat.

ROYALE — A moulded custard cut into stars, squares, diamonds etc. and used to garnish clear soup. It may be flavoured with a meat or vegetable purée or be plain. A la Royale is applied to poached poultry coated with a creamy truffle-flavoured velouté sauce. Salpicon à la Royale is truffles and mushrooms bound with chicken purée.

ROYAL ICING — Hard cake decoration of icing sugar and egg white.

RUBBING IN — One of the three standard methods of cake making. the fat is rubbed into the flour until crumbs are formed (as in pastry making) then the sugar, eggs and other ingredients are added. Cakes made by this method usually have diced fruit and/or nuts added to relieve the dry texture, and keep well.

RUGELACH — Traditional Jewish pastry made with a cream cheese pastry dough rolled into a circle and cut into wedges. It is spread with a sweet spicy nut mixture, rolled up and shaped into a crescent before baking. Jam or poppy seeds may also be used as fillings.

RUMAKI — A piece of chicken liver marinated in soy sauce with a piece of water chestnut and a spring onion wrapped in bacon, secured with a toothpick and grilled or baked. It is served hot as an appetizer and is of Polynesian origin.

RUMP STEAK — Cut from the rump (rear end) of a cow. It is less tender than fillet but has more flavour.

RUMTOPF — Traditional German way of preserving different summer fruits in layers in a large stoneware jar, covering each layer with sugar and rum. As each new crop comes along it goes into the pot with the rum and sugar until the pot is full and the summer is over. The rumtopf is served at Christmas. The special jar used for this technique is also known as a rumtopf.

RUPTURE — French term meaning the kneading of bread that has risen once.

RUSK — Twice baked biscuit made of milk bread or cake dough. It is baked first in a large square tin then cut into slices when cold and cooked again in a slow oven until crisp through.

RUSSE — Name given to mayonnaise when mixed with caviar, lobster coral and mustard. Also a garnish of beetroot, soured cream, chopped hard-boiled egg and pickled cucumber. A salad of diced vegetables including beetroot, apple and peas in mayonnaise. Service à la russe describes the way of serving food at a banquet by having a waiter bring the dishes to seated guests in the order in which they are to be eaten. Before 1860 when this form of service was introduced all the dishes were spread out on a table before the guests came into the room and made a choice from the large selection.

RUSSIAN — Russian dressing is mayonnaise mixed with chilli sauce. Russian mayonnaise is cold velouté sauce, sour cream, horseradish and tarragon vinegar. Russian salad is a mixture of cooked vegetables including potato, carrot and beans coated with mayonnaise.

RUSTICANA, ALLA — Sauce for spaghetti of garlic, anchovies and oregano. It is served with Pecorino cheese.

S

SABAYON — Egg yolks, sugar and white wine whisked over a gentle heat to a light mousse, then poured into glasses and eaten hot as a dessert. The same mixture may also be used as a sauce, either hot or cold, though it is best eaten as soon as it is made. Occasionally kirsch or another liqueur may replace the wine. The Italian version, zabaglione, uses marsala.

SABLE — A rich, shortbread type biscuit, originally from Caen in Normandy. The name means sandy in French, which is a comment on the crumbly texture. It is made with a pâte sablée dough. The cooked biscuits are often served sandwiched with jam, cream or crème pâtissière. A savoury version is also found with a creamy savoury filling.

SABLEE, PATE — Short pastry used by pâtissiers. Its high butter content makes it difficult to handle, but results in a texture more like shortbread than pastry which makes a delicious flan case.

SABLER — French term meaning to rub in fat to flour.

SACHERTORTE — Austrian chocolate cake invented by Franz Sacher, chef to Prince Metternich, in 1832. It is a dark chocolate sponge, sliced in half, filled with apricot jam, then covered with a rich, dark chocolate icing. It was the subject of a famous court case between the Hotel Sacher (who won) and the celebrated Viennese pastry shop, Demel.

SACRISTAIN — French pastry. It is simply a twisted strip of puff pastry.

SADDLE — The whole back of a lamb complete with kidneys. It is roasted.

SAG — Indian spiced purée of spinach.

SAGAN, A LA — Garnish for small cuts of white meat consisting of rice, mushrooms, truffles and a purée of brains.

SAIGNANT — French for bleeding, meaning rare in cooking terminology.

SAIGNEUX — French butchery term for neck of mutton or veal.

SAINDOUX — French term meaning pork lard.

SAINTE-ALLIANCE, FAISIN, A LA — Roasted pheasant stuffed with woodcock forcemeat. Served on a croûton wiht slices of bitter orange.

SAINTE-MENEHOULD, A LA — A way of cooking pig's trotters, and also less often, sheep's trotters, or breast of veal or lamb. The meat is braised for a long time, then boned and cut into strips, which are coated in egg and breadcrumbs and grilled. The result is juicy if fatty meat inside a crisp coating. The method is named after a town in Verdun where it originated. The pig's trotters may be served with Ste-Ménéhould sauce: a demi-glace with onion, vinegar, mustard, gherkins, parsley, chervil and cayenne.

SAINT GERMAIN — Term used commonly to denote the presence of peas in the dish. Crème St Germain is a green pea soup. A la St Germain can mean one of three classic garnishes. For sweetbreads it will be pea purée in artichoke bottoms, served with béarnaise sauce. For cuts of meat it will be a more solid pea purée turned out of a dariole mould, glazed carrots cut into olive shapes, fondant potatoes and béarnaise sauce. Fish à la St Germain, however, is simply fish fried in egg and breadcrumbs with noisette potatoes and béarnaise sauce.

SAINT HONORE — Saint Honoré was a bishop of Amiens. He is the patron saint of bakers because once whilst he was celebrating mass a divine hand sent down a loaf of bread. Rue St Honoré in Paris was a street famous for its pastrycooks and in 1879 one of them, a man called Chiboust, created Gâteau St Honoré. This famous cake has a base of pâte sucrée, surrounded with tiny choux paste balls which are covered with caramel, and filled with an elaborate crème pâtissière into which whisked egg whites have been folded. Over the years variations involving puff pastry bases and cream fillings have become popular. Spun sugar may be used to decorate the gâteau.

SAINT HUBERT — Saint Hubert is the patron saint of hunters and many game dishes are named after him. Two classic game soups bear his name. One is a consommé with Madeira, garnished with game royale, julienne of mushrooms and cream. The other is a pheasant potage garnished with pheasant meatballs.

Sa

SAINT JACQUES, COQUILLES — This is what the French call scallops. According to legend, the body of St Jacques (the apostle James) travelled in a boat without sails or oars around the Iberian coast, finally coming to rest in Compostela in Northern Spain. Various miracles occured to those who came into contact with the boat, including a man who was saved from drowning and emerged from the sea covered in scallop shells. The shell was taken as a badge for pilgrims to the shrine of St Jacques at Compostela, which became one of the most important places of pilgrimage in medieval Europe. Although Coquille St Jacques can refer to scallop cooked in any fashion, the most usual method is in a béchamel sauce and served on its shell with a border of duchess potato piped round.

SAINT MICHEL — A French cake made of three layers of genoese mixture and a coffee and vanilla butter cream icing.

SAINT REGIS — A salad from the New York hotel the St Regis. It consists of pineapple, grapefuit, celery, potato and asparagus in a cream and vinaigrette dressing.

SALAD — Any cold dish composed mostly of a selection of vegetables which are cut up and mixed lightly. The vegetables are more often raw then cooked (except potato). A salad is usally served with a dressing such as vinaigrette or mayonnaise. It may be a side dish, a starter, a light main course or eaten after the main course to refresh the palate. A fruit salad is a mixture of fruit (cooked or raw) in a light syrup. The word salad is derived from the latin sal (salt).

SALAD RELISH — An American cabbage and tomato pickle.

SALAD SHAKER — Collapsable metal basket with two handles to dry salads by shaking out moisture.

SALAD SIMPLE — A salad of one type of vegetable dressed in vinaigrette.

SALAD SPINNER — Device for drying salads mechanically. Salad is placed in a basket inside a box. The lid is put on the box and string pulled or handle turned to make the basket spin inside the box.

SALAMANDER — A fire iron used to brown the surface of sugar-coated desserts or gratins to make a crisp coating without heating the food underneath. It is like a poker with a thick circle on the end and it is heated until it is red hot before use.

SALAMANDRE — French term meaning breadcrumbs fried in butter and sprinkled over food.

SALAMBOS — Small balls of choux paste filled with orange flavoured crème pâtissière and topped with caramel.

SALAME — Originally a highly seasoned and salted Italian sausage, there are now many varieties available including salamis (the commonly used term salami is in fact the plural) from Denmark, Poland, Hungary and Germany. Usually made with pork and/or beef, the dark red meat (which is artificially coloured) is speckled with white fat. It is served cold in thin slices and the fine skin is peeled off each slice and discarded.

SALLY LUNN — A round bun of yeast dough popular since the eighteenth century when Sally Lunn sold them in a shop which still exists today in the town of Bath. Originally they were made in special Sally Lunn rings and split open while hot and filled with cream and sprinkled with sugar. Nowadays they are eaten with butter or clotted cream.

SALMAGUNDY — Traditional English meat salad arranged in an elaborate pattern on the serving plate.

SALMIGONDIS — French dish of leftover mixed meats reheated as a ragoût.

SALMIS — Usually duck or goose roasted then cut into pieces and braised in a rich wine-flavoured brown sauce.

SALOMTER — A device for measuring the amount of salt in a brine. It is a weighted glass tube like a thermometer which is read according to how far it sinks into the brine: the more salt the more it floats.

SALPICON — A mixture of shredded or diced ingredients, bound in a rich sauce. This can be used as a garnish, a filling for pastry cases or made into croquettes. Occasionally a fruit salpicon is used in pâtisserie.

SALSA — Mexican accompaniment of chopped chillies, tomato, onion and coriander. The degree of spiciness varies.

SALSA VERDE — Green sauce in Spanish. Made of garlic, parsley and peas, it is served with fish.

SALT — Verb meaning to preserve food by adding salt. This practice dates back the neolithic age. It was found that salt draws moisture from food so the organisms which would normally spoil the food cannot grow. For the method to be successful the salt must penetrate the food thoroughly and evenly so small flat shapes are easier to preserve in this way than large joints.

Sa

SALTENA — A Bolivian mid-morning snack consisting of a pastry turnover filled with meat, eggs, vegetables, olives, raisins and aspic, which is eaten cold.

SALTIMBOCCA — Italian for "jump in the mouth". This is a famous dish of thin slices of veal rolled up with thin slices of ham and a sage leaf, then cooked in butter and marsala.

SALZBURGER NOCKERL — Literally Salzburg dumpling, this Austrian dessert is a very light pudding in a vanilla and lemon sauce. It is traditionally made in three moulds and was invented by the chef at the archbishop's palace in the eighteenth century.

SAMBAL — A side dish served with a main course in India or the Far East. A selection is served, each in a small bowl. In South East Asia a sambal means meat or fish dishes fried with chilies or any chili-based sauce.

SAMOSA — Indian savoury pastry, triangular in shape, stuffed with a vegetable or meat mixture. It is a tea-time delicacy.

SAMOVAR — Russian metal tea urn heated from an inner tube, in which charcoal is burned.

SAN BERNARDO — A tomato, pea and tuna sauce for pasta, usually tagliolini.

SANCOCHO — Caribbean spicy stew of chicken, meat, sausage, beans, vegetables and herbs. The cooking liquor is often served first as soup.

SANDWICH — A way of serving almost any food between slices of bread. It is named after the fourth Earl of Sandwich who was a great gambler and would not leave a game for a meal, so his meat was brought to him in a form that he could eat while continuing to play cards. The idea of enclosing food in two slices of bread, however, was the custom for peasants working the fields long before the Earl gave the idea a name. A sandwich normally has two slices of bread, both spread with butter. An open sandwich involves just one slice of bread used as a base for the other ingredients. A double decker sandwich uses three slices of bread with two different fillings.

SANDY POT — Chinese cooking pot made of a mixture of sand and clay which is fragile and needs a reinforcement of wire round the pot. It is used for cooking meat or fish very slowly in stock, either on top of the stove or in the oven. It has a domed lid and a handle at the side.

SANGLER — To pack ice round a mould to freeze the contents.

SANGLIER, EN — Meat, often pork, marinated and cooked to taste like wild boar.

SARAH BERNHARDT — The famous nineteenth century French actress Sarah Bernhardt has been honoured with four dishes named after her. A chicken consommé garnished with chicken quenelles, julienne of truffles, asparagus tips, poached beef marrow and crayfish butter. Eggs stuffed with a chicken mixture, covered in perigueux sauce and baked. A vanilla soufflé with layers of curacao-soaked macaroons, decorated with strawberries and crème chantilly. A salad of chopped artichoke bottoms, asparagus tips and quartered hard-boiled eggs on lettuce with vinaigrette.

SARATOGA CHOP — American cut of lamb from the shoulder, skewered to form a round shape like a noisette.

SARDE A LA — Garnish for meat of rice croquettes

SARDO — Sardinian pork and chili salame.

SARLADAISE — From Sarlat, a town in the Dordogne which is famous for its truffles. Pommes de terre à la Sarladaise is layers of sliced potato, truffles and foie gras, baked in butter until browned. Sarladaise sauce is hard-boiled eggs, cream and sieved truffles blended with oil, lemon juice and Armagnac brandy. It is served cold. A la Sarladaise is a classic garnish for lamb of truffles, sliced potatoes and demi-glace sauce.

SARRASINE, A LA — Garnish for large cuts of meat of rice tartlets filled with tomato and sweet pepper fondue, small buckwheat cakes and fried onion rings.

SARTU DI RISO ALLA NAPOLETANA — Rice mould filled with meatballs, bacon, chicken livers, sausages, ham, mushrooms, hard-boiled eggs and cheese. It is covered in tomato sauce, cheese and breadcrumbs and baked.

SASHIMI — Japanese dish of fillets of raw fish, sliced very thinly and soaked in lime or lemon juice to kill any bacteria. It is served with shredded vegetables and a ginger, soy and vinegar sauce for dipping.

SATE — Also known as satay. Indonesian kebabs of pork or chicken on short wooden skewers and served with hot peanut sauce.

SAUCE — A form of liquid seasoning. As well as being used to enhance flavour, sauces can be used to bind ingredients together. There are over two hundred sauces in classic French cuisine, and many hundreds more in the world of cookery. They may be sweet or savoury, hot or cold, light or dark, and they can make or mar the dish they accompany.

187

SAUERBRATEN — German dish of topside or silverside of beef, marinated for several days and pot roasted. Though the marinade ingredients may vary from region to region, the end result always has a sweet-sour flavour.

SAUERKRAUT — This means sour cabbage in German, but although the dish is usually supposed to be German in origin, the idea came from China and was brought to Germany by invading tartars. The cabbage is fermented in brine for several weeks and this makes it more digestible. The sharp taste makes a good contrast with fatty meats like goose and pork which play a prominant part in German cuisine.

SAUGRENE — French method of cooking vegetables very slowly with a little water, butter, herbs and seasoning.

SAUMURE — Brine or pickle.

SAUPIQUET — A sauce of the blood and mashed liver of a hare, with shallots, red wine and vinegar. It is served with venison.

SAURE — French term applied to food such as fish which has been both salted and smoked.

SAUSAGE — A mixture of finely minced lean and fat pork and/or beef, breadcrumbs and seasoning, made into a cylindrical shape and cased in gut. There are many varieties large and small, over one thousand in Germany alone. Sometimes the breadcrumbs are replaced by another binding starch such as rusks or rice. The degree of spiciness can vary considerably. The word comes from the latin salsus (salted). Sausages have been eaten all over Europe since the time of the Ancient Greeks.

SAUSSOUN — A French sauce of mint, anchovies, ground almonds, olive oil and water, which is spread on bread.

SAUTE — From the French verb sauter, to jump (ie. to make jump or toss). To sauté is to cook food in a small amount of very hot fat, constantly keeping the food on the move. It is important not to try to sauté too much food at a time as if the pan is overcrowded the food will steam and the juices will burn.

SAUTEUSE — Heavy long-handled metal pan with low straight sides at right angles to the round base.

SAUTOIR — Like a sauteuse but with higher, outward sloping sides.

SAVARIN — Large cake made with a yeast dough in a special ring mould. It is soaked in rum or kirsch flavoured syrup after cooking. It is named after Brillat-Savarin the nineteenth century French gastronome.

SAVELOY — A smoked pork sausage with a characteristic thick bright red skin (coloured with saltpetre), which is removed for eating. It is sold cooked and eaten cold in slices.

SAVOURY — A light savoury course served after the dessert.

SAVOURY DUCK — See FAGGOT.

SAVOYARDE — Term applied to dishes from the Savoy region of France or containing some of their typical ingredients – gruyère cheese, bacon or ham, potatoes and cream.

SCALD — To plunge food into boiling water for easy peeling or to heat a liquid to just under boiling point.

SCALLOP — This word has several meanings in cookery beside the shellfish. It is an American term for an escalope of veal. Also it is a verb meaning to bake in a sauce with crumbs on the top or bake in thin slices layered in a shallow dish with a sauce on top.

SCALOPPINE — Italian cut of veal, similar to escalopes but cut against the grain of the meat.

SCHAU — Sorrel soup from Eastern Europe. It is served cold with sour cream.

SCHLEMMERTOPF — A modern version of an ancient cooking pot. It is a baked clay pot with the lid the same size as the base. It is oval and unglazed. The pot is soaked in water before use and is put into a cold oven. The oven is then turned on so the clay heats up gradually. The wet clay keeps the food from drying out and also partially steams the food while it is baking. No fat is needed for basting, which makes this a healthy alternative to roasting. The idea comes from Germany.

SCHMALTZ — Yiddish term for rendered chicken fat, which is used as an alternative to butter as a frying medium in kosher households where no milk products can be eaten with meat.

SCHNITZEL — German name for escalope of veal dipped in egg and breadcrumbs and fried. Wiener schnitzel means Viennese schnitzel and this is the original, though there are now several variations with regional garnishes.

SCHNITZ PIE — Double crust pie filled with dried apple from the Pennsylvania Dutch region of America.

SCHUSTERPFANNE — German for shoemaker's pot. This is a stew of pork with vegetables and pears.

SCHWABISCHES SCHNITZEL — Schnitzel fried with lemon juice and cream and served with spatzle.

189

Sc

SCHWARZWALDER KIRSCHTORTE — Chocolate cake filled with cream and kirsch-flavoured cherries. From the Black Forest of Germany which is famous for its cherries.

SCONE — Very simple small cake from Scotland made by the rubbing in method. It can be savoury or sweet (sometimes with sultanas) and is split open and served with butter soon after it is made.

SCORE — To make a series of shallow cuts on the surface of food.

SCOTCH BROTH — Sustaining soup from Scotland made with mutton, barley and vegetables.

SCOTCH EGG — Hard-boiled egg surrounded by sausagemeat, coated with egg and breadcrumbs and deep fried. It is eaten cold.

SCOTCH PANCAKE — Small, dense pancake cooked on a griddle. Also known as a griddle cake.

SCOTCH WOODCOCK — A savoury of scrambled eggs with a cross of anchovies on top.

SCRAG — A stewing cut of lamb or veal from the top of the neck.

SCRAMBLE — To prepare eggs by stirring while cooking over a low heat until the mixture is lightly set.

SCRAPPLE — A Pennsylvania Dutch dish from America of pork mixed with onions, spices, herbs and cornmeal. The cooked mixture sets on cooling and is then sliced and fried for a hearty breakfast served with maple syrup. Originally this dish was devised as a way of using up otherwise unwanted parts of a pig. Nowadays it is sold ready prepared.

SEA PIE — Traditional English dish of a beef stew topped with a suet crust. It was made for sailors on board ship, hence the name.

SEAR — To fry at a very high temperature to brown the outside (eg. of meat) prior to slower cooking by some other method. The idea is to seal in the juices.

SEASONING — Adding salt and pepper to a dish. The word also means the salt and pepper itself.

SEFTON — A savoury custard made with veal stock. It was named after the Earl of Sefton, employer of its inventor, Eustache Ude.

SEIN DE VENUS, COUPE — A vanilla ice cream, with a poached peach on top and a strawberry in the centre, decorated with whipped cream. The name means breast of Venus.

SELKIRK BANNOCK — A fruit bread from Scotland.

190

SEMI-FREDDO — Italian frozen cream dessert.

SEMI-SWEET — In America semi-sweet chocolate is what the English call plain chocolate.

SEPARATE — To part the yolk of the egg from the white. This is done by gently cracking the egg shell, opening the shell and letting the white fall out while retaining the yolk in the shell.

SERGE, A LA — A garnish for veal escalopes or sweetbreads of shredded ham, small artichokes and Madeira.

SERVIETTE, A LA — Food served wrapped in a napkin.

SEVIGNE — Steak garnish of braised lettuce, grilled mushrooms and potatoes sautéed in butter.

SEVILLE — Elaborate garnish for tournedos of pastry shells filled with artichoke bottoms, masked in béchamel sauce and sprinkled with Parmesan cheese then browned in the oven. The tournedos are served on croûtes the same size as themselves with sherry-enriched pan juices poured over. A pat of garlic butter goes on top.

SFOGLIATELLE — Italian tart of flaky pastry filled with ricotta cheese and candied fruit.

SHABU-SHABU — Japanese dish similar to fondue. Paper thin slices of beef and vegetables are cooked in boiling liquid and dipped in a hot sauce. When all the meat and vegetables are eaten, noodles are cooked in the cooking liquor and this is served as a soup.

SHARK'S FIN SOUP — Chinese speciality which takes four days to prepare unless processed, dried shark's fin is used. The flavour comes from the other ingredients: chicken, rice wine and soy sauce. To serve each person, put some bean sprouts and matchsticks of ham into their bowl before pouring on the soup. Little bowls of vinegar and mustard are offered for additional seasoning.

SHASHLIK — Russian dish similar to a kebab. Pieces of meat are threaded on a skewer then grilled. Originally the skewer would have been a sword and the grill a camp fire.

SHAWARMA — Arab name for Doner kebab.

SHCHI — Russian cabbage soup.

SHEPHERD'S PIE — A British dish which is similar to Cottage Pie except that lamb or mutton is used as the meat.

SHERBET — Arabic origin of the sorbet. It was filtered through silk and kept in snow.

Sh

SHICHIMI — Also known as seven flavours spice. Japanese mixture of hot spices used as a flavouring or garnish. Contains pepper leaf, rape seed, poppy seed, hemp seed, tangerine peel and sesame seeds.

SHIN — Cut of beef from the leg of the carcass. It is the cheapest and toughest beef joint, but has a very good flavour when cooked gently for at least four hours. It is coarse grained and gelatinous. Shin of veal can also be sawn across the bone for osso buco.

SHIO-YAKI — Japanese method of cooking fish by covering it with salt, leaving it for half an hour then grilling it over charcoal.

SHIRRED EGG — The egg is broken into a small flat dish and cooked under a hot grill until the white is set but tender and yolk is liquid but covered with a transparent film. Eggs baked in individual ramekins with a little butter and cream are also known as shirred eggs.

SHIVERING — A temperature of 180-190°F, 82-88°C, which is slightly lower than simmering, for very gentle cooking.

SHOOFLY PIE — Traditional dessert from the Pennsylvania Dutch community of the USA. It is a spicy, gooey mixture of molasses, brown sugar and eggs inside a pastry case and topped with a crumble mixture. The name is said to derive from the efforts of the cook to shoo away the flies attracted by the sweetness of the pie.

SHORTBREAD — Scottish biscuit made with butter, sugar, semolina and flour and baked in a round tin then cut into pieces to serve. It has a rich, crumbly texture.

SHORTCAKE — A cake-like pastry, or pastry-like cake made with flour, sugar and butter from the USA. Also known as shortnin'bread. It is sometimes split open and filled with cream and strawberries.

SHORTCRUST — The oldest and most widely used type of pastry, it is made by the rubbing in method, with half fat to flour and as little water as possible.

SHORTENING — American term for any fat used in pastry making.

SHORT THREAD — The stage reached when sugar is boiled to 215°F, 105°C.

SHOULDER — Cut of lamb or veal suitable for roasting. It is often rolled and stuffed. It is also used for a blanquette.

SHOYU — Japanese condiment made by fermenting soya beans and barley.

SHRED — To slice or grate finely.

SHREWSBURY — The town of Shrewsbury in Shropshire has given its name to two culinary creations: a large, round, lemon-flavoured biscuit invented in one of the town's bakeries, and a dish of lamb cutlets from the best end of neck, cooked in a sauce of redcurrant jelly, red wine and mushrooms, was named after an Earl of Shrewsbury.

SHRIKAND — Indian cold dessert made with yogurt flavoured with saffron and rose water.

SHUCK — American term for the shell of oysters and clams, also the outer husk of corn. It is also used as a verb meaning to remove the shell, husk, pod (of peas). Shucked oysters are those already shelled.

SICILIANA, ALLA — Describes a pizza topped with tomato, capers, anchovies and black olives.

SICILIENNE, BOMBE — Ice cream bombe dessert with an interior of vanilla flavoured praline ice cream and grilled almonds and an exterior of lemon sorbet.

SIDE BACON — American for streaky bacon.

SIDEMEATS — American for offal

SIEVE — Fine mesh net attached to a rigid ring, usually with a handle. The mesh may be curved like a basket or stretched across the bottom of a wooden drum. The word is also a verb meaning to remove any lumps from food pushed through a sieve. The lumps are left behind on one side of the mesh.

SIFT — Similar in meaning to the verb to sieve, but when sifting the sieve is shaken gently to introduce air and to mix dry ingredients (eg. in cake making the flour is sifted with salt and baking powder).

SILD — Young herring and sprats. They swim together in a mixed shoal and so are caught and processed together.

SILVERSIDE — Lean boneless cut of beef from the hind quarters. It is usually salted and boiled.

SIMMER — To cook food in liquid just below boiling point.

SIMNEL CAKE — British cake traditionally eaten at Easter or on Mothering Sunday. It is a light fruit cake layered with almond paste and decorated with almond paste eggs.

SINGE — To put a naked flame to the outside of poultry and game to burn off any feathers that remain after plucking.

Si

SINGIN' HINNIE — A girdle teacake from the North of England. The name comes from the sizzling sound it makes on the griddle when cooking. A hinnie is a term of endearment. To serve it is split and buttered.

SINGLE CREAM — Cream with a minimum fat content of 18%. It is used as a pouring sauce and in cooking.

SIPPET — A small piece of bread.

SIRLOIN — Whole meat and bone of one side of beef, between the fore-ribs and the rump. It contains the fillet and is usually cut into steaks for frying or grilling, but may also be roasted on or off the bone. It is one of the most expensive cuts of beef. Originally it was refered to as loin but was 'knighted' by King Charles II of England after a good dinner.

SIU MAI — Chinese steamed dumpling filled with meat and lobster coral. Served heaped in a bamboo basket as part of Dim Sum.

SKILLET — American frying pan with deep sides. It was originally an English saucepan with three feet and a handle.

SKIM — To remove scum, fat, froth etc. from the surface of liquid. Froth and scum are removed with a perforated spoon. Fat is skimmed by allowing the liquid to cool so that the fat sets on top and can be removed easily. Skim milk, meaning skimmed milk, is the lowest fat milk available, though it is no longer 'skimmed' as described here.

SKIRLIE — Scottish dish of oatmeal and onions cooked in dripping.

SKIRT — Inner cut of beef which has a good flavour but needs long, slow cooking to tenderize.

SKORDHALIA — Greek sauce of garlic, breadcrumbs, olive oil and lemon. Potatoes or nuts may sometimes be used to thicken it in place of breadcrumbs. It is served with chicken or fish or as a dip for cooked vegetables. It may also be blended into soups.

SLAKE — To blend a thickening agent such as arrowroot or cornflour with a small amount of liquid before adding it to the soup or sauce it is to thicken.

SLICE — To cut in one direction only. A slice of food has a long thin shape unless it is cut from a round cake or pie, in which case it will be wedge-shaped.

SLIPPER — English cut of pork or ham from the corner of the fillet.

SLOPPY JOE — American sandwich made with a long, crusty roll filled with a spicy mixture of minced beef, baked beans, onions and green pepper. It is served hot.

SLOW COOKER — Covered electrical pot resembling a casserole, which keeps food at a steady temperature as low as 200°F, 83°C, for slow gentle cooking.

SLUMP — American fruit dumplings served with cream.

SMETANA — Russian dessert of sour cream and sweetened thick cream mixed with fruit. Though the word means sour cream in Russian, the product sold as smetana in the UK is much lower in fat than regular sour cream.

SMITANE, SAUCE — French sauce of Russian origin, made with onions, white wine, sour cream and lemon juice.

SMITHFIELD HAM — Surprisingly not from London's Smithfield Market, but from Smithfield in Virginia, USA, where the pigs are fed on peanuts and corn. It is smoked with hickory and apple and is served hot, baked with a sweet glaze.

SMOKE POINT — The temperature at which heated fat or oil gives off a blue vapour. The more refined the fat or oil the higher the smoke point will be.

SMOKING — A way of preserving meat and fish by drying in the smoke of a wood fire, which has been popular since the days of the Ancient Egyptians who are thought to have invented it. The type of wood burned affects the flavour of the food smoked. Oak, juniper, hickory and beech are the most common. Sawdust is often sprinkled over the fire to create more smoke. There are two kinds of smoking, hot smoking and cold smoking. For hot smoking the temperature is high enough to cook the food and it therefore needs no further cooking. Cold smoking uses a lower temperature smoke so light cooking is needed afterwards.

SMORGASBORD — Swedish for sandwich table. In fact it is a large selection of food (usually cold hors d'oeuvres). It originated when guests would be asked to bring a dish to a party and all the dishes would then be displayed on a long table, which the guests would walk round, helping themselves, beginning with the herring dishes and ending with the cheese.

SMORREBROD — Danish for open sandwich. It is usually made with thinly sliced rye bread and topped with a variety of savoury foods.

SMOTHERED CHICKEN — American method of baking chicken in milk.

SNACK — The word comes from the Middle Dutch snacken, meaning to snap up. It is something either uncooked or simply cooked and eaten quickly.

SNICKERDOODLE — American-German cookie with a light texture and a cinnamon sugar crust. It is best eaten still warm from the oven.

SNITZ KLOES — Very spicy, steamed fruit pudding from the Pennsylvania Dutch community of the USA.

SNOW — Fruit purée folded into whisked egg whites. Snow cream is a snow enriched with whipped cream or evaporated milk. Snow eggs is another name for Oeufs à la Neige.

SOBRONADE — Very thick soup containing pork, salt pork, haricot beans, potatoes, carrots, celery and leeks. It is a peasant dish from the Perigord region of France.

SODA BREAD — Irish bread made without yeast. Bicarbonate of soda and soured milk act as the raising agent and give the bread its characteristic crumbly texture.

SOFRITO — Thick purée of onion and garlic, cooked in olive oil with tomato and sometimes parsley, which forms the basis of many Spanish dishes.

SOFT BALL — Stage reached when sugar is boiled to 240°F, 115°C. If a drop of the boiling sugar were to be dropped into cold water it would form a soft ball.

SOISSONAISE — Indicates haricot beans in the recipe.

SOPPRESSA, SALAME — Pork and beef salame from the Veneto district in Italy.

SORBET — A strongly flavoured and very smooth textured water ice, made by freezing a fruit syrup. It is an idea from the Middle East introduced to the west by the Crusades. Originally it was served between courses at a banquet to refresh the palate. More often it is now a dessert served in a glass with crisp biscuits to accompany. Sometimes flavours other than fruit may be made into a sorbet, for example champagne or peppermint.

SORGES, SAUCE — French sauce made from vinaigrette, spring onions, shallots, mashed soft-boiled egg yolk, parsley and diced hard-boiled egg white. It is served cold.

SORPRESA, PETTI DI POLLO — Italian boned, stuffed, deep fried chicken breasts.

SOSATI — South African mutton or lamb kebab, marinated in a mixture of curry powder, onion, chutney and vinegar before grilling.

SOT-L'Y-LAISSE — This is what the French call the parson's nose of a fowl. It translates as " a fool leaves it".

SOUBISE — A purée of onions, rice and butter, invented by Marin, chef to the Marquis de Soubise. Sauce Soubise is a béchamel sauce flavoured with onion and cream.

SOUCHET — Method of poaching fish, especially trout, in stock, onions and parsley. Sauce souchet is a white wine sauce with julienne of potatoes, carrots, leeks and celery, cooked in butter and fish stock.

SOUFFLE — There are two quite different dishes called soufflé: one is hot and the other is cold. They are made differently but both rely on whisked egg white for the characteristic light, raised effect and both are served in the traditional soufflé dish. A hot soufflé is a yolk-enriched white sauce, either sweet or savoury, into which a high proportion of whisked egg whites are folded. It is then cooked and during the cooking the mixture rises several inches above the top of the dish. It must be eaten immediately before it has the chance to collapse on cooling. A cold soufflé, however, is uncooked. It is made like a mousse and can be sweet or savoury. The sole difference between a cold soufflé and a mousse is that a cold soufflé is served in a soufflé dish slightly too small for its quantity: a collar of greaseproof paper is tied round the outside of the dish to artificially build up its height. When the soufflé is set the collar is removed and the exposed sides of the soufflé are often decorated.

SOUFFLE DISH — A round bowl with high, straight sides which have a regular grooved pattern on them. It is usually made of white china.

SOUFFLE GLACE — This is a parfait made in a soufflé dish with a collar to build up the sides.

SOUP — A general term for liquid in which other food is cooked. Soups may be thick, clear, jellied, puréed, hot or cold. Unless it is very substantial a soup is usually served before a main course, its moist heat stimulating the salivary glands and the flow of gastric juices. Fruit soups can be served before or after a main course. Where hors d'oeuvres and soup are served at the same meal the hors d'oeuvres come first.

SOURDOUGH — American bread dating from pioneer days but now associated with San Francisco. For early settlers, fresh yeast was unobtainable and often replaced by a homemade starter made by leaving a mixture of flour and milk to ferment. A quantity of the starter was always saved for the next batch of bread and pioneers even slept with it when necessary to protect it from the cold. It is a round white loaf with an open texture and distinctive tangy flavour.

SOURED CREAM — Single cream (minimum fat content 18%) to which a special culture is added for a pleasantly sharp taste.

SOUSE — To pickle in vinegar or brine. This is a popular method of preparing fish, especially mackerel and herring. Souse is also the name of a spicy caribbean stew made with pig's trotters, ears, snouts and tongues.

SOUVAROV — A la Souvarov describes a method of cooking poultry and game birds in a sealed casserole with foie gras and truffles, and just enough stock to moisten. A souvarov is a petit four consisting of rounds of pastry sandwiched with apricot jam.

SOUVLAKIA — Greek kebab of cubes of lamb marinated in oil and lemon juice. Herbs are often used for flavouring, and chunks of onion and green pepper may be added between the pieces of meat.

SOY SAUCE — Condiment made from soya bean extract and caramel which is important in Chinese cooking. It has a very salty flavour.

SPACERS — Device used for ensuring that pastry rolled out is of a uniform thickness. Spacers are a pair of square sectioned rods which are placed at right angles to the rolling pin just below each end. The pastry goes between the two rods and the rolling pin is kept at a constant level by the spacers.

SPAGHETTI — Italian pasta made from durum wheat and eggs in long, thin strings.

SPANISH OMELETTE — More solid than a French omelette and served flat on the plate, this egg dish from Spain contains cubes of potato fried in olive oil and garlic. Onion, peppers and tomato are optional extras.

SPANOKOPITA — Greek phyllo pastry pie filled with a spinach and feta cheese mixture. It is usually prepared in a large tray and cut into squares, triangles or diamonds to serve.

SPARE RIB — There are two cuts of pork known as spare rib. There is an English cut comprising the first four ribs which may be sold as a joint or cut into chops. However the American cut of ribs nearest the loin (side ribs) is more popular both sides of the Atlantic nowadays. It may be sold in one piece or cut into ribs, and is always marinated before barbecuing. There is little meat on these ribs and it has to be chewed directly off the bone. Fingerbowls replace the knives and forks.

SPATCHCOCK — Poultry or game bird which has been split down the back and spread flat before grilling. The name means "with dispatch" ie. cooked in a hurry.

SPATULA — A blunt edged knife used for lifting, turning, cutting in, folding and spreading food. It may be made of wood, rubber, plastic or metal depending on its intended use.

SPATZLE — Small dumplings made of flour, eggs and milk or cream. The dough is forced through a special press with perforations, simmered until cooked, then tossed in butter and served with meat or soup. They are from Germany.

SPECULAAS — Dutch biscuits traditionally made in a windmill shape. They are flavoured with almonds, lemon, cinnamon, nutmeg, ginger and cardamom.

SPECK — Also known as spek depending on which Northern European country you are in. It is fat bacon with very little lean used for adding flavour to dishes.

SPEZZATINO — Italian veal stew with tomatoes, red peppers and wine.

SPICE — An aromatic substance used to flavour food. Spices have been used from the very beginning of cookery and medicine. The spice trade was vital to world economy in biblical times and was an important factor in the exploration of the world. More often than not spices were used to disguise the flavour of food that was not as fresh as it might be. Hot spices (like chili) may still be used for this purpose in some parts of the world.

SPITCHCOCK — An eel split down the back and opened out before grilling.

SPLIT TIN — Long tin-baked loaf giving a large number of slices. It is slashed along the centre of the top before baking to give a crusty top.

SPOLETINA — Spaghetti sauce from Spoleto in Italy. It is made from white truffles, anchovies, garlic, olive oil and tomato purée.

SPONGE — A very light cake made with eggs, sugar and flour – and no fat. The eggs and sugar are whisked together until frothy, then the flour is carefully folded in. Because it contains no fat it does not keep well and is best eaten on the day it is made.

SPOOM — Similar to a sherbet but with a higher density of sugar.

SPOONBREAD — A savoury pudding made of cornmeal, eggs and milk from the USA. The ingredients are the same as for cornbread, but the proportions are different and spoonbread has to be spooned out of the dish it is baked in, hence the name. It is eaten straight from the oven with lots of butter. It has a moist texture and can be flavoured with crackling, ham, bacon or cheese. An alternative theory as to its name is that it derives from the American Indian word suppawn, meaning porridge.

SPOTTED DICK — Traditional British pudding. Suet pastry is rolled out, sprinkled with currants, rolled up again, wrapped in a cloth and steamed.

SPRING CHICKEN — A chicken which is slightly older than a poussin.

SPRINGFORM MOULD — A cake tin with hinged sides held together with a clamp which is opened to release the cake. Thus a delicate mixture can be unmoulded without being inverted.

SPRING ROLL — Also known as pancake roll or egg roll. Chinese stuffed savoury pancakes which is deep fried and served hot. Fillings vary but invariably contain beanshoots. It is traditionally served at the Chinese New Year which is roughly at the start of spring.

SPUMONE — Italian frozen mousse.

SPUN EGGS — Egg strained through muslin over boiling consommé. Threads of egg are made by moving the muslin backwards and forwards. The threads are drained and used to garnish soup.

SPUN SUGAR — Sugar and water are boiled to the crack stage, then threads of the sugar syrup are twisted over a rolling pin. The syrup threads harden and can be used to decorate cakes and desserts. Spun sugar has to be eaten within an hour of making as it starts to crystallize as it absorbs moisture from the air.

SQUAB — American term for a young (four to five weeks old) pigeon.

SQUAB PIE — Farmhouse dish from Devon, made to imitate pigeon pie. The filling contains no pigeons, but lamb, apple and onion instead. It is eaten hot with clotted cream.

STARCH — A form of carbohydrate made of units of glucose. Starch swells when heated and is used as a thickening agent in cooking. Foods containing starch (cereals, rice, potatoes) need to be cooked to open the starch cells otherwise they are indigestible.

STARGAZY PIE — Cornish pie of pilchards or herrings. The heads of the fish are left on and stick out of the middle of the pastry lid, their dead eyes gazing at the stars, hence the name.

STEAK — Cut from a lean, meaty part of an animal. Also a thick slice of a dense flesh fish.

STEAM — To cook by moist heat. This is a slow method of cooking as the food does not come into direct contact with boiling water, only its steam. Instead of using a steamer, food can also be steamed between two plates over a pan of boiling water. Steamed vegetables lose less of their vitamins than if boiled. Steamed food is easily digested and often used in cooking for invalids.

STEAMER — A container with a perforated base which fits on top of a saucepan. The saucepan contains boiling water and the food to be cooked is placed in the top container. Steam passes through the holes to cook the food.

STEEP — To soak food in an aromatic liquid for a long time. Also to soak food in cold water to remove salt.

STEW — To slowly cook food in liquid which, at the end of cooking, forms part of the dish. It is useful for tough but flavoursome cuts of meat and poultry. Stewing is done in a covered pan either in the oven or on top of the stove. A stew is the dish which is prepared by this method.

STICK — American term of a 4oz (125g) quantity of butter.

STIFADO — Greek stew made from beef or hare with tiny onions, currants, vinegar, pickling spices and tomato.

STIR FRY — A Chinese cooking technique similar to sautéing except that it needs a higher temperature and very little oil. Constant vigorous stirring is essential for even cooking while retaining the individual textures of the foods: it is normal to cook several different ingredients at once. Meat, fish or vegetables can be stir fried, but the pieces of food must be small as the cooking time is rapid – five minutes at the most. The ideal pan for stir frying is a wok.

201

St

STOCK — Liquid obtained by simmering meat or fish bones and trimmings or vegetables in water with herbs and seasoning. When all the flavour has been extracted the liquid is strained and reduced to concentrate the flavour. Good stock is vital in the preparation of soups and sauces. White stock comes from white meat. For brown stock the bones are browned in fat before water is added. Stock is not a dish in itself, but a basic ingredient to many others.

STOCK SYRUP — Heavy syrup used as a base for water ices etc. 1lb (500g) to ½pt (¼l) water boiled at 220°F(104°C) for one minute makes 1pt (½l).

STOLLEN — German fruit bread flavoured with cinnamon, mace and cardamom, which is traditional at Christmas. It may also contain marzipan and be iced with glacé icing.

STONEGROUND — Describes flour which is ground in the traditional way between two stones. It is unrefined and therefore contains all the wheatgerm and bran.

STOVIES — Potatoes and onions cooked in beef dripping and water until mushy.

STRACCIATELLA — A clear soup from Rome, made by stirring a mixture of beaten egg, semolina and Parmesan cheese into boiling chicken stock. The mixture breaks up into threads and is cooked by the soup itself.

STRACOTTO — Italian beef stew with sausage, vegetables and white wine.

STRAIN — To separate liquid from solid by passing through a sieve or muslin.

STRAINER — A sieve of liquids only. It is usually made of stainless steel and conical in shape.

STRASBOURGEOISE, A LA — Name given to a consommé flavoured with juniper, garnished with red cabbage and Strasbourg sausage (lightly smoked pork sausage). Also a garnish for poultry of sauerkraut, slices of salt pork and foie gras.

STRATA — Savoury bread pudding made in a flan dish. It provides a base for a variety of fillings and toppings and is served hot in slices. Though Italian in origin it is popular in the USA.

STRAW POTATOES — Potato cut into the finest possible strips, three inches (eight cm) long and deep fried.

STREAKY — Bacon rashers cut from the belly. It has alternating streaks of fat and lean. Prime streaky is from the front and is leaner.

STREUSEL — German crumb topping for cakes and flans, made with flour, butter and sugar.

STROGANOFF — Famous Russian dish of thin strips of beef fillet in a sauce of mushrooms, onions and sour cream, which is always served with rice. It is named after Count Stroganoff whose chef discovered when stationed in Siberia that his beef was frozen so hard that it could only be cut into strips. There is also a Russian dish of herring baked in layers with potato, onion and sour cream known as Stroganoff.

STRONG FLOUR — Type of flour used in bread making for its high gluten-forming protein, which reacts with yeast to form a well-risen dough.

STRUDEL — Classic Austrian pastry made of a special dough of flour, oil and egg, rolled out to a paper thin rectangle and filled with fruit, usually spiced apples and sultanas. Other fillings include cream cheese or a vegetable mixture. The strudel is rolled up, twisted into a horseshoe shape and baked.

STUFATO DI MANZO — A rich beef pot roast from Italy.

STUFFING — A preparation used to stuff an item of food to give flavour, correct fattiness or dryness, or to eke out a small joint of meat. It may be made of almost any ingredients, the most common being sausagemeat, minced meat, breadcrumbs, rice, vegetables and fruit. Sometimes the stuffing is more important than the item being stuffed, as is the case with stuffed vegetables.

SUCCES, LE — Cake of almond flavoured meringue layers filled with iced butter cream.

SUCCOTASH — American dish of lima beans and corn kernels in cream which dates from pioneer days. Indians showed settlers how to plant corn and lima beans in rows together so that the cornstalks served as poles for the beans. They also introduced the settlers to the dish which they called misickquatash and which was flavoured with bear fat in place of cream.

SUCRE COULE — French for poured sugar. A mixture of sugar, glucose, water and food colouring is boiled then poured in a continuous stream into a cut out template and left to cool. It is used in pâtisserie for models and displays at banquets.

SUCREE, PATE — Sweet short pastry used mainly for fruit tarts which have been baked blind before filling, as it is crisper and less fragile than other short pastries. It holds its shape well and does not go soggy. It is made with flour, butter, sugar and eggs.

SUCRE FILE — This is a form of spun sugar, also known as angel's hair. It is spun into fine threads using two forks.

SUCRE ROCHER — A decorative sugar used by pâtissiers. It has a rocky appearance and unlike other sugar decorations it keeps well.

SUCRE SOUFFLE — Blown sugar in French. It is used by pâtissiers as a decoration. The sugar is blown up like a balloon and can be shaped and moulded. Sometimes it is painted with food colouring.

SUCRE TIRE — French for pulled sugar. For this decorative sugar, the sugar is pulled like toffee and moulded into shapes.

SUCROSE — Double sugar (half glucose and half fructose) found in cane or beet sugar, root vegetables and fruit.

SUEDOISE — A sweet fruit purée set with gelatine in a mould. Sauce suédoise is apple purée mixed with mayonnaise, horseradish and mustard, and is served with cold goose or pork.

SUET CRUST PASTRY — Spongey textured pastry which is used for puddings rather than pies and is often steamed instead of baked. Suet and self-raising flour in proportions of two thirds fat to flour are used. Sometimes breadcrumbs replace some of the flour.

SUFFOLK HAM — Ham which is cured with honey and spices, smoked and left to develop a blue mould. It has a sweet, full flavour.

SUGAR PIE — American open tart with a rich filling of cooked down double cream, butter, sugar and cinnamon.

SUIMONO — Traditional Japanese clear meat or fish stock garnished with cooked vegetables.

SUKIYAKI — Japanese dish of meat and many vegetables cooked in one pan at the table. The name means roasted on a plough.

SULTANE, A LA — This name indicates that pistachio nuts are in the dish in question.

SUMMER PUDDING — British dessert made with raspberries, redcurrants (and sometimes other berries or currants) and sliced white bread. It is assembled the day before eating and a weight is put on top of the bowl so that the fruit juices thoroughly impregnate the slices of bread, staining it pink and ensuring that the pudding does not collapse when it is turned out to serve.

SUNDAE — Composite dessert based on ice cream. Other ingredients may include fruit, fruit syrup, chocolate or butterscotch sauce, nuts and whipped cream. It is served in a tall glass with a long spoon. It was invented when the state of Massachusetts forbade the sale of soft drinks such as ice cream sodas on Sundays, so by leaving out the soda water the sundae was legal.

SUNNY SIDE UP — American way of describing fried eggs served yolk side up.

SUPPLI — Italian rice croquettes. If they are flavoured with cheese they are known as suppli al telefono as the melted cheese resembles telephone wires. Ham or sausage may also be used to flavour them.

SUR LE PLAT, OEUFS — Two oven fried eggs served in the fireproof dish in which they were cooked. The dish has handles on each side.

SURPRISE, EN — Indicates a surprise to be had on eating, usually an item of food filled with a different item of food eg. oranges en surprise are oranges hollowed out and filled with glacé fruit and liqueur in the orange flesh before topping with meringue cuite.

SUSHI — Japanese rice paste rolled around a filling and served with pickles as a snack.

SUSHI-MESHI — Japanese dish of vinegared rice with small pieces of fish, vegetables and seaweed arranged on it.

SUSSEX POND PUDDING — Steamed suet pudding with a whole lemon in a mixture of butter and sugar inside.

SUSSEX SAUCE — Sauce for fish of egg and cream flavoured with anchovies, mustard, cloves and mace.

SUZETTE, CREPES — Celebrated sweet pancakes which are flambéed at the table. Tangerine juice and curacao is added to the crêpe batter, then tangerine butter is spread in the cooked crêpe, which is then folded in four. It is thought to have been created by Escoffier and named after a courtesan of the day.

SWEAT — To tenderize vegetables in fat without browning. This is done in a covered pan, over a low heat.

SWEET AND SOUR — Chinese sauce of suagr, vinegar and soy sauce which goes well with fatty meat and fried food.

SWEETBREADS — Thymus glands of calves or lambs. They are soft and white with a mild flavour.

SWISS ROLL — Also known as jelly roll. A cake made with a sponge or genoese mixture, baked in a shallow tin, then spread with jam and rolled up.

SWISS STEAK — Thick cut of round steak coated with flour then pounded to tenderize it before braising.

SYLLABUB — Traditional English dessert made by whisking cream and wine, dating back to Elizabethan times. Originally it was a bubbly drink (a bub) of still wine (sill or sille) mixed with frothing cream.

SYLTE — Pickled belly of pork rolled around crushed peppercorns and mustard seed. It is served in thin slices and comes from Scandinavia.

SYLVIE — Name given to a dish of veal or pork marinated in wine then stuffed with ham and cheese before roasting.

SYMPHONIE D'OEUFS — Omelette filled with chopped hard-boiled eggs and whole poached eggs.

SYRUP — Solution of sugar and liquid, boiled to a sticky consistency.

TABASCO — Hot chilli sauce said to be Mexican in origin.

TABBOULEH — Syrian salad of cracked wheat with onion, tomato, lemon and mint.

TABIL — Tunisian paste of garlic, red peppers, caraway seed and coriander leaves, used as a relish.

TABLE D'HOTE — French for the host's table. It means a set meal for a fixed price: this is less expensive than à la carte as the dishes are not cooked to order.

TABLER — French term meaning to work a chocolate coating on a marble slab with a palette knife so that it cools but does not harden, prior to spreading it on a cake.

TACOS — Mexican snack. It is a crisply fried, folded tortilla with a spicy meat filling.

TAFELSPITZ — Viennese dish of boiled beef, usually topside, with boiled potatoes, root vegetables and grated horseradish.

TAFFY — Confection made with sugar, vinegar and water, which is boiled at a very high temperature, then turned onto a cold marble slab and pulled until thick. It is twisted into a rope shape and cut into pieces.

TAGINE — Moroccan stew, often of lamb, with fresh and dried fruit, beans or chick peas and honey. It is cooked over an open fire or a bed of charcoal in a special pot, also called a tagine. This is a wide earthenware dish with deep sides and a lid like an inverted funnel.

TAGLIATELLE — Italian pasta in the form of very narrow (⅛th inch, 2mm) wide noodles.

TAGLIERINI — Italian name for pasta dough.

TAGLIOLINI — Very thin noodles usually found in soup.

TAHINI — A Middle Eastern paste made from sesame seeds. It has a nut like flavour and is used in the making of hummous.

TALLEYRAND — The early nineteenth century French statesman had three dishes named after him. A chicken velouté sauce with stock, Madeira and cream added, garnished with truffles, diced pickled tongue and a mirepoix of vegetables. A garnish for meat and poultry of elbow macaroni bound with butter and Parmesan, mixed with foie gras, julienne of truffle and sauce perigordine. Also a chicken consommé with sherry, garnished with truffles.

TALMOUSE — A cheese tartlet, triangular in shape, served as an appetizer.

TAMALE — Mexican stuffed pastry made with corn dough and steamed inside a corn husk (which is not eaten).

TAMALE PIE — American indian dish consisting of layers of cornmeal, minced beef, onions and tomatoes baked in the oven.

TAMARI — Soy sauce made only from fermented soya beans and salt. It has a rich, full flavour.

TAMBOUR — A fine sugar sieve. Also a small dessert biscuit.

TAMIS DE CRIN — Hair sieve on a wooden frame.

TAMMY — To pass a sauce or cream soup through a cloth. The process binds the fat and flour particles together giving the sauce a glossy finish. A tammy cloth is the name given to a thick cloth used for straining liquids.

TANDOORI — Indian method of preparing meat and poultry by marinating it in spices then roasting it in tandur – a primitive brick oven.

TANSY — The name given to any cake, batter or pudding flavoured with the leaves of the plant tansy. This was a favourite herb in the seventeenth and eighteenth centuries.

TANT POUR TANT — French expression used in pâtisserie to describe a basic mixture of equal quantities of icing sugar and ground almonds.

TAPENADE — A paste of black olives, anchovies, capers and oil from the Provence region of France. It is used as a spread for bread and also may be spread on meat halfway through the cooking to add a distinctive flavour.

TARAMASALATA — Greek paste of fish roe (originally salted grey mullet –tarama– but more often smoked cod's roe) with olive oil, garlic, breadcrumbs and lemon juice. It is served as an appetizer with pitta bread.

TARATOR — Turkish sauce, often served with cold fish or vegetables. It is a creamy paste made with breadcrumbs, nuts (almonds, pine nuts, walnuts or hazelnuts), oil, lemon juice or vinegar and garlic. It is served cold. It is also the name of a Bulgarian soup of cucumber, yogurt, walnuts, dill and garlic, which is served chilled.

TARHONYA — Pasta in the form of tiny pellets which is fried then boiled.

TART — A flat open pastry with fruit or other mixture on top. Tarts can also be made in individual sizes. In the US it only means an individual sized pastry with no top crust. The word comes to us from the French tarte which came from the Italian torte, which in turn came from the Latin torquere meaning to twist or torture: the crust was twisted on the original tarts. Tart has another use as an adjective; it means sharp in taste when applied to sweet things.

TARTAR, CREAM OF — Potassium tartarate, a mildly acidic compound which reacts with bicarbonate of soda (sodium bicarbonate) to lift a cake mixture.

TARTARE — Tartare sauce is mayonnaise with hard-boiled egg, capers, anchovies, pickles, chives and parsley. It is served with fish. Steak tartare is top quality beef steak minced and served raw in the centre of a dish; an egg yolk is placed on top and small piles of chopped gherkins, capers, shallots and hard-boiled egg white are arranged around the meat. The diner then mixes in the egg yolk with the other ingredients, adding seasoning, oil and vinegar to taste before sprinkling the dish with chopped hard-boiled egg yolk and parsley and eating it with brown bread and butter.

TARTE TATIN — French upside down apple flan, supposedly created by accident in a restaurant belonging to two sisters whose name was Tatin, when the waitress dropped it.

TASSY — An American name for an individual size tart.

TAVA — Indian griddle pan with wooden handle for cooking bread.

T BONE — A steak or cut of beef sliced across the sirloin between the vertebrae of the backbone.

TEMPURA — Japanese speciality consisting of at least six items of food dipped in batter and quickly fried. It is served with chopped raw vegetables and sauces for dunking.

TENDERIZE — To make food tender by one of the following methods: beating meat to break up the fibres; by hanging game; cooking slowly; marinating.

TENDERLOIN — Lean, tender cut of pork from the inside of the loin bone.

TEPPAN YAKI — Japanese style of cooking where wafer-thin slices of food are cooked on a hot plate at a very high temperature.

TERIYAKI — Japanese method of cooking using a simple soy sauce and rice wine marinade before grilling over charcoal.

TERRINE — A substantial pâté served from, and named after, the earthenware casserole in which it is cooked. The casserole can be rectangular or oval and has a lid. After cooking it is weighted down to compress the pâté and make it easier to slice.

TETRAZZINI — Way of cooking pieces of turkey (or it could also be chicken, veal or lobster) in a velouté sauce flavoured with wine, layered with spaghetti and mushrooms, then scattered with almonds and Parmesan cheese and baked au gratin. It was named after the Italian opera singer Luisa Tetrazzini, but is American not Italian.

Th

THALI — Indian presentation of food: small metal bowls containing different food are served on a round metal tray, one tray per person.

THERMIDOR, LOBSTER — Lobster in a sauce of shallots, tarragon, chervil, wine, butter, cream, egg yolk and mustard. The tail meat of the cooked lobster is mixed with some of the sauce and then returned to the tail sections, the remaining sauce is spooned over the whole lobster, grated cheese is sprinkled over and the lobster is then browned in the oven. It is named after a controversial play *Thermidor* by Victorien Sandov which opened and closed on the same day in 1894. It was created at Chez Marie in Paris.

THIAMINE — Vitamin B1. Good sources are wheatgerm, nuts, oatmeal, liver and kidneys. It is important for the nervous system.

THICKENING — There are six ways of thickening liquids: by reduction, by adding starch in the form of beurre manié, cornflour or arrowroot, by adding egg yolk, by adding blood, by adding nuts in the form of peanut butter, coconut cream etc, by adding a setting substance such as gelatine.

THONNE — A method of preparing veal by marinating it in oil. lemon juice, bayleaf and spices, then cooking it with tuna.

THOUSAND ISLAND DRESSING — A cold sauce for salads and seafood made with mayonnaise, tomato purée, chopped capers, celery, hard-boiled egg, mustard, cayenne and Worcestershire sauce.

THUNDER AND LIGHTNING — A Cornish dish of black treacle and clotted cream, often served on splits or scones.

TIAN — Provencal earthenware deep dish with two handles for gratin dishes. A vegetable mixture cooked in a tian is also called a tian.

TIANG-ZU — Szechuan method of food preparation using cold sauce of grated root ginger, soy sauce, vinegar and sesame seed oil.

TIAO-MA — Szechuan method of food preparation, using a sauce of peppercorns, tahini, soy sauce, ginger, sugar and shallot.

TIKKA — Pakistani kebab of chicken or lamb, marinated in yogurt, ginger, coriander, and chillies and grilled over charcoal.

TIMBALE — A thimble-shaped mould. The name comes from an Arabic word thabal meaning drum – a reference to the shape. Also the food cooked in such a mould, which is a savoury mixture and often in a pie crust.

TIMBALLO — Italian general term for pasta baked in cheese sauce.

TIPSY CAKE — An old name for a trifle.

TIRAMISU — Popular Italian dessert of sponge fingers soaked in coffee liqueur, topped with mascarpone cheese, egg yolks and cream. The name means pick-me-up.

TIRE-BOUCHON — A small, oval, crusty, white roll with a slash on top. The name means corkscrew in French.

TIROPITA — Also known as Tyropitta. It is a Greek cheese and egg pie made with phyllo pastry and cut into squares, triangles or diamonds to serve.

TISANE — Herb or flower infusion, which may be mildly soothing, stimulating or restorative according to its ingredients.

TOAD IN THE HOLE — A British dish of meat, especially pork sausages in a savoury batter pudding. The sausages poke out of the pudding like toads in holes.

TOAST — A slice of bread browned on both sides either under a grill, in front of a fire or in an electric toaster.

TOCINO — Spanish cured pork fat used as flavouring.

TOFFEE — British confection made by boiling sugar, water and butter then leaving it to harden on cooling. Its origins go back a long way and there are many types of toffee from hard treacle toffee to the soft caramel, the result being determined by the temperature reached during boiling and the type of sugar used.

TOFFEE APPLE — A toffee apple as sold at an English seaside resort is an apple on a stick which has been dipped in red-coloured toffee. There is also a Chinese dessert called Toffee Apples or Apples Pulling Golden Threads. Chunks of apple are dipped in batter, deep fried twice, then dipped in caramel and sprinkled with sesame seeds, finally they are plunged into a bowl of cold water to set the caramel. Bananas are given the same treatment.

TOFU — Soya bean curd which is sold in blocks and cut into cubes. It has a bland flavour and is an important source of protein in oriental and vegetarian diets.

TOKANY — Hungarian dish of any meat or combination of meats cut into slices and cooked with the minimum of liquid.

TOLL HOUSE COOKIE — An another name for a chocolate chip cookie. Since 1709 a toll house stood midway between Boston and New Bedford. In 1930 Ruth Wakefield and her husband converted the toll house into an inn and she invented the cookie. However this story is disputed and other Toll Houses claim the honour. Walden Ridge Toll House near Chattanooga also had a cookie named after it but it is quite different, being a rolled, refrigerated and cut sugar cookie with no chocolate chips.

TOM TROT — Also known as Plot Toffee. Yorkshire dark treacle toffee traditional on Bonfire Night.

TOM YAM KUNG — Hot sour soup with prawns from Thailand.

TONGUE PRESS — A round metal pan with a lid which can be screwed down to any level inside the pan. The whole cooked tongue is curled inside the pan while still warm, the lid is screwed down as tightly as possible and the tongue is chilled until firm, then unmoulded in a neat round.

TONNATO, VITELLO — Italian dish of cold veal in tunny fish sauce. Chicken is sometimes prepared in this way too.

TONNELLINI — Matchstick-like noodles from Italy.

TOP RUMP — Cut of beef from the lower belly of the animal which is suitable for stewing.

TOPSIDE — Cut of beef from the hind quarters of the carcass, suitable for braising or pot roasting. It is fleshy with little bone. It is also known as buttock or round of beef.

TORRIJAS — Spanish pudding of bread which has been soaked in milk, dipped in beaten egg and fried, then baked with honey and water.

TORTE — German term of cake.

TORTELLINI — Stuffed pasta discs folded so that both ends meet, from Bologna in Italy.

TORTILLA — Thin, flat pancake made with cornflour, from Mexico.

TORTILLADORA — A tortilla press. Two metal discs, one with a handle, are hinged together and the dough is pressed between the discs until paperthin.

TORTONI — Iced pudding made with cream, macaroons, almonds, sugar and egg white. It is made in a loaf tin and served in slices. It is named after an Italian who had a famous café in eighteenth century Paris, where ice cream was the speciality.

TORTUE — French for turtle. Sauce tortue is a demi-glace sauce with white wine, tomato sauce, Madeira and herbs. It is served with offal, particularly calf's head (en tortue). Herbes à tortue is a commercially prepared mixture of basil, thyme, bay leaves and marjoram.

TOSCANA, ALLA — Name for rice served with minced beef, veal kidney and liver, tomato and cheese. It is Italian and means Tuscan style.

TOSCANE, A LA — This is French for Tuscan style and refers to a garnish for escalopes of veal, chicken breasts or sweetbreads of macaroni, foie gras purée and diced truffles.

TOSS — To turn over food in the pan with a quick, jerky movement. It refers especially to tossing, ie. inverting, pancakes.

TOSTADAS — Crisply fried cornmeal pancake from Mexico. It is served with a spicy sauce.

TOULON, A LA — Describes fish stuffed with whiting forcemeat poached with mussels and served with a rich fish velouté sauce.

TOULOUSAINE, A LA — Three different dishes carry this name which means Toulouse style. A ragoût bound with a white sauce and used either as a pie filling or as an accompaniment to poultry. Potatoes browned in goose fat and olive oil, then cooked in a casserole with parsley, garlic, flour and water. Also a classic garnish for chicken, sweetbreads and vol au vent of chicken quennelles, diced sweetbread, mushroom caps, cock's combs, and truffle slices in sauce allemande flavoured with mushroom.

TOUPIN — Earthenware bean pot from the Béarnaise district of France. It has a bulbous base narrowing to a cylindrical neck, a close fitting lid, one straight handle (for holding while stirring the contents) and two curved handles (for lifting). The shape of the pot means very little moisture is lost by evaporation. Besides bean dishes, soups and stews may be cooked in it.

TOURANGELLE — This is the name of a garnish for tournedos, consisting of prunes stuffed with foie gras and a Madeira sauce with pieces of truffle in it. Salade Tourangelle is several different vegetables, raw and cooked, served in separate piles on the same plate. It is also the name of a chicken, turnip, pea, leak and carrot soup.

TOURER — French pâtisserie term meaning to fold the dough in two or three after rolling it out.

TOURIN, LE — Onion cream soup from the South of France.

To

TOURNEDOS — Small, thick, round, slice cut from the heart of a fillet of beef.

TOURNELLES, DES — A garnish for noisettes of onion purée, which is grilled to glaze and served with a vermouth and sherry sauce.

TOURTE — A French term meaning a round tart. The word comes from the Latin tortus meaning round.

TOURTEAU — A cheesecake in a pastry case from South West France. The filling rises so much during baking that it is almost spherical.

TOURTIERE — The dish in which a tourte is cooked. It has higher sides than a flan dish. A tourtière is also a French Canadian deep pie with a filling of minced pork and beef, onions, breadcrumbs and garlic.

TRANCHE — French term meaning a thick slice.

TRASTEVERINA, ALLA — A sauce of tomato, tuna and anchovy mixed with another sauce of mushrooms and served with bavette or other pasta. It comes from Rome.

TRAVAILLER — French word, literally meaning to work, in cooking terms means to beat with a wooden spoon or spatula.

TREFAH — Not kosher ie. food not permitted to orthodox Jews.

TREMPETTE — A slice of bread which has been dunked in a liquid such as coffee or soup.

TRENETTE — Very thin noodles from Genoa in Italy.

TRIANON, SAUCE — Hollandaise sauce to which sherry has been added. The name refers to Queen Marie Antoinette's smaller 'family' palace at Versailles.

TRIFLE — Also known as Tipsy Cake and Whim Wham. It is a layered, cold dessert of sherry-soaked sponge, fresh fruit, egg custard and whipped cream, decorated with nuts and glacé fruit. Flavourings vary. It is usually made in a large glass dish so that all the layers can be seen.

TRIPE — The stomach of an ox.

TRIPIERE — A special pot for cooking tripe. It is shaped like a car tyre with a small lid in the hub and two handles.

TRIVET — A metal ring or an ornamental plate on legs used underneath cooking pots on a range. It slows the cooking by distancing the bottom of the pot from the flame. It can also be used to improvize a steamer: a trivet placed in a large pan of boiling water can hold a basin with food in it to be steamed.

TROCADERO, BOMBE — Frozen dessert in a spherical shape. Outside is orange sorbet with diced orange peel in it. Inside is layers of whipped cream and Genoese sponge soaked in curacao, with diced orange peel.

TROIS FRERES — Sponge cake made of rice flour, sugar, butter and eggs, flavoured with maraschino, set on a pastry base, soaked in apricot syrup and sprinkled with angelica and chopped almonds. It is made in a special tin like a shallow, wide kugelhopf tin. It was invented in the nineteenth century by the three Julien brothers (the name means three brothers in French).

TRONCON — French word meaning a thick fish steak on the bone. Also a chunk of food which is longer than it is wide.

TROU NORMANDE — Conical lemon sorbet. Inside is a hole filled with Calvados. The name means Norman hole in French. Normandy is famous for its Calvados.

TROUVILLAISE — A garnish for fish of shrimp, poached mussels, fluted mushrooms and shrimp sauce.

TRUFFADE, LA — A cheese, bacon and potato cake, made in a frying pan, from the Auvergne region in France.

TRUFFLE — Underground fungus, either white or black, greatly esteemed for its flavour. Normally only used as a garnish due to its high cost: truffles cannot be cultivated and so the demand far exceeds the supply. There is also a rich chocolate confection named Truffle. It is a dense mixture of chocolate, cake crumbs, butter and sugar, often flavoured with rum, rolled into a ball and covered in either cocoa powder or chocolate vermicelli.

TRUSS — To secure the legs and wings of poultry and game birds with needle and string. This is done to keep the bird's shape during cooking.

TRY OUT — American expression meaning to render down, as in fat.

TSARINE — A fish garnish of olives of cucumber cooked in butter, fluted mushrooms and Mornay sauce.

TSUKEMONO — Japanese pickled vegetables.

TSUKEYAKI — Japanese cooking method which involves marinating the food in a spicy sauce, grilling it and basting it frequently.

TTORO — Basque soup of shellfish, fish, peppers, tomatoes, chili, onions and garlic.

TUBE PAN — American for a ring mould or ring shaped cake tin.

TUILES — French for tiles. Crisp biscuits which are rolled around a rolling pin while still warm, giving them a resemblance to curved tiles.

TUN — Chinese cooking term which means the food in question has been steamed slowly in the Chinese equivalent of a double boiler.

TURBIGO — A garnish for kidneys of chipolatas and mushrooms, with a white wine and tomato sauce.

TURBOTIERE — Square fish kettle with a removable grid. It is used for poaching large, flat fish such as turbot.

TUREEN — Large deep covered dish from which soup is served at the table. Often it has two handles and stands on a raised base or has four legs.

TURKISH DELIGHT — Also known as Rahat Lokum. Turkish confection made of sugar, water and cornflour, flavoured with rosewater and often pistachio nuts. It has a soft, chewy consistency and is sold in cubes dusted with icing sugar.

TURK'S HEAD PAN — American name for a round cake tin with straight or spiral fluting on the sides which leave a distinctive pattern on the cake cooked in it.

TURNOVER — Any pastry, sweet or savoury, made from a circle of pastry folded over a filling to form a semi-circle.

TURRON — Spanish confection made with whole nuts (usually almonds). It is similar to nougat.

TUTTI FRUTTI — All fruits in Italian. Originally it was a selection of fruit arranged in layers and preserved in brandy, which was used as a sweet sauce. All too often nowadays it indicates the presence of candied peel and glacé cherries finely chopped.

T.V.P. — In full this is Textured Vegetable Protein. It is made from soya beans and is intended to replace meat in dishes for vegetarians or for reasons of economy. It is available as 'mince' or 'stewing steak'.

TWICE-COOKED PORK — Szechwan dish in which a piece of belly pork is simmered to partially cook, cooled and then cut into very thin strips and stir-fried with leeks and garlic in a sauce of hot soy bean paste, soy sauce, rice wine and sugar.

TWIST — Another name for a bloomer loaf of bread.

TYROLIAN — Choux pastry balls covered in chopped almonds and filled with an almond, sugar and egg yolk mixture.

TYROLIENNE, A LA — A garnish for grilled meat and poultry of quartered tomatoes cooked in butter and fried onion rings.

TYROPITTA — See TIROPITA.

TZIMMES — Jewish slow cooked casserole of brisket sweetened with carrots, golden syrup and dried fruit, and topped with potatoes and dumplings. It is traditional for the Jewish New Year. The carrots are cut into rings to resemble coins as the Hebrew word for carrot also means more wealth: in this way the Jews wish themselves and those who eat with them a prosperous new year. The word Tzimmes is Hebrew for fuss or excitement.

U.H.T. — Ultra Heat Treated. This is a preservation method for milk and cream which has a slight effect on taste.

UITSMIJTER — Popular Dutch snack dish consisting of a slice of buttered bread covered with ham or cold roast beef and topped with two fried eggs. The name means bouncer in Dutch.

UMBLES — Also known as Humbles. These are the internal organs of a deer which were often made into a pie for the servants after a hunt – while venison was eaten upstairs. Hence the expression eating humble pie.

UMIDO, IN — Italian for moist or damp. It means stewed with vegetables and herbs.

UNGHERESE, SALAME — Italian for Hungarian salame. It is made with pork and beef and is flavoured with paprika, garlic and white wine.

UPSIDE DOWN CAKE — A cake in which fruit (often rings of pineapple) is arranged at the bottom of the cake tin, then covered with cake mixture and baked. It is turned out to serve and eaten, hot or cold, as a dessert.

URBAN-DUBOIS, A L' — Three different but related dishes were named after the nineteenth century French gourmet. Poached, boned fish put in a dish with sauce aurore, crayfish tails and truffles poured over, then a crayfish soufflé mixture on top and baked. A variant on this is to put lobster soufflé in place of crayfish souffle, and sauce normande and white quennelles in place of the sauce aurore and crayfish tails. Also scrambled eggs with lobster tails and lobster sauce.

URSULINE, A L' — Soft boiled eggs on a bed of salmon forcemeat with mushroom purée, a truffle on top, then Mornay sauce before being grilled au gratin.

UZES, SAUCE — Hollandaise sauce flavoured with anchovy essence and Madeira.

VACHERIN — Large meringue made by piping circles of meringue on top of each other. It is filled and decorated with cream and fruit. Almond paste may sometimes be used instead of meringue. It comes from Alsace and is named after a local cheese whose shape it resembles.

VALDOSTANA, ALLA — Italian name for any dish containing fontina cheese.

VALENCIENNES, A LA — Garnish for small cuts of meat or poultry of rice mixed with ham and peppers, served with tomato-flavoured gravy or sauce suprême. Also a chicken consommé with chicken quennelles and chervil.

VALLEE D'AUGE — Chicken Vallée d'Auge is sautéed chicken with a cream sauce flavoured with Calvados. The Auge valley is in Normandy and is famous for its cream, cheese (Camembert and Pont L'Eveque) and apple brandy (Calvados), so the term can mean any dish prepared with some or all of these local produce.

VALOIS — A la Valois can be a garnish for fish of soft roes, crayfish, potato balls and Valois sauce, or a garnish for meat of sliced potatoes and artichoke bottoms, with an enriched gravy. Valois sauce, which is also known as Foyot sauce, is a béarnaise flavoured with melted beef extract, which is good with boiled chicken. Valois was the family name of the French royal family during the sixteenth century.

VANDYKE — To vandyke the tail of a fish is to accentuate the line by cutting an acute V-shape into the tail, thus making two distinct points. This decorative finish is named after the seventeenth century painter, Anthony Van Dyke, who made small pointed beards fashionable. The decorative serrated edging for tomatoes and citrus fruit is also referred to as Vandyking.

VANILLA SUGAR — Sugar flavoured with vanilla. This is done by storing sugar in a closed jar with a vanilla pod.

VANNER — French term meaning to stir a sauce constantly so that no skin forms.

VARENNE, LA — Mayonnaise flavoured with duxelles.

VARIETY MEATS — American term for offal.

VEAL — The meat of a calf between four and six months old. It is pale in colour and bland in taste.

VELOUTE — A blond roux sauce. Also the basis for a rich, thickened soup.

VENEZIA — Venetian style, usually means with onions. Liver cooked in this way – Fegato alla Venezia – is cut into juliennes and sautéed with sliced onions.

VENISON SAUCE — A brown sauce flavoured with pepper, redcurrant jelly and cream. It is a sauce for venison and does not contain any venison itself despite the name.

VENITIENNE — A salad of olives, celery, diced truffles, orange segments, sieved chicken livers and green mayonnaise.

VERDE, SALSA — Italian green sauce which has many uses, made with lemon juice, olive oil, and finely chopped capers, anchovies and parsley.

VERDURETTE SAUCE — Vinaigrette with hard-boiled egg yolk, chives, parsley, chervil and tarragon.

VERMICELLI — Italian for little worms. Thin noodles often used in soup.

VERONIQUE — Name given to dishes having grapes as a garnish, the most famous being Sole Veronique.

VERT, AU — French term for food served with a green sauce.

VERTE, SAUCE — Mayonnaise flavoured with green herbs.

VERT-PRE — French for green meadow, as a cookery term it can mean several different things. A garnish for meat of watercress, matchstick potatoes and maître d'hôtel butter. Fish or poultry dishes coated with green mayonnaise. Food coloured green by the presence of watercress or parsley.

VESIGA — The marrow of sturgeon.

VICHY — Vichy is a spa town in France where carrots were often served as part of the dietary cure, so the name can just mean carrots in the dish. Carrots à la Vichy, however, means carrots braised in butter, sugar and very little water.

VICHYSSOISE — A soup of leeks, potatoes and cream which is correctly served cold, but is also very good hot. Despite being named after the French town of Vichy, it was created in America by Louis Diat of the Ritz Carlton Hotel in New York.

VICTOR HUGO SAUCE — Hollandaise sauce flavoured with meat extract, onion juice and grated horseradish. Named after the nineteenth century French writer.

VICTORIA — Queen Victoria has had many dishes named after her. A la Victoria is a garnish for fish of crawfish, truffles and Sauce Victoria. It is also a garnish for meat of tomatoes stuffed with mushroom purée and gratinéed artichokes, with port-flavoured gravy. Coupe Victoria consists of a brandy soaked macédoine of fruits, with strawberry and pistachio ice creams. Salad Victoria contains crawfish, cucumber, truffle and asparagus tips. A Victoria Sandwich is a cake made by the creaming method, cooked in two layers and sandwiched together with jam. Victoria Sauce is an espagnole sauce flavoured with cloves, oranges, cinnamon, peppercorns, port and redcurrant jelly: it is served with venison. There is also a lobster-flavoured sauce with diced truffles, which is served with fish, called Sauce Victoria.

VIDELLE — Two pieces of equipment share this name: a French pastry wheel and a tool for removing stones from fruit.

VIENNA — A long, crusty loaf to which milk is added at the kneading stage. It is shaped either into a short bâton with tapering ends or a horseshoe. It is highly glazed with a thin, crisp crust and may be covered with poppy seeds.

VIENNOISE, A LA — Garnish of chopped hard-boiled egg yolk and white (kept separate), anchovy fillets, olives, slices of peeled lemon, capers and parsley. These items are arranged around the rim of the plate. It means from Vienne, a French town on the Rhone, and has nothing to do with the Austrian capital.

VIERGE — French for virgin. It is whipped butter, flavoured with salt, pepper and lemon juice, which is served with boiled vegetables.

VILLEROI, A LA — Method of preparing food by first coating in a reduced sauce allemande flavoured with stock and mushroom or truffle fumet, then egg and breadcrumbs before frying.

VINAIGRETTE — Emulsion of oil and vinegar, seasoned with salt and pepper and used as a salad dressing. Other flavourings, such as mustard and garlic, may be added.

VINCENT SAUCE — Mayonnaise with a purée of green herbs and chopped hard-boiled egg yolk.

VINCIS GRASSI — A version of lasagne where the meat sauce is made of chicken livers, sausage and mushrooms.

VINDALOO — A very hot curry from South West India, which uses vinegar to moisten instead of the more usual coconut milk. It is traditionally made with pork.

VIROFLAY — Garnish for roast lamb of braised spinach, artichoke hearts cut into quarters and sautéed potatoes. Viroflay, near Paris, was famous for its spinach.

VITAMIN — Substances found in food which are essential for good health. Vitamin A is important for the growth of the cells of the eye, mouth and intestines: cod liver oil is the best source. Vitamin B (of which there are several subdivisions) are vital for the effective performance of muscles and nerves: meat and wholemeal bread are good sources. Vitamin C is needed on a daily basis, as it cannot be stored by the body, to form connective tissue between cells: blackcurrants, citrus fruit and green vegetables are full of it but it is destroyed by heat and soluble in water. Vitamin D is necessary for bone formation and growth: it may be obtained by sunlight on skin, also by eating oily fish.

VIVEURS — Term which refers to the presence of cayenne or paprika pepper in the dish in question.

VLADIMIR — Garnish for small cuts of meat of cucumbers cut into ovals and diced courgettes cooked in butter. Also a sauce suprême with a little demi-glace added.

VOISIN, POMMES DE TERRE — Potatoes baked in layers with grated cheese between each layer.

VOL-AU-VENT — French for puff of wind. A puff pastry case which rises two or three inches or more during baking. The uncooked centre is scooped out and the vol-au-vent is filled with a savoury mixture.

VOLIERE, EN — Way of presenting a game bird by placing the head, tail and outspread wings (all still feathered) in the appropriate position on the cooked bird.

VOLKORNBROT — German bread made with a mixture of wheat and rye.

VOLTAIRE, OEUFS EN COCOTTE — Eggs on a bed of chicken puree, covered with cream sauce and Parmesan cheese,then gratinéed. Named after the eighteenth century French writer.

VOSGES PIE — Two crust pie with a filling of pork, Madeira and cream.

WAFER — A thin, light biscuit served with cold desserts, especially ice cream. It developed from the waffle, originally being made in irons.

WAFFLE — A batter mixture cooked in a waffle iron, which is two hinged metal plates, usually rectangular, decorated in a criss-cross pattern. The waffle is very crisp and eaten piping hot. It may be sweet or savoury, filled or plain. The word comes from the German wabe, meaning honeycomb, a reference to the pattern made by the iron. Waffles have been eaten since the early Middle Ages.

WALDORF — The Waldorf Salad is an American mixture of chopped apple, celery and walnuts in mayonnaise, which was invented at the Waldorf Astoria Hotel in New York. From the same source comes Waldorf Sweetbreads, sautéed sweetbreads on artichoke bottoms, covered with sauce allemande.

WALEWSKA, A LA — Denotes a method of preparing fish, especially sole, with a lobster and truffle garnish and a Mornay sauce. It is named after Countess Marie Walewska, the Polish mistress of Napoleon Bonaparte, in honour of their son who was a minister in the French government in the 1860s.

WARKA — Moroccan pastry used for bistayla, brik etc. It is very thin and dry, similar to phyllo and strudel pastry.

WASABI — Hot green horseradish sauce used as a condiment in Japanese cuisine.

WATER BISCUIT — A plain, crisp biscuit with a flaky texture, eaten with cheese.

WATER ICE — A frozen dessert made by mixing frozen sugar syrup and fruit purée with whisked egg white then refreezing.

WATERZOI — A light casserole from Belgium. It was originally called Waterzootje, a fish stew, but it is now better known as a chicken cooked with vegetables, wine and parsley roots, which are puréed after cooking and returned to the casserole. The sauce is then thickened with egg yolks and cream as well as arrowroot.

WEENIE — Popular name for Wienerwurst.

WEISSWURSTE — German white sausage of veal and pork flavoured with nutmeg. It is light and delicate and already cooked, so it can be served cold, although it is often served fried.

WELLINGTON, BEEF — Fillet of beef spread with pâté de foie gras and mushrooms, baked in a puff pastry case. Named after the Duke of Wellington, hero of Waterloo.

WELSH RAREBIT — A mixture of grated cheese, beer and mustard is spread over bread which has been toasted on the underside. It is grilled until bubbly and eaten as a savoury snack.

WESTPHALIAN HAM — German ham smoked with juniper.

WHEATGERM — Embryo of the wheat grain which is removed by the milling process of flour making as it contains oils which go rancid in storage. It may be added later in cooked form to make wheatgerm bread.

WHEATMEAL — 85-90% extraction flour. This means that some (10-15%) of the germ has been removed by chemicals. The bread made from this flour is wheatmeal bread.

WHEY — Liquid which separates from the curd when milk curdles. It is used in cheese-making.

WHIM-WHAM — *See* TRIFLE.

WHIP — To beat air into a mixture (such as cream or egg whites) using a whisk until it is stiff and thick. A whip is a fruit purée folded into whisked egg whites, which is then baked and served immediately (as it quickly sinks).

WHIPPING CREAM — Homogenized cream with a minimum fat content of 35% It is suitable for whipping, but does not hold its shape for more than an hour or so, unlike double cream.

WHISK — Tool for whipping egg whites, cream, batter, sauces etc. There are several types. A rotary egg beater whereby a handle is turned to make two beaters revolve. A flat whisk, which is good for sauces, has a spiral wire shaped into a oval on a long handle. A balloon whisk, which is best for egg whites, has flexible wires in a long balloon shape on a handle. As a verb the term to whisk applies only to beating egg whites.

WHOLEFOOD — Any natural food with nothing added and nothing taken away.

WHOLEMEAL — 100% extraction flour and the bread made from it.

WIENER BACKHENDL — Viennese chicken, It is jointed, rolled in egg and breadcrumbs then fried until crisp.

WIENERBROD — Viennese bread. What the Danes call a Danish pastry. It is made with a yeast dough which is reminiscent of puff pastry. It is made in many different shapes (windmill, cartwheel, Tivoli), with a variety of sweet fillings (almond paste, crème pâtissière, spiced fruit) and topped with glacé icing and nuts.

WIENERSCHNITZEL — Veal escalope, coated in egg and breadcrumbs and fried in butter. Speciality of Vienna.

WIENERWURST — Viennese sausage. It is a small frankfurter most often seen in a Hot Dog.

WILTED — Cucumber is wilted by soaking in salted water or sprinkled with salt before serving. Lettuce is described as wilted when served in a hot sauce of vinegar, sugar, bacon and onion.

WINDSOR SOUP — Also known as Brown Windsor Soup. This traditional British soup is made from beef and lamb stock and is flavoured with Madeira. It was a favourite of Queen Victoria.

WINTER MELON POND — Chinese soup served in a hollowed out winter melon. The ingredients include crabmeat, duck, pork, mushrooms and bamboo shoots.

WINTERTHUR, A LA — Describes poached lobster or crayfish, stuffed with a salpicon of shrimps and crayfish, and covered with shrimp sauce.

WISHBONE — First double bone from the ribcage at the neck end of poultry.

WOK — Chinese all-purpose cooking pan with a lid, which can be used for braising, sautéeing, frying, stewing and steaming. It is shaped like a wide, deep bowl and is available in several sizes. The rounded base is designed to fit into Chinese cookers, but a separate ring base can be bought to adapt its use to gas and electric hobs. Woks with flattened bases suitable for Western cookers are also available.

WONTON — Chinese for swallowing a cloud. A wonton is a savoury dumpling, often served in soup. Wonton paste, or wonton skin as it is sometimes called, is a Chinese pasta. It is usually cut into rounds, the filling is wrapped up in it, then it is deep fried.

WOOD EAR — Large Chinese dried mushroom.

WORCESTERSHIRE SAUCE — A commerically bottled sauce of soy sauce, vinegar, molasses, chilli, anchovies, shallots, garlic, fruits and spices. It is used in small quantities to add bite to dishes. The legend of its origin is as follows: an ex-governor of Bengal asked Lea & Perrins, a Worcester grocer's shop, to make up a sauce for which he had a recipe, but he did not like the result and refused to pay for it. Years later the sauce was rediscovered in the cellar, found to be excellent and launched on a grateful public.

WURSTCHEN — Small German sausages held in bunches which are poached then grilled to serve. They contain meat from a pig's throat.

XAVIER — Two soups bear this name: a beef and Madeira consommé, garnished with strips of pancake, and a chicken velouté soup, garnished with diced chicken and royale.

XERES — This is the old name for Jerez in Spain, where sherry comes from, so this appellation applies to dishes containing sherry.

YAHNI — Popular Greek method of cooking by braising in olive oil, tomatoes and a little water. The word means stew in Turkish.

YEAST — Living organism which produces a gas while fermenting. It is this gas which lifts bread dough. Yeast is killed by extremes of temperature and therefore by cooking. Sugar is usually used as the agent to start the fermenting process. The Ancient Egyptians accidentally discovered the properties of yeast: before then all bread was unleaven.

YEMISTA — Greek stuffed, baked vegetable (pepper, aubergine, courgette, tomato, cabbage leaves or vine leaves). The stuffing is usually a meat and rice mixture. It is served with a thin tomato sauce.

YORK HAM — Thought to be the finest cooked ham, with a mild, subtle flavour and pale pink flesh. It has a dry salt cure and is smoked.

YORKSHIRE PUDDING — Savoury batter pudding, baked in a shallow baking tray and cut into squares to serve. It is traditional with roast beef, but in Yorkshire it is served before the beef rather than with it. Originally it was baked under the meat, which was on a trivet. The meat juices ran down into the batter as it cooked.

YORKSHIRE SAUCE — Espagnole sauce flavoured with orange, port, redcurrant jelly, cinnamon and cayenne, and decorated with strips of orange peel. It is served with ham and duck.

YUFKA — Turkish version of phyllo pastry.

YUNNAN STEAM POT — Round Chinese casserole with a cone shaped chimney in the centre of a tight-fitting lid. When it is placed in a pan of boiling water, steam rises through the chimney to cook the contents. The result is moist and full of flavour. The idea comes from Yunnan, a province of Western China.

YU-XIANG — Szechuan method of food preparation in which the food is stir fried or deep fried, then cooked with garlic, ginger, hot soy bean sauce and spices. The result is reddish brown in colour and spicy or sweet and sour in taste, depending on the proportions of the ingredients.

YVETTE — Name confusingly given to six quite different dishes. Poisson Yvette is poached fish in thickened stock, garnished with tomatoes which are stuffed with a purée of sole. Oeufs Yvette could be either poached eggs on corn fritters with archiduc sauce, or scrambled eggs with crayfish tails, asparagus tips and shrimp sauce. Potage Yvette is a lobster velouté soup with fish quennelles, chopped lobster and truffles. Consommé Yvette is chicken consommé flavoured with turtle herbs, garnished with chicken quenelles and spinach. Pommes Yvette is also known as Pommes Annette.

ZABAGLIONE — Also known as Zabaione and sabayon. Italian dessert made by whisking egg yolks, sugar and Marsala until thick and served immediately in a glass. It may also be served cold or used as a sauce for a hot pudding.

ZAKOUSKI — A selection of hot and cold dishes served as an appetiser or as an accompaniment to vodka.

ZAMPINO — Italian dish of stuffed leg of pork, wrapped in a cloth and simmered for several hours. The stuffing is pork sausage meat.

ZAMPONE — Italian dish of boned pig's trotter stuffed with spiced, minced pork and cooked slowly for several hours.

ZENSAI — Japanese hors d'oeuvres. They are always cold, very small and beautifully decorated.

ZEPHIR — Mousseline forcemeat of game, poultry or veal with beaten egg white. It is baked in small soufflé dishes. The name, which is a reference to the wind, may be given to any light or frothy dish in France.

ZEST — The oil from the rind or skin of any citrus fruit. It is extracted by rubbing a cube of sugar over the outside of the fruit.

ZESTER — Tool for removing the zest of citrus fruit. The blade is an inflexible strip of metal with a hole cut into it. The end of the blade is bent into a peak, which is sharpened on one side so that it will cut a shallow strip of peel when it is pulled over the surface of the fruit.

ZEWELWAI — Onion tart from Alsace.

ZIGEUNER SCHNITZEL — Escalope of veal with tomato sauce mixed with mushrooms and smoked tongue.

ZINC — Essential mineral found in oysters, herrings, wheatgerm and bran.

ZINGARA — Italian for gypsy style. Scallopine alla Zingara describes scallopine fried in breadcrumbs, Marsala, sliced ham and mushrooms. Zingara Sauce is a demi-glace sauce to which strips of ham, pickled tongue and mushrooms, truffles, tomato sauce and paprika are added. It is served with meat and poultry.

ZITE — Long tubular pasta which is cut slightly oblique.

ZOLA — Name given to a beef consommé garnished with small cheese and white truffle dumplings in honour of Emile Zola, the nineteenth century French writer.

ZOUAVE — Name given to a demi-glace sauce with tomato purée, garlic, mustard and tarragon added.

ZUCCHINI — American and Italian term for courgette.

ZUCCOTTO — Alcoholic Italian chocolate ice cream cake.

ZUNGENWURST — German tongue sausage.

ZUPPA INGLESE — Italian for English soup, it is in fact a dessert based on trifle which originated in Italy in the nineteenth century when British tourists demanded trifle. It contains sponge fingers soaked in liqueur or sweet wine, fresh or candied fruits and whipped cream. There is also a chocolate version.

ZUPPA PAVESE — Italian for Pavia soup, but it is popular throughout Italy. It is consommé in which eggs are poached and it is served with crostini as a light meal. It was allegedly first made for King Francis I of France after he was taken prisoner at the battle of Pavia.

ZWIEBACK — German rusk. It means twice baked.

.